A DROP IN THI

Lawrence MacEwen and th.

Polly Pullar has worked with animals all her life, as a sheep farmer, wildlife guide, field naturalist, photojournalist and wildlife rehabilitator. She writes and illustrates articles for numerous magazines including the *Scots Magazine*, *Scottish Farmer*, *Tractor* and *People's Friend* and is currently the wildlife writer for the *Scottish Field*. She has written a number of books including *Dancing with Ospreys*, *Rural Portraits Scotland's Native Farm Animals and Characters*, and is co-author of the acclaimed *Fauna Scotica: People and Animals in Scotland*. She lives in Highland Perthshire.

For my wonderful son Freddy, and for Iomhair, who both made this possible

Polly Pullar

This story is dedicated to my wife, Jenny, who for 30 years has worked tirelessly to build the community on Muck.

Lawrence MacEwen

Contents

List of Illustrations

ix

Acknowledgements

xi

Map

xiii

Foreword

xvii

A DROP IN THE OCEAN

1

Lawrence's Parents

205

Timeline

207

The Isle of Muck – a Brief History,
According To Lawrence

211

List of Illustrations

Landing feeding stores from the puffer in Laurie's launch, 1931

Unloading Coal in the 1940s

Putting cow in sling from Caledonian MacBrayne Steamer, c. 1950

Loading Sheep onto Estate Boat, 1940s

Commander MacEwen

Alasdair, Lawrence, Ewen and Catriona

The Commander, Mrs MacEwen, Alasdair, Lawrence, Catriona and
    Ewen Lawrence c. 1960

Shepherd Archie MacKinnon with Alasdair, 1960s

Lawrence and Jenny's wedding, Soay

Jenny with Colin

Jenny, Mary, Colin, Lawrence and Sarah

Puffer Eilean Easdil at Port Mor

Haymaking at Gallanach, 1970s

Lawrence's mother in the farmhouse kitchen

2000 *Wave* arrives in Arisaig with lambs

Gallanach, farm, lodge looking to Eigg

Muck sheep with Rum

Highland mare and foal

Calves with Rum behind

Colin and Ruth's wedding

Jenny with Mattie, April 2014

Amy waiting for the ferry

Coming off Lamb Island

Lawrence in the byre door

Lawrence with his beloved Fergie and beloved cows

Lawrence feeding ewes, 2014

Lawrence with Molly

Ruth and Hugh

Muck school with teacher Liz Boden and islanders doing litter pick

View from Beinn Airean

The Bronze Age Circle and MacEwen Grave with Rum behind

Rainbows over Gallanach

Camus Mor

Acknowledgements

Firstly, I want to thank Freddy and Iomhair for their advice, enthusiasm, invaluable input, patience and support.

Sincere thanks and gratitude go to the Society of Authors; in particular, the Authors' Foundation and K. Blundell Trust for their generous help with this venture. Also to Caledonian MacBrayne, for support and sponsorship.

Special thanks to Mark Stephen for his incredible encouragement and enthusiasm, and to Debs Warner, who has done a wonderful job with the editing and made so many hugely helpful suggestions.

Further thanks go to the following: Jenny MacEwen, for putting up with it all, and for providing endless sustenance and advice; Ruth and Colin MacEwen, for their generosity in lending me Gallanach and Seilachan cottages – perfect places to find peace and creativity – and also for rooting out photographs and newspaper cuttings.

To Clare Walters, for her time, stories and photographs; Zoe Moffat, for her creative input and hard work to produce the map; Dougie Irving, the itinerant dyker, whose input was hugely appreciated; Mary and Toby Fichtner-Irvine, for their support, and for doing a great deal of printing; Sarah Maitland MacRae, for photographs and general help; Julie MacFadzean, for meals, kindness and accommodation; Dave Barnden, for his well-timed Rusty Nail, and his encouragement and general unsurpassed support; Sandra Mathers, for extremely wise advice; Sandy Mathers, for fixing the door; Ewen

Bowman, for really great craic; Cathy Vaas, for her help and comments; Ewen MacEwen, for kindly rooting out the missing diaries; Richard Bath of *Scottish Field* magazine, for the inaugural trip that sowed the seed; Molly Fitch, for archive images; and to Ian McCrorie, Les and Chris Humphreys, Fiona MacEwen, Ian Bell and Martin Beard. And to wee Willow Moffat, for her effusive welcomes at the pier.

Finally, thanks to the maestro: father, grandfather, farmer, forester, retired coastguard and Special Constable, Muck ambassador, unofficial grave digger, master of ceremonies, etc. dear Lawrence, who has been such a joy to work with and who ironically does not seem to think he has the 'MacEwen' determination. If this were not the case, then this story would never have been told.

Polly Pullar

Many islanders appear in the text and need no mention here, but there is another group of people who played a vital part in running the farm and have received scant attention: the students. First fed and watered by my mother, and later by Jenny, it is my hope that they left this island with experiences that will serve them well for the rest of their lives: James Alexander, Alec Boden, Charles Blundell, Jamie Brett, Nicki Brett, Lucas Chapman, Peter Douglas, Duncan Geddes, Alan MacBroom, Donald John MacDonald, Calum MacRae, Helen Nimmo Smith, John Slater, Kate Sutton, John Symon, Andrew Todd, Miles Tompothelthwaite, Mark Wang, Simon Ward, Andrew Watts, Philip Watts, Adrian and Justin. And, from Switzerland, Anna, Florian, Lorenz, Mitja and Roger.

Lawrence MacEwen

Map

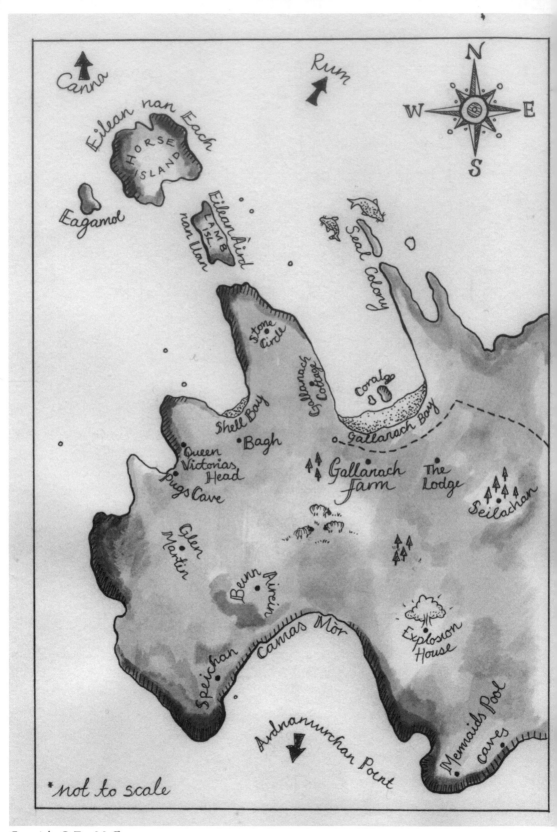

Copyright © Zoe Moffat

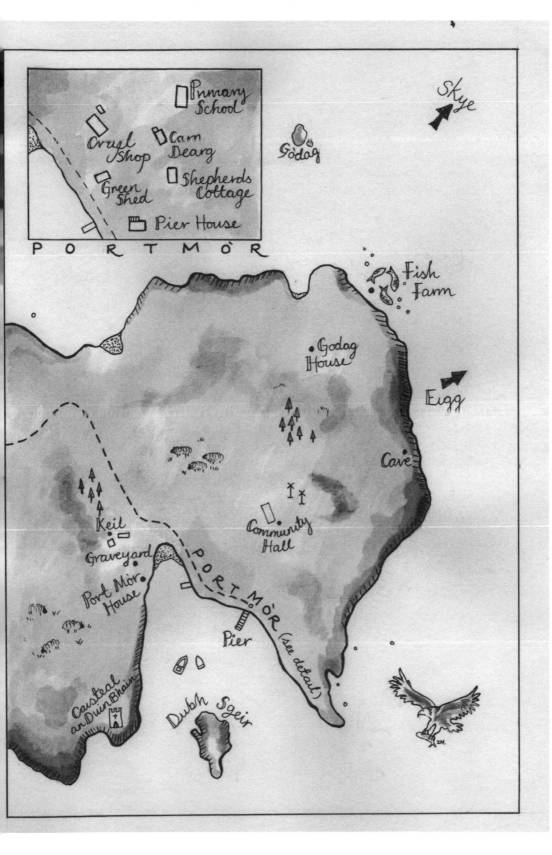

Foreword

All islands suffer from a sort of romantic overlay, the application of a heedrum-hodrum filter that softens the edges, prettifies the reality and disguises all warts or blemishes; it's a sort of geographical beer-goggles. That's what makes writing about Muck so difficult. Muck is one of the smaller Small Isles, the others being Rum, Canna and Eigg.

The problem with writing about Muck is this. The light here *is* actually diffuse, naturally soft-focus; you're not imagining it, that's the way it is. It is beautiful, the views from it are superb and it's a haven for wildlife – last night I stood under the thinnest of fingernail moons listening to snipe drumming in the dark, while geese grumbled and squeaked in the field above me and seals sang in the bay. Muck is no Shangri-La, but the folk here seem, on the whole, pretty happy and content. There is new building going on, children playing, projects being planned; a real sense of purpose. The houses are lived-in, worked from. This island has managed to avoid the pernicious spread of holiday homes that has hollowed out so many other west coast communities. The land is fertile and in good heart, the fields have that groomed look usually associated with the wealthier mainland farms, boggy sections and rushes are at a minimum. The sheep, cattle and ponies are all breeds that fit well into the landscape and thrive here naturally.

Much of this is due to the man who, together with his family, owns the island: Lawrence MacEwen.

If anyone ever gave Lawrence the manual on 'How to Be a Landowner', I can only assume that he used it to catch oil drips from his beloved vintage tractor; he certainly never read it. On the telephone you might mistake Lawrence for a toff – those gentlemanly Gordonstoun-trained vowels, the measured statements, the reflective pauses. In the flesh he looks like an elderly Viking jarl, cast out of time and into a boiler suit and wellies. His body is bent with 60 years of hard labour; his huge hands are maps of the island, the contour lines drawn deep into his flesh with soil and lanolin. A gentle man, he seems as comfortable hand-milking cows as he is playing with his grandchildren or chatting to his neighbours.

This is a man who dearly loves his flocks, both animal and human.

He is modest, hugely knowledgeable and undoubtedly infuriating to his family, who probably wish that he would act his age and stop being so bloody outspoken. He is a fount of stories, a few of which cannot be included or else they might land author Polly Pullar in court for years to come.

(In fairness, having described Lawrence I should also describe Polly.)

A slim, attractive redhead with a depressing ability to outrace larger, stronger men on the hill – I speak as one of those men – Polly is a countrywoman to her bones, curious about all things and closely familiar with plants, birds and animals. And she has a rare gift. She can listen, *really* listen, to what people are saying, their stories, memories and anecdotes. Her genuine admiration and respect for the storytellers shines through and, like a glass lens on a sunny summer's day, she focuses each tale to a point of brightness and helps warm it, bring it to life. Her extensive bibliography and the respect in which she is held by country folk speak for themselves.

Scotland is fortunate to have people like Lawrence and Polly, but doubly so now that they have come together. It was a pleasure watching them work on this project; it seemed to me to be more than a friendship, something more akin to a father/daughter relationship.

It may seem to you, on reading this, that Polly will have, *must* have, fallen into the classic Brigadoon trap I mentioned earlier, painting a man and his island, and its people, with a shortbread-tin gloss. She hasn't. Yes, there are lives and experiences on these pages to envy, much to smile or laugh at, but this book also makes it abundantly clear that nobody 'escapes' to an island. If you have problems in the Home Counties, you'll still have them here, and if anything they'll be even more noticeable.

Polly has produced an extraordinary, unique portrait of a quirky, hard-working, fun-loving community and its democratically minded leader, who hates being called 'the Laird'. It's a fascinating, at times sad and frequently hilarious tale, as well as a valuable instalment in Scotland's social history.

These are folk who voted for a less reliable ferry service so that the best view on the island wouldn't be ruined: a generous, friendly un clannish clan, constantly on the hunt for new members.

Can life on Muck really be like this? Well, on the basis of an admittedly brief acquaintance, I think so, but please don't take my word for it, visit for yourself.

It's two hours by ferry, but the scones alone are worth it and you can sing back at the seals if you want to . . . I did.

Mark Stephen, presenter of BBC Radio Scotland's Out of Doors
Isle of Muck,
Spring 2014

A Drop in the Ocean

A watercolour painting hangs above my bed. A treasured possession, it depicts a Hebridean shoreline: turquoise, black, grey and moody, a surging sea with foaming waves leads the eye to the distinct shapes of Rum's forbidding peaks. In the foreground there is another island. Muck, a place that has punctuated my thoughts since I was a child growing up on Britain's most westerly mainland peninsula, Ardnamurchan.

Whilst wandering at Achateny beach, looking for otters, I often sat daydreaming on a rock, gazing out to the islands as rain fell fizz-like on sea the colour of pewter, or clouds chased one another across an azure sky over Rum's Askival, Sgùrr nan Gillean and Hallival, the nearby Sgùrr of Eigg, and the distinctive Cuillin Ridge on Skye. Muck, approximately six miles by sea from Ardnamurchan: it came and went through the weather, so near yet so far. Its name and erratic moods fascinated me.

From Ardnamurchan's north coast, Muck's outline is often a silhouette, akin to the shape of a melting iceberg. Its highest hill, Beinn Airein, just 451 feet, and the steep sea-girt cliffs bordering its southern coast, appear prow-like.

Other than a brief foray in my stepfather's boat at the beginning of the 1970s, Muck remained largely a figment of my imagination. I knew so little, yet it is a fascinating place, with a passionate story. When I found myself there by sheer chance on a working mission, I

[1]

lingered an extra day and fell heavily under the island's spell and the ethos of its owners, the MacEwen family. That extra day was dismal: I endured the kind of rain that assures thankfully that the west coast of Scotland will never compete with a Spanish holiday resort. The horizontal rain seeps right into the skin, laying waste to the finest outdoor clothing on earth. And it was cold, too. I wanted to spend some time with the island's owner, Lawrence MacEwen, a familiar name in farming circles, a man who has gained the greatest respect, a true countryman, an eccentric and benevolent character, and most importantly someone who, with his incredible wife Jenny, has been largely responsible for making Muck and its small community the success it is.

My photography work for *Scottish Field* magazine the previous day had thoroughly whetted my appetite for life on Muck. There had been a shoot, and an encompassing involvement from the islanders, including most of the children, something seldom seen elsewhere. The pheasant, partridge and duck shoot on Muck is a relatively new venture and the visiting guns told me that the event is unsurpassed; fabulous sport, fabulous home-produced food and great craic, so much so that they plan to make the foray an annual event. I had witnessed that camaraderie myself.

I briefly chatted with Lawrence and liked him instantly. We had quickly found common ground – a shared passion for hill farming and native breeds. Sheep have opened many doors for me, and once again they quickly did so. We passed a cheery morning gathering and then dosing and marking ewes in the fank in one of the sheds, while the rain battered the roofs with a vengeance. Following soup with Jenny, he took me on an island tour. It was not the best day for this, yet it mattered not; his stories were fascinating.

At one mile by two, and with only a short stretch of road, Muck may be small but it has plenty to offer. When I left in a worsening gale next morning, I couldn't decide whether it was actually harder to leave or be stranded. If the forecast was accurate, then this was going to be the last trip for a few days for Ronnie Dyer, the skipper of the *Sheerwater*. I was already secretly planning my next visit. Over the following months, there were several.

It was a day of squalls lavished with brilliant shafts of low autumn sun. Fulmars flew low over the swell, waves massaged long wings and rainbows momentarily painted dark clouds with hope. From Arisaig, the crossing to Muck in the *Sheerwater* takes approximately two hours. It's a *turus mara* – a sea journey – of heart-stopping beauty, as the play of light on the islands is sometimes almost too much for the human soul to bear.

The boat stops briefly at Eigg – if Ronnie has not been sidetracked en route by his passion for cetaceans, then passengers can land for half an hour. In summer, he frequently runs a little late. A minke whale is spotted. He prides himself on getting his passengers up close enough so that they may even smell the cabbage-like breath of a breaching whale. He may point out a pomarine skua, or some common dolphin; this journey is as much about wildlife as it is about reaching island destinations.

Eigg was a bustle of activity – asthmatic Land Rovers and a throng of islanders met new arrivals, as backpack-clad tourists stepped ashore to be sniffed at by wagging collies. A bossily bristling Jack Russell terrier endeavoured unsuccessfully to mount a flirtatious collie bitch, then defiantly hupped his leg onto an unattended suitcase instead. There were reunions and new meetings, hugs and handshakes, laughing voices; everyone dived in to sort out provisions, luggage and supplies, from light bulbs to loo paper, spanners to sugar. *Sheerwater* and Caledonian MacBrayne's *Loch Nevis* are lifelines. Boat arrivals are a social occasion, a gathering of long-awaited booty amidst a haze of revelry, and perhaps the aromatic whiff of wacky baccy.

We headed for Muck. The sea had turned inky blue-black, a storm cloud hid Eigg's craggy sgùrr; a venomous shower was burdened with hail. The channel into Muck's new pier is tricky. In severe weather and difficult tides, the small *Sheerwater* can often manage when the larger Caledonian MacBrayne boat cannot. Ronnie is intrepid but never puts his passengers at risk; Muck can be cut off for long periods.

Muck's pier also buzzed with activity. Bedraggled dogs and antiquated vehicles were gathered. Unlike Eigg, on Muck bitches are sensibly the only resident canines, so avoiding unwanted pregnancies, hassles and heartbreaks. Small rosy-cheeked children raced about on bikes. In the midst of the melee stood Lawrence, a man entering his early 70s. He was chatting, slightly stooped. Like the island's small trees, he appears almost wind-sculpted by the prevailing gales, honed by years of sheer hard graft and the vagaries of the climate, still handsome. Clad in a boiler suit and wearing yellow oil rig-style wellies (and usually no socks), this is no tweedy absentee landowner but a driven soul who participates in everything from farming to his grandchildren's tea parties, from drain clearance to butchering pigs, from holding business meetings to biking off to meet new arrivals at the pier. He and Jenny have always worked interminably long days and seem to be everywhere all the time for everyone.

Lawrence MacEwen is, in fact, the laird of Muck, but you would never think it. A distinctive figure with incredible blue eyes and bushy ginger eyebrows, a shock of greying, blond hair and a ginger beard, some describe him as like a noble Viking. He smiled, as huge work-hardened hands warmly shook mine. Soon my belongings and provisions were loaded into the transport box of his vintage Ferguson tractor, together with me and my collie, and it spluttered into life, carrying us in style to our accommodation. Two island collies galloped beside us, as the reek from the tractor dispersed and we gently proceeded along Muck's highway – just a mile of tarmac with a grassy fringe down its centre. The squalls had calmed, the air was sharp, clearing from the west. Rum looked spectacular.

At the end of the road, my chauffeur barrowed my belongings

from the farm up a narrow path around the bay to an airy cliff-top cottage overlooking a view to die for. We chatted about the price of sheep, the forthcoming cattle sale in Fort William and the final electrification of Muck. Despite a dodgy knee and a painful limp, he was insistent on pushing the heavy load. As I was about to discover, it is this very dogged determination that has kept this man at the helm of Muck for all these years. I had arrived and was now starting a journey with one of the most extraordinary people I have ever met. Lawrence MacEwen's story, the story of the remote Hebridean island of Muck, was about to unfold.

Muck, like all Hebridean islands, has a character all of its own. It's part of a group known as the Small Isles which, though they may be relatively close to one another, all have a very different tale to tell: Eigg, with its chequered history of difficult landowners, is now owned by the community; Rum, a National Nature Reserve, with its minutely studied red deer population, is owned by Scottish Natural Heritage, as well as the local community; Canna, a farming isle bequeathed to the National Trust for Scotland by the Gaelic scholar John Lorne Campbell; and Muck, owned by the MacEwen family since 1896, the smallest and most fertile.

Muck is approximately 1,500 acres and has always had an excellent farming enterprise. The MacEwens are born stockmen and have farmed *with* the elements rather than *against* them, choosing highly suited native breeds with infusions of other blood to produce prime livestock. The good grazing supports 600 ewes, predominately dark-fleeced Jacob-Cheviot, plus 40 Luing and Luing-cross cattle. Recently Lawrence handed over the farm to his son, Colin, a man infused with the same MacEwen work ethic, and his equally hard-working wife, Ruth. Muck can produce surprisingly good crops, and over the years haymaking has been an important part of the agricultural calendar, though in recent increasingly wet summers silage has proved a less stressful option. Many of the island's ancient drystone dykes have been recently rebuilt, adding greatly to the landscape features. There has been some new building – a new guesthouse/shooting lodge and a smart new community centre – and there are usually about eight children in a fairly modern school. The island population is currently around the 40 mark. Small woods planted since the mid-1900s have stood the abuse hurled at them by the climate, and have miraculously survived, providing vital shelter for birds and beasts.

The MacEwens made two smallholdings to accommodate the islanders, but Muck is not honeycombed with crofts; Lawrence and his family are about as far removed from the archetypal 'feudal laird' mould as it is possible to be, but their leadership and guidance has greatly helped the island's stability. Despite this, problems and tragedies have been aplenty, some of them so heartbreaking and hard to deal with that they have doubtlessly led to a deep inner sadness.

In savage weather Muck can be one of the hardest places to live, but on days when sky and sea are as blue as topaz, and the bogs are red and emerald green with verdant mosses spiked with the delicately green-veined white waxy flowers of Grass of Parnassus, and the curlew calls over the sandy beaches, it is also heaven on earth. The flora and fauna of Muck is richly varied. In spring bluebells carpet the small woods and grassy banks, and stunted orchids dot bog and headland, while snipe drum high in the sky serenaded by cuckoo, skylark and a host of newly arrived migrants. In the sheltered bays the amorous cooings of dapper pied eider drakes posing to prospective mates also heralds the beginning of another busy tourist season. Though the wildlife is varied, there are few land mammals – otters are occasionally seen, common seals are numerous and haul out onto the skerries at Gallanach every day, and some grey seals come ashore to breed on Horse Island in the autumn. Their melancholy singing mingles with the wind and on moonlit nights adds an eerie dimension to the backdrop of silhouetted islands. Whales, in particular the minke, basking sharks, dolphins and porpoises can also be seen. It has been suggested that the Gaelic name for porpoise – *muc mara*, sea pig – is perhaps the origin of the island's name. Both golden and sea eagles appear, though do not nest, on Muck. During one particular stay at Gallanach Cottage, a young sea eagle passed several times each day, sweeping so low and close around the headland that the sky noticeably darkened. I stood in a garden vibrant with fuschias and montbretia and watched it drift over in the direction of the duck pond – sea eagles are lazy hunters; it had clearly learned that an easy takeaway could be found courtesy of the Muck shoot. Toby Fichtner-Irvine, husband of the MacEwens' daughter Mary, who runs the shoot, was philosophical about it: 'The visitors will love it and I am sure we can spare a few duck and partridge for the sea eagle.' Nature is quick to take advantage. Peregrines, too, were a daily sight and I found a plucking post on a prominent rock near the shore, with remnants of rock pipit's feathers. Since the advent of the shoot and the arrival of numerous game birds, and the associated feeding of grain, numbers of passerines have increased dramatically, but so too have the rats. Occasional passing rarities cause a flurry of excitement, as 'twitchers' flock from near and far to add another tick to their lists, despite the logistics of the journey. As Lawrence wryly put it: 'When we had a very nondescript bird, a veery, a North America member of the thrush family, hanging around the silage pit, they came in droves and stood there with telescopes and massive lenses – I suppose they must record it on Twitter.'

Muck has never had a shop or post office. There is no doctor or nurse, and until 2013 there was no round-the-clock electricity. In fact, it was one of the last places in the UK to be electrified. Jenny MacEwen, who Lawrence describes as the 'human side of Muck', runs a thriving tearoom; it bulges at the seams in summer with day-trippers calling in on either of the two boats. Island fisherman Sandy Mathers, one of few remaining residents bred here, keeps her stocked with shellfish. She is up at dawn baking delicious bread and cakes, as well as vast vats of soup with home-produced ingredients. Many visitors will walk no further than the tearoom close to the pier and, satiated with Muck's fine fodder, leave to tell friends and family how lovely it all is, though relatively they will have seen nothing.

Muck, like neighbouring Rum and Ardnamurchan, is important geologically and is largely composed of basalt lava flows. The dramatic shoreline and cliffs at Camus Mor on the island's south-west side are a Site of Special Scientific Interest; fossils found here are confined to stunted oysters forming layers amongst other material. Surrounded by a dramatic panorama of islands, views sweep to the rugged hills of Knoydart, Torridon and Ardnamurchan Point; this tiny drop in the ocean captivates all who visit but not only for the scenery, flora, fauna and peace.

Growing Up on Muck

Lawrence's debut on the island was perhaps a little unceremonious. In July 1941, when Mrs MacEwen was returning from hospital to Muck with the latest addition to her family, she travelled as usual from Mallaig on the *Loch Mhor*, skippered by the well-respected and fearless West Highlander Captain 'Squeaky' Robertson. He descended from the bridge with aplomb and greeted her whilst peering into the Moses basket, where the new infant was lying peacefully. 'Ah, Mrs MacEwen,' he said smiling broadly, 'he looks chust like a boiled lobster.'

The second of four children, Lawrence, due to the age gap, was closest to his late brother Alasdair. Catriona and Ewen are respectively three and five years younger.

'In the beginning, Mother was running the farm, as Father was in Shetland, where he would have been having a relatively cushy time looking after the harbour in Lerwick; Mother had a lot to do. Father had Wrens to iron his shirts, while Mother had to look after us hooligans, as well as doing the farm. Father did send a naval rating over to help us, who had come from a Lewis croft, so he was quite good – he used to carve us little wooden boats as well. I suppose at that stage there was no paperwork on the farm and you just had to look after the livestock. She had quite a reasonable staff, as agriculture was still important: if you were working in that line, you weren't called up. Sometimes I remember, she sent some washing over to a Mrs Campbell, who was a washerwoman on Eigg, though it was just linen, as a note from her read, "No body clothes."

'During the war, even Muck had a blackout, though we must have been well out of range. However, it was important that the German bombers would not see us. They reached as far as Fort William and dropped a few bombs there. We only had double burner lamps, which hardly gave any light, but even with these insignificant lights we were supposed to have brown paper over all the windows. Then we had ration books with vouchers valid for the Co-op in Eigg; it was amazing how well we all survived on hardly any food. Not everything was rationed, but to acquire most items little squares were torn from a ration book. We were fortunate to be fairly self-sufficient. We had our own meat on the farm, and eggs. In fact, we used to sell the latter on the black market in Tobermory and got paid a good price for them. Driftwood often used to wash up on the shore and this was a big thing for us in the war. The Atlantic was rife with German U-boats busy sinking merchant ships by the dozen, so deck cargos of timber from Canada and all sorts of other treasure came ashore. The MacDonald family, who lived in Pier House, always kept watch and patrolled around the shores day and night with hurricane lamps. Timber was piled high on the shore, but sometimes amongst it bodies were found – two were British and had come from HMS *Curacoa*. It had been hit by the *Queen Mary* in fog and was literally cut in half; it was a huge tragedy, with over 350 killed, though it was all hushed up at the time. There were two Germans from a submarine and their bodies were transferred from a grave in Muck and eventually in the 1980s sent down to Cannock Chase, but the British are still up there in the graveyard.

'One of my early memories is of a mine going off. There were extensive minefields between Scotland and Iceland. Six mines came ashore and one appeared into Port; everyone was very frightened. There was no telephone at that time and only a weekly boat, so forms had to be filled in and sent off so that eventually the mine disposal team came out in a Motor Launch, an ML, and disposed of it. I remember being very impressed by them, as they had all sorts of shiny things hanging from the belts on their uniforms. I was with Father when one mine went off. There was a huge bang, but no one was hurt. Once a bit of mine casing hit a tup and killed the poor beast.

'Right at the end of the war we had a bit of excitement when Alick MacDonald, one of the men who worked on the farm, came rushing over to tell Mother that there was a raft coming ashore. We were eating our revolting porridge at the time – during the war the oatmeal was really horrid. We raced out and saw this square raft coming into Gallanach. I would have been about four. We gingerly explored it and found tins of wonderful ship's biscuits. Alasdair got an anchor and tied the raft to the shore, but the rope was rotten and eventually after only a few days it floated off again.

'In 1947, two major events took place. First, a tractor arrived. It totally transformed farm life. It was a grey Fergie TE20 and we still have it. Our son Colin tried unsuccessfully to get it going again when he was about ten. It arrived on top of a load of coal on the puffer. Father drove it off the pier because Alick, the farm steward at the time, was not very good with machinery and had tried to dance up and down on the clutch; Charlie, who also worked on the farm, managed it no problem. Sadly, the tractor meant that most of our five workhorses were replaced, though we still had Dan, a pure Clydesdale, and Dick, a Highland Clydesdale cross.

'We shared a load of coal with Kilchoan in Ardnamurchan; the puffer always went there first so that some of the coal had been offloaded. We tried to arrange for her to come in during spring tides at high water and then she could sit grounded all day whilst we unloaded the coal. If the flat-bottomed puffer was too heavily laden, she would be too low in the water even at high tide and would ground astern. Ideally for Muck we needed a boat that was no bigger than 180 tonnes. As the weight in a puffer tended to be all in the stern anyway, it was important that there was enough left in the bow to ensure that, as it came into Port, it could cope with the shallow water and get alongside the pier to unload. Shovelling the huge pieces of coal into a five hundredweight bucket was hard work.

'The second momentous thing to happen in 1947 was school. Mother had taught us a reasonable amount of reading and writing, and even a little French. She used to draw little pictures to illustrate new words – I remember *la maison* and the picture of a house. But she could not illustrate the important things, such as the verbs *to be* and *to have*, and we all got totally bored with it. I was never any good at French. School was in Port Mor – we usually walked there barefoot in spring and summer. It began in earnest in January, but by February 1947 we were experiencing one of the coldest spells we ever had. I remember walking to Port and sadly finding lots of dead curlews on the track. We never had bikes then because the road was so rough, with large potholes, and our parents were clearly worried about us falling off and damaging ourselves. Soon after this we all developed scarlet fever and were in bed for weeks, so that put paid to school.

'School really was so boring. We had a reader, and a jotter that we had to fill with "pot hooks" – these are lines and lines of tedious curves supposed to teach good handwriting. Goodness, it never worked for me, unlike Father who had super copperplate-type writing. When things got tough at school, one of the problems was the teacher's son, Francis MacLeod. Needless to say, he really did not have much respect for his poor mother; he was not a bad boy, but he and I used to gang up on poor Alasdair, who was a very good boy by comparison. We used to call the teacher Mrs Mouse. When we got fed up with lessons, we just got her to read to us. The book I remember most was about whaling, *The Cruise of the Cachalot*. To begin with, school was just from nine till noon. Mrs MacLeod complained she did not have enough time to teach us so it was extended. Then we had to take our lunch and I really did not enjoy being there for a longer time each day. We had dip pens with inkwells and they were horrid, as they were so messy. When we were at school till early afternoon, Mother was pleased if we did not arrive back till about five because if we were out of sight we were out of mind. After we left the school we went off on wee expeditions and Francis sometimes came with us. He seemed to have access to boxes of matches and we loved lighting little fires in the heather, and occasionally did this in the lunch hour, too.

'The island had no telephone or radios at that time. If someone took ill and our boat was away, it could be quite serious. Father had arranged that if there was an emergency we would light a fire as a beacon on the island and then help would come from Eigg. It was a good system. The post office was on Eigg, and if we had an important telegram they would light a fire there and we would see it and go over to collect it in the island boat. Father used to be away collecting telegrams quite often, and even more so between the two wars, when he had his own private yacht. With his naval background, he was a very competent sailor.

'Anyway, we lit this fire during lunch and it rather took off. It was spotted and caused mayhem. Then the Eigg boat, the *Dido*, came over to the bay. Well, by the time we got back home to Gallanach, Father was waiting for us, looking furious, and he had a bunch of birch twigs in his hand. We really thought we were going to get a beating.

Miraculously, he seemed to accept all the excuses we made about not knowing about that system and we had a very narrow escape.'

Another fire adventure could have been far more serious. Leaving school one day, the children went off towards Camus Mor and found another good place for some pyrotechnics, lighting heather growing in an old ruin. There was something wooden sticking out and after a few minutes there was a loud bang. They panicked, thinking it was a gun belonging to Charlie. It turned out that Hector and Charlie had stored a box of detonators there that had washed ashore and they were letting them off by degrees when the coast was clear.

The freedom of Muck provided the 'feral' MacEwen children with an idyllic childhood: running barefoot all summer, toes were frequently bashed on the rocks but their feet soon became hardened. In winter they wore tacketty boots.

'We used to escape to go camping and sneaked out of one of the windows after bedtime. We would take quilts from the house, lowering them out. We did have a ground sheet, but I cannot say it was a formula for a good night. Sometimes we slept under a big rock known as Pug's cave – it was a tight fit, but we were very small and somehow managed to wriggle our way in. Our parents must have known, but they just let us go – probably because they knew how tired we would be from lack of sleep: it was funny how we could never do it two nights on the trot. We never got into too much trouble and often would camp under just one quilt together.

'Picnics were the great thing and Mother was very keen on them. We had excursions all around the island, particularly on Sundays, when we would gather driftwood.'

Mrs MacEwen's hayfield teas were also famous. She made large batches of scones and cut them into four, covering them in jam or cheese and tying it up in a clean dishtowel to take out to the fields together with a large kettle of tea. Lawrence remembers Ewen being in the pram in the hayfield as his mother came out and how she always made special tea for her husband, as he did not like tea so strong that the spoon stood up in it. She was always adamant that the men got their tea before anyone else; the children worried that there would not be any scones left for them, especially the jammy ones. Mrs MacEwen appears to have been the farmer for much of the time and she always ensured that she looked after the workers – an important trait she clearly instilled in Lawrence and his brothers and sister from a young age.

When Lawrence was only 11, already a daring maverick and showing his leadership skills, he decided to scale the craggiest cliff face of Ben Airein with his eight-year-old sister Catriona. His brother Alasdair had gone to prep school, so he had no one to keep him under control. It is an impressive cliff face even for a seasoned climber. They clung onto the rock and heather for grim death. Lawrence, being scared of heights, looked down at his sister and kindly asked if she was all right. 'Of course I am,' she replied crossly. 'Now, hurry up and get on with it, will you?' She was clearly not suffering from vertigo as he was. Once he reached the top, he raced away from the edge and collapsed on the grass, so relieved to have achieved it. Led by her unruly brothers, Catriona was a tomboy whom they nicknamed 'Girl'.

Collecting aluminium fishing floats from the shore provided the children with a source of pocket money, for they could get half a crown for a good one and even a shilling for one in less than perfect condition. They wandered around the coast looking for them and when they had enough they were sent to Mallaig, where Willie Fyall from St Monans, in Fife, collected them. Once, their mother took them over to Ardnamurchan for a few days' camping and Lawrence remembers how much he enjoyed it; they had found plenty of floats there, though it was almost impossible to carry them. They would also go over to collect floats on Rum; the south-west side at Papadil was the best.

There would be plenty of opportunities for swimming, and when they were still very young they all climbed Askival and Sgùrr nan Gillean on Rum, despite Lawrence's fear of heights. Their mother loved brambles and, though at that time there were few growing on Muck, they would sometimes go with a load of lambs en route to the mainland and get dropped off on Eigg, where they were plentiful, then the boat would collect them on its way home.

'Another thing I spent a great deal of time doing was watching the tide in the evenings. None of the others did it, but I would stand for hours just glued to it, particularly as it was coming in during spring tides. I was totally mesmerised by it. Mother would eventually shout and tell me it was teatime and I would drag myself away. I now ask myself, was this the equivalent of Facebook or PlayStations? I suppose it was, though I cannot help thinking it was a bit more useful. Alasdair's great passion was naval history and when we went to bed he would regale me with all this. Looking back, it is quite amazing how much he knew even for just a wee boy. Of course it just went in one ear and out the other, at least most of it did. I was always thinking about farming, even then.

'I remember we could earn pocket money by helping to carry the thrashed straw to the stirks in their sheds. It was un-baled and was very bulky, and we heaved it up in a big hessian sheet; it was very heavy for us. Father paid me 1s per day and I subcontracted this out to Catriona for 3d and Ewen for 2d. We also had to bed the pens with straw chaff as well. The cattle were fed linseed cake and bruised oats; Ewen could carry buckets of this, as it was not too heavy, and he was just big enough to fill the troughs. Catriona liked climbing up on the hay. She was very acrobatic and used to hang by her legs from the beams, sometimes with a 20-foot drop below her.

'As Alasdair had been sent away to boarding school and could no longer accompany father, the perks of the job for me were to go with him to the Oban sales – I loved this and went for two years before I too was sent away.'

Lawrence's first trip away from Muck was to the Salen Show on Mull when he was just seven. It was there, in the streets of Tobermory, that he first saw cars. He and his father stayed at the Western Isles Hotel, overlooking the bay. The best part of this was that at dinner there was ice cream, a treat that Lawrence clearly remembers.

'I used to think about the ice cream – and sausages, too – for weeks before we went, as these were things we seldom had at home. We would stay in the hotel and then early next day set sail again, heading for the show with the sheep in the boat. We went straight to a private pier owned by a Miss Heriot-Maitland. There we offloaded the sheep and then drove them about a quarter of a mile to the show. We sometimes did very well, but there was staunch competition from Boots the Chemists, who owned Ardnamurchan Estate; the Department of Agriculture, who owned Glen Forsa on Mull; and another big Mull estate, Killiechroanan.

'One year, I remember there was an announcement over the tannoy. We were all busy with the bustle of the show and this voice said: "Could the parents of Ian Clifton please come to the secretary's tent, as he is about to cry?" One of our friends who had come with us was very inquisitive and rushed over to see the distraught little boy. When she got there, she found our poor little brother Ewen, who we had not even noticed was missing. Of course he must have been upset and, as he was on the verge of tears, they had misheard his name as he had tried to pronounce his first two names, *Ewen Christopher*. It was so funny.'

Though the MacEwens loved showing, the logistics of getting animals on and off the island by boat made it a serious challenge, particularly as the weather so often spoilt plans. However, Lawrence's early determination and tenacity, which some describe as foolhardiness, have meant that he has defied all odds on numerous occasions and got beasts to their destinations come hell and high water, often in the most dubious conditions.

The houses on Muck were sadly wanting. In 1951 under a special Hill Farming Scheme to help modernise facilities and boost productivity for farmers, all the dwellings on Muck were finally given a makeover. Until that time most had not had running water or inside toilets; the women had carried all their water from wells at Port. Rayburns that ran continuously and heated the water were fitted and were a major advance on the ancient 'black' stoves. A new house was also built, with materials arriving precariously by puffer. Not surprisingly some of the builders were cowboys; the island was full of Glaswegians who stayed in huts and ate in the bothy, where Jessie MacDonald cooked for them. However, a three-ton lorry brought to help soon expired and clearly could not tolerate Muck's terrible road.

'I remember watching all this stuff arriving on puffers and being very excited about it. I was so naive then. The contractor was called Spiers, Dick and Smith and as they had put in a tender of £17,000 – £10,000 below their nearest rival – it is hardly surprising that they cut a few corners. Poor Charlie MacDonald spent the next ten years rectifying all the botched jobs but never complained about it until finally the builders had all gone. I suppose he did get a good new house out of it; he had lived in a tin shed up to that point.'

Stealing My Own Chocolate

Lawrence's school years were not particularly happy. He was sent to boarding school at Aberlour when he was 12 and felt like a fish out of water. It was all a far cry from the freedom of his island home. Lining up to have hands and shoes inspected before meals and not being able to chat after lights out, to say nothing of the strict regime, went against the grain for a child who was as wild as the wind that frequently swept over Muck. Lawrence, who was already mad on farming, quickly made friends with other farmers' sons; Martin Weir from Loch Fyne became his best friend, and they at least chatted about the things they loved. When Lawrence bumped into him many years later in Mallaig, he was shattered to find out that Martin was a sales rep for a biscuit company and not a farmer. He explained that poor health had prevented him from following his chosen career.

One of many attributes that I recognised in Lawrence very early on in our friendship is the fact that, though he may be very stubborn, he is an incredibly fair person. However, at prep school one particular incident seemed so unfair to him that he has never forgotten it.

'My aunt used to send me boxes of chocolate from Melrose's in Edinburgh and when these wonderful parcels arrived I was suddenly very popular. The headmaster's wife was a bossy sort of woman and when someone was handing around the parcels, she intercepted mine. I then got a message to go to the headmaster's study and was told that I could not have it; instead, it would have to go into a common pool for everyone. Well, I was rather philosophical about this. But the stupid woman left the box in the surgery where we had to go each evening to have a revolting mixture of cod liver oil and malt. I walked in and there was my parcel open, so when everyone had gone I took out a couple of bars of what was in effect my own chocolate. I heard steps coming down the corridor and there she was; there must have been a wee bit of chocolate sticking out of my pocket. She was beastly and I was sent straight to the headmaster to be punished. They clearly thought I was a bad influence and at the end of that term I was moved on to Altyre, part of Gordonstoun. I always reckoned it was all down to stealing my own chocolate that I was moved on early.'

Lawrence, who still takes a cold bath every morning, did not find the icy showers and spartan aspect of Altyre an issue. The MacEwens had grown up with almost daily swims in the sea and were well used to cold water. But there were plenty of other things that Lawrence found hard. Thoughtful Alasdair took him under his wing. Collectively known as Big Muck and Little Muck, the pair made their mark early on.

'I was not very academic, however I did love things like hillwalking, even though I was scared of heights when it came to serious rock climbing. By the time I left, I had done 78 Munros. We used to travel to the Cairngorms, the Nevis Range or Glencoe in horrible, smelly green school buses with crunching gearboxes and everyone always got sick.'

Sometimes they persuaded their rather un-outdoorsy music teacher, Mr Tony White, to take them hillwalking; on those occasions, they travelled in style in an open-topped car instead, which was wonderful in summer. However, it was the boys who did the leading on these expeditions, as they knew far more about the hills than their music teacher did.

When Lawrence was in his early 20s, there was a rather bizarre expedition to climb Ben Nevis again, but this time he insisted on doing it barefoot.

'All the way?' I ask him.

'Why certainly,' he replies, smiling broadly. 'I think I put my boots on again to come down.'

It is at this point, as we sit with a gale raging around the house, rudely rattling the slates and firing abusive horizontal sleet-laced rain at the windows, that I notice his bare feet, newly devoid of wellies. Perhaps his childhood barefoot ethos is the reason why his pins are perhaps not his finest assets and, like many men, a set of sheep's foot clippers for his toenails would not go amiss.

Altyre was part of the Gordon-Cummings' estate and the head forester proved inspirational to Lawrence. One afternoon a week he helped him plant trees, as well as with a range of other forestry-related jobs. Even though woodland enterprise on Muck has always been a serious challenge, with the severity of the salt-laden gales, it is due to this early influence that Lawrence and the rest of his family persevered and there are continual new planting schemes to this day. Commander MacEwen, Lawrence's father, had sought the advice of Sir Osgood Mackenzie at Inverewe Gardens in an endeavour to find salt-tolerant species. One school holiday Lawrence ordered 1,000 beech trees and 1,000 Sitka spruce for Muck and, in what I am quickly learning is very typical of his behaviour, he decided to try and plant 1,000 in a day.

'I realised that I had to put a wee patch here and a wee patch there and it all took an impossibly long time, so I had to give in and even at the end of the holidays I had not finished and had to heel them into the vegetable patch in the garden till I could get back to plant them. I was very disappointed.'

There were other opportunities for Lawrence while he was at school, including working on local farms digging potatoes and helping with livestock, and in particular milking, something that was to become a particular passion. Though he loved the farming aspect, there was also the lure of tea with cakes and scones, much required as fuel for an adolescent schoolboy's engine. Though he tolerated school, he was pleased to leave, but he had clearly made fond friends. A letter from one of his schoolmates to congratulate him on his wedding many years later reads as follows: 'I read the announcement of your nuptials and want to congratulate you both – I will never forget the "Muck MacEwens" and how often you were not there at the start of term. We would say to each other, "The Muck MacEwens are not back yet . . . Well, don't worry, they will be here just as soon as the weather changes." ' As Lawrence already knew, living on Muck, the weather and its erratic moods was always set to rule his life.

Johnnie and Hector Macdonald

Lawrence found forging friendships at school difficult, something he puts down to the fact that at home on Muck he saw few children other than his siblings. 'I had problems being a prefect and I seemed to fail to keep order in the house; I always felt I was a bit of a square peg because I did not always fit in with the things that were going on around me. However, I was perhaps better able to adapt to the academic side, but even then, while I was extremely good at geography and fairly good at history, French was a disaster, as was algebra. I managed to leave school without my biology A level but wanted to go to university, so there was no avoiding a crammer in Edinburgh – Basil Patterson's. As I was taking London University exams, I had to go south to do the practical. This was my first visit to London and it proved very stressful. I had to dissect the cranial nerves of a dogfish and probably failed that side of it. I then had a few months to kill and ended up in a hostel on a farm at Mersington, Greenlaw. The owner, Robin Forrest, was a college governor, but he did not take much part in our lives. His dour steward had to find jobs for us and for the whole of February I was in a line of about six students lifting large stones into a trailer. We were paid £1 12/6d per week, though that was probably not too bad for that time. The steward barely seemed willing to impart any farming information, so it was boring. Then in pairs we were seconded to the dairy, where there was an abreast milking parlour and Ayrshire milkers. Before the cows were milked we washed their udders, but we were also allowed to put the cups on the teats. In those days only fully trained dairymen were allowed to do this, so I felt very privileged. I have loved milking ever since. I also learned about rearing calves on a commercial scale and how to extract semen from the young pedigree Ayrshire bulls. Robin Forrest hoped to sell these to the Milk Marketing Board. In the end, back at the dreaded BP's, I passed various exams and finally went to university in Aberdeen.'

Lawrence appears to have excelled at the practicalities, even if the written side of the work bored him rigid, and he claims he was a 'quiet student'. He particularly loved the year's practical with Haig and Peggy Douglas at Glen Dearg, near Galashiels, where he forged a friendship that was to last until their deaths.

'Haig was a big character with a very short fuse and he was interested in everything. He was related to the Black Douglas – Sir James Douglas, a Scottish warlord and landowner who was one of the chief commanders of the Wars of Independence. Haig's and his ancestors would have been amongst the Border Reivers. He came from a long line of Border farmers. He also loved forestry work and further encouraged my interest in the subject. There was already a connection with Muck, as they bred South Country Cheviots and Father had bought tups from them for the island. Though I was largely unpaid, I stayed in the house and Haig took me to sales and shows and even racing. He did have a bad temper and could not keep his staff, but he taught me the importance of keeping mine and had a great influence on me, teaching me to take an interest in wherever or whatever the situation. He did take it to extremes by fighting with lots of official bodies, not for financial gain but always for what he thought was right. I became very keen on horses, as he had two lovely hunters, a thoroughbred called Princess and a Connemara-cross called Misty. As his groom had just left, I rose at 6 a.m. each morning to muck out, groom and exercise. I really swotted up on the theory of horsemanship, as I longed to go hunting; I even had to have a cap made for me, as my head is so large I could not get one off-the-shelf. Haig was a very small man, however, and he felt that I was too heavy for both Princess and Misty, so instead he bought me an Irish draft cross called Jock; within a month of his arrival, very deep snow fell and the farm was almost completely isolated.

Hunting ceased altogether, but I did manage a little jumping where the snow had formed ridges.'

When Lawrence finally completed university, in 1964 he set off to Australia and New Zealand, where he was to work for two years on farms. It was during this trip that he spent time with Janet Blundell and her family in Tasmania. She had given birth to her son Richard in Inverness at the same time as Lawrence was born and the two babies had been in adjacent cots. Janet, who Lawrence describes as a 'great lady', met him on his arrival and was very kind to him. She also realised soon after that he had measles. He remembers that she even made him a haggis for New Year so that he felt at home. No sooner had Lawrence disembarked in Australia than he was dealt a cruel blow, hearing devastating news from Muck.

'I had set off for Australia on the *Canberra* and within one month of my departure tragedy struck at home. We had boatmen at that time – two brothers, Johnnie and Hector MacDonald. Johnnie was head boatman, but he was not a drinker, something that is important for a boat skipper, and he was very good at his job, very safety conscious. However, Hector, who was the assistant boatman, enjoyed a good dram or two and on occasions had accidentally fallen into the sea. Incidentally Johnnie had strong socialist leanings and was reputed to read *The Daily Worker*. He used to instigate strikes but when Alasdair was in charge of the island, he used to go and fetch the mail from Eigg himself so that this put a stop to any nonsense. There were 11 members of the MacDonald family living in Pier House, including various nieces and nephews. They were collectively known as the Sandies because their grandfather was called Alexander.

'The system then was that the boatmen would come around to Gallanach and would anchor our boat *Wave*, or her predecessor, and then row ashore in the dinghy to fetch Father or anyone else leaving the island. Father could not walk to Port to meet the boat there, as he always had a heavy suitcase to carry, and that is why they came round to Gallanach.

In those days there were no steamers to Muck; we had to collect everything from Eigg, including the post. On occasions Father was taken to Eigg to get a steamer from there. He was a county councillor, so he travelled quite a lot, but he did not go to many meetings as he found them too boring and slow. He represented all the Small Isles in the days of Inverness County Council and often had to meet important people to make decisions.

'It was a very cold December day and Johnnie and Hector had rowed ashore to fetch Father, with his immaculate brown leather suit-case, smart suit and his handmade shoes. He always had the best and certainly did not skimp. I cannot be doing with all that nonsense.' Lawrence pauses. I note his elbow peeping out of the work-worn jersey and the strong aroma of cattle pervading the room. His wellies and dung-clarted waterproof trousers lie at the door. I also remember his plastic feed sack tied up with bailer twine to transport his outdoor gear when I met him off a train at Crianlarich; there was certainly no leather suitcase.

'Anyway, they used to take the dinghy on board, rather than towing it, and despite its heaviness lifted it on the boat. Father was standing in the hold forward and the dinghy was half in and half out of the boat. Hector must have had a heart attack, as he suddenly toppled over into the sea. There was a panic and Johnnie, who had probably never been in the sea before, didn't let go and went in too, pulling the dinghy over on top of himself. Father, who was in the hold as this terrible incident took place, rushed forward to try to let the anchor chain out so that the boat would drift back and he could then get hold of the two victims.

'Mother, who would have been 61 at the time, was standing on the shore about 60 yards away and saw it all happening. Quick as lightning, she leapt into the water and swam out fast to where Hector was lying on the surface; Johnnie had disappeared under the dinghy and was nowhere to be seen. She managed to swim back to the shore with Hector and pulled him out onto the beach. But it was too late; he was probably dead when he hit the water. Later they found that he had no water in his lungs, proving that he'd had a heart attack and had not died from drowning. They eventually found Johnnie too, but he was long dead, drowned right there in the bay in front of the house.

'It hit the island badly and everyone fell into the depths of despair. There was a story that Johnnie and Hector, both in their 60s, had had a premonition while anchored in the South Harbour on Eigg a few days earlier and had delayed their return home because they felt frightened. Perhaps they had the second sight. It's entirely possible, though we will never know. They had told their family and it played into the doom and gloom that followed.

'When I finally arrived in Australia, I was greeted by this shattering news. At Christmas time the following year, the Royal Humane Society gave mother an award. The chief constable of Inverness came to present it to her. She was an extraordinary, tough woman. Even though she was a strong swimmer, getting Hector's body ashore and in such icy conditions must have been a real challenge. I was still away when they had the little ceremony in the school. They'd had no idea what to do to entertain the chief constable after it was finished. In the end they had a table tennis match and he won.'

Lawrence laughs, but a gesture I am soon to become familiar with, his enormous hand brought up to the side of his face and the blue eyes cast down, indicates his depth of feelings.

Though both men were lost, during a Fatal Accident Inquiry in 1965 the sheriff congratulated the modest heroine. But the dire sadness of this shocking accident was to cast the first of several dark clouds over Muck.

Lobster Fishing

When Lawrence returned from his travels, no one was fishing on the island. Lawrence used the 10-foot dinghy that Johnnie had previously rented from his father for 12 shillings a week before his tragic demise. Johnnie had worked with 70 creels. When the weather was bad, he'd had to make several journeys into safer waters, as the dinghy could only carry a maximum of ten creels. Lawrence made himself six creels to start off with. He had fished since he was about five years old, when they had gone out in a little Shetland-type sailing skiff that they had to row all the time as they trolled long lines out from behind her. Darrows were not used at that point. One evening he remembers catching 108 fish, cuddies as well as mackerel.

The first day Lawrence went lobster fishing he used four creels and caught six lobsters. Nearly every day he went out at 6 a.m. to check his pots and then was back in by 8 a.m. to work on the farm. The waters around Muck have never been overfished, so have always been extremely good for lobsters.

'I used to bait the pots with salt mackerel. There were crabs too, but though I caught plenty there was then no market for them unlike today, so they just went back into the water. We had to make our own pots but often cheated a bit, using canes instead of hazel, as that was much easier to work with. One of the lobster buyers that I dealt with was a Mr Pickles. He seemed to be very fair and he also got cane for me. He paid 7/6d per pound for the lobsters in the summer, and I got 12 shilling for them at Christmas time. In 1969 I bought myself a new 12-foot dinghy from Orkney that cost me £79. I also purchased a Seagull outboard engine, but even now that I no longer had to row I didn't seem to catch any more lobsters.

'One beautiful August day we decided to do a trip to Dibidil on Rum. There was quite a strong wind from the north, with white caps to the waves, and I made an arrangement with the rest of the family that they would bring *Wave* around from the Port side of the island and we would shortly meet up. However, they were delayed and I set forth, heading towards Rum. It was fine when I was heading straight into the wind, as the dinghy had a good bow on her, but when I had to refuel the Seagull outboard, the boat tended to turn sideways and there was a real risk of her going over. It was very frightening. The family did not show up, but miraculously I finally reached Rum. When *Wave* arrived at long last, everyone on board was greatly relieved to see me, as they had really thought the worst. Eventually, when Alasdair moved to Hardiston, I had far too much to do on the farm so did not go out very often after that, but it was something I always enjoyed.'

Alasdair

'Alasdair was at school on the island with me for some of the time. However, Francis MacLeod and I, despite being younger, used to gang up on him. I think together we were more than a match for him. I know at times I was a real nuisance because on one occasion he came home from school and was so fed up with me that he bashed me on the head with a tin can and there was a copious quantity of blood. I am sure, though, that it was justified.

'He was perhaps less adventurous than me, and he was very much a health-and-safety man. When we were given a pram dinghy, Mother, who had insisted we were good swimmers, always put Alasdair in charge, and we were allowed to potter about close to the shore. Father and Mother had great confidence in him and trusted him totally. He was always allowed to go to bed up to a couple of hours later than me, and this annoyed me, but it was justified. I think he was an old head on young shoulders; he was always very responsible. The four of us children fought quite a lot, usually in pairs. Mother would boot us out of the house and tell us to continue on the lawn, but that was not so exciting, as there was no furniture to knock about.

'Alasdair was away at school when Catriona and I had done the cliff-climbing stunt – there is no way that would have happened if he had been there. He was always interested in sheep, probably more so than cattle. When he was about ten, he was allowed to go to the Oban sale with Father. By the time he left school, he only had one A level and that was in history, which was a subject he adored from the very beginning. Like Father, he had a probing mind towards the subject. If you read a book called *The Influence of Sea Power* when you are only 11, you have to be fairly intense about the matter. I am always astonished that he read that book and many others similar.

'After school he did not go to university. I think this was a big disappointment to him, particularly as we all went. He never said so, but it was sad because he was someone who would really have excelled there. He had probably not been channelled right at school, though at Gordonstoun he really excelled at hillwalking and climbing, and was a superb navigator, even in the depths of winter. The climbing master, John Rae, who was a great friend of his, gave him plenty of responsibility. Alasdair often led parties and for his age had gained some good experience. I remember one very cold day in May going up Ben Nevis and on the way down John Rae put Alasdair in charge of one party and I was allowed to go with him. There was no visibility whatsoever, with dense mist, but he knew exactly the place between the high cliffs where we should descend and he was absolutely spot on. I was always in awe of how he did that. Over the years, I was often very impressed by Alasdair.

'He'd also spent time doing practical farming with Haig and Peggy Douglas at Glen Dearg in the Borders a few years before I went there. He got on really well with them and loved being in the heart of sheep country. Then he went to the East of Scotland College of Agriculture in Edinburgh before returning home to Muck in 1961 after a year-long trip to New Zealand, by which time Father was beginning to step down. Though it was four months late we laid on a 21st birthday party for him, and some people from Eigg came over for it. It turned into quite a big event. A few days later the tail end of a hurricane arrived in Muck and caused havoc with the hay. We had a real struggle that year to make hay due to the awful wet summer. While he was away, I was keen to prove myself, to show him what I could do on the farm, but the haymaking really had been tricky. More than 100 hayricks blew down and most of the hay ended up on the fences; some went straight into the sea.

'Once he was home Alasdair set out to modernise the farm a little, and though he was very competent I would not have said he was as competent on the mechanical side as Colin. He got rid of the tumbling tam and we got a tractor-mounted buck rake, and he bought Sprackman sides for making clamp silage in the field. In our climate it makes far more sense to concentrate on silage rather than hay. So there were quite a few changes. Then he was also instrumental in bringing Archie MacKinnon, the shepherd, to the island; they got on incredibly well together. At that point sheep prices were very good, so that we could afford to have a shepherd. Alasdair lambed the blackfaces west of Gallanach, while Archie lambed the Cheviots on the east side. They were both very keen on showing and this was far more successful during Alasdair's short period of stewardship than it had been since the 1930s.

'Alasdair also wanted to build up the tup-selling business. We had always sold the tups that the Department of Agriculture did not buy at the Fort William sale, where we had a good support from local crofters who liked our stock and paid a decent price because it was acclimatised against tick-borne diseases. However, when he and Archie decided to also try to sell them in Oban, there was a totally different type of buyer, mostly farm managers and farmers from further south, and they were not prepared to pay so well without a decent luck penny so they came unstuck.

'There was a girl called Catherine Haggerty who came to the island with her friend, Jean Hammond, who was incredibly quiet. Catherine managed somehow to get Jean installed on the island as schoolteacher and told her, as she was going to be the only single girl and Alasdair was available, she should set her cap at him and she should not miss him at any price. He was not remotely interested, so nothing came of that; however, I do think Alasdair worried it would be hard to find a suitable wife whilst living on Muck.

'On the other hand, in 1968 the Style family from the south booked Boatman's Cottage for a holiday and came with their children, including an older daughter, Fiona. It was haymaking time and as always we commandeered any island visitors to help, as this was a very big, important event and if the weather was fair we really had to take advantage. We were working hard in the Tank Park behind the house and Fiona was beavering away, too. I must admit I noticed that she seemed particularly good with the hayfork and Alasdair must have spotted this, too. A few days later we all went on a day trip to Soay, but Alasdair refused to come and stayed behind. Clearly, he wanted to be with Fiona. When someone asked me where he was, I said that my brother had other fish to fry. Soon after that Jean left as schoolteacher.'

Following the summer holiday, Alasdair and Fiona wondered how to continue seeing each other. Alasdair had the bright idea to get Fiona to apply for the teaching post, as Jean had gone and it was still vacant. An interview in Inverness then secured the position and Fiona returned to the island at the end of August.

'Alasdair used to go down to see her on a motorbike. He would park it at Port wood, then creep down so no one would hear him, but of course everyone knew he was off there to see Fiona anyway. I have no idea why he persisted, but it made us all laugh. I don't think we were very welcoming to poor Fiona.'

The MacEwens during that era were often hard to please and expected a lot from prospective spouses, but let us not forget Fiona was *good with the hayfork* – something that Lawrence used a great deal when weighing up a person's potential.

During her time as teacher on Muck, Fiona got her pupils to make small island news magazines. These were type-written by the children and provide a wonderful vignette of some of the day-to-day events:

WAVE

Our boat is called the Wave. *It is a 36' motor launch, varnished with white paint and red paint. The* Wave *can take sterks & sheep and people and it hasn't got long ends. I like to go in it to Eigg and Alasdair, Lawrence and Peter go too!*

And it has an anchor.

— Archie MacKinnon — January 1969

The dentist came on Wednesday to pull out our teeth. He pulled out seven of mine. He brought a funny nurse with him.

On Tuesday the MacEwens found a baby seal at Gallanach.

On Monday we made a guy. We screwed up lots of paper to put inside him. We put on him Mummy's old trousers and shoes and Charley's old shirt. One day when Miss Style was going to get some sheets she got a terrible fright when she saw a face looking at her.

— Alasdair MacKinnon —November 1969

JET

One of Daddy's dogs is called Jet and she is five years old. Jet is nervous and shy. She is mostly black with one white leg.

She eats porridge and milk. On Sunday she gets it in the afternoon and during the week she gets it at night.

Jet doesn't run as fast as Floss. She is bad at rounding up sheep but Daddy takes her out whether she is naughty or not to train her.

— Donald MacKinnon — 1969

[31]

'Once I was back home from my own travels, things at home were very tense because it was never really very clear who was actually going to run the farm. Father had various irons in the fire and had been away looking at mainland farms with the view to working the two together, something that is quite common for west coast farmers. He had also considered trying to find a farm on Eigg for me, as Alasdair would be running the farm at home. However, a consortium including Father, County Councillor Fergus Gowans and a Glasgow hotelier failed in their bid to buy the island; Major Robert Evans from Shropshire bought it instead and bred Hereford cattle there. Behind the scenes there were major private family discussions going on about Muck's future. One awful idea was mooted that we should evacuate the island and then use it as a "summer only" operation, with a holiday cottage business. So things were not very stable at that point. This was totally unacceptable to me because Muck was very precious.'

As Lawrence showed no inclination to leave Muck to farm elsewhere, Alasdair apparently worried greatly that the island could not support both of them. Though it may have seemed that Alasdair's announcement to move to the mainland came totally out of the blue, according to Fiona he had spoken to her about it and had been agonising over it for a long time.

There is obvious sadness when Lawrence speaks about his brother: 'Soon after Father's death, Mother bought Hardiston at Cleish in Fife and I ran that for a short while. Fiona was still the schoolteacher and in 1969 they were married. Eventually, it seemed far more appropriate for him to leave the island to farm at Hardiston permanently.'

Mrs MacEwen, often nicknamed Ma, told Fiona that after his return from New Zealand each time she put Alasdair's suitcase away he brought it back to his bedroom. She tells me: 'Ma said she felt that Alasdair was uncertain about his future on the island. He told me that on his 21st birthday Pa had wanted to hand over the entire island to him, but he was not happy about that and insisted it should be shared between the other three siblings and this was duly done.'

Suddenly, having never been prepared for the idea of taking over the island, Lawrence was thrown in at the deep end, and was shocked and rather worried about whether he was up to the job.

'It had always been assumed that the eldest son would do it, and I was certainly overawed at the prospect, but perhaps more than a little excited by it too. It is extraordinary how fate played its hand and where that has led Jenny and I.

'Alasdair and Fiona had three children, Philippa, Will and Louise. He brought the family to Muck sometimes, but perhaps I felt that his heart seemed to be on the mainland, though sadly, looking back, maybe this was not the case. Hardiston was a good stock farm and he improved it immensely, put in field drainage and built indoor cubicles for his suckler cows. He also used to take some of our lambs for growing on, to then be sold at Hawick. He sometimes sent me good tups he had bred. They were real escape artists and seemed to manage to spread their genes around the flock before they were meant to. Everything seemed to be going fine at Hardiston, but suddenly in 1981 Alasdair announced they were moving south to Stickland Farm in Dorset.'

Fiona explains that following Ma's death, the three siblings continued to each own a share of Hardiston; Alasdair knew that if all three ever perhaps wanted to realise their money he would not be able to continue there. She tells me: 'Our children were then ten, eight and four, and we both felt that a more secure future for us seemed preferable. Hardiston was sold in 1980 and a year was spent in Kinross whilst Alasdair looked for a farm. He felt farming was destined for very hard times and therefore he wanted a farm that he could run single-handed, so decided to look further south and we moved to Dorset.'

There is doubtless a great sadness surrounding a situation that must have been far from easy for all them 'Though none of us ever threatened to withdraw our shares, it is understandable that my brother wanted to be independent. From there, he bought lambs for finishing and rented extra ground on dairy farms in the area. He used to come north to Scotland to buy lambs, too. Once he was in the south we saw them all less frequently. Then on 6 May 1990 we were hit by another dreadful tragedy when we got the really shocking news that my brother, the person I had really looked up to and admired so much, had taken his own life. He was only 51.' There is a silence, and Lawrence brings his hand up to the side of his face.

Wave

'*Wave* was the third of three boats that the estate had had with engines. The first one was acquired and used between 1917 and 1930; it had an engine in a box, so to speak. It was about 27 feet long and it was amazing, as at that time my family would take bulls over to Sanna in Ardnamurchan in it and even went off to places such as Soay to collect cattle. About 1930 Father traded up and got a firm in St Monans in Fife to build a Kelvin cargo launch. She had a petrol paraffin engine. But by 1953 she had a bit of shipworm, so it was time to move her on and he went to Henderson's boat builders in Mallaig and asked them to build him another boat. At that time they were still building a few fishing boats there. Father employed a naval architect to design something for him and *Wave* was the end result. She is a much more seaworthy boat than her predecessor because she has a finer bow so she throws off the seas. She is 36 feet long, with a hold 13 feet long, and she can carry between four and six tonnes of cargo, or 15 calves, or about 70 lambs. In 1985, I recorded that we took off 12 boatloads of livestock in her. There was a period when everything went in *Wave*.

'Transporting livestock in boats always took a great deal of time and we had to wait for good days, but she really was very heavily used before the steamer slipways were made. She has a diesel engine and she cost £1,950 and is largely made of larch and oak. It took two years to build her and some of the oak frames got so dry that they cracked and had to be doubled-up before she was launched.

'I clearly remember the day she was brought home. We had just been on holiday in the old boat up to Staffin on Skye. We came down to Mallaig on 7 August 1955 and there was *Wave* ready and lying alongside. It was very exciting. Father and the boat's builder, Charlie Henderson, took her out up to Sleat Point on Skye to do a sea trial, but as she had no ballast she was very lively and I was horribly sick. So before we took her home to Muck we lifted a whole pile of stones off the shore to use as ballast and we got back home fine. She has lasted all this time, though has had three engines and a bit of re-fit. Initially she had an engine house and a tiller, and now she also has a wheelhouse. We used to camp in the hold and had a green canvas cover to keep off the rain. We put the sheep and cattle in the hold and have to use a ramp to get them on and off. However, there is one hazard with placid older cows. Sometimes getting them off can be really hard. It's fine with the wilder ones, as often once we are at a pier they will just leap ashore, but the quiet ones are not too keen and stay put, even a big slap on the rump won't work. There was one famous time when Jenny, Davy Jones and Bryan Walters apparently had an awful time at Glenuig; it took them well over an hour to get them off. The ramp was just too steep and they were just too quiet.

'In the early days we always used head ropes with a knot to prevent the loop from tightening around the animal's neck and tied this to rings bolted to the gunwale. Later we put them in loose and, though the boat listed if they all moved to one side, it was never too serious. Actually, we have never had a beast jump overboard at sea, and at least by tying them we ensure that won't happen either. When we are transporting horses and ponies, we put gates down each side and then they are safely tied between them. With *Wave* being a wooden boat, she does need a lot of maintenance. We have to scrape the bottom, put on anti-fouling and remove the old varnish before putting more on each year. Colin is now in charge of all that.

'I always enjoyed all our boat trips so much and I have always loved going to see other places. *Wave* has gone ashore three times; once she went ashore below Sandra Mather's house and she was left high and dry. Henderson's, the boat builders, had to come and get her off, and then patched her up and took her back to Mallaig for repair. She survived and we were very lucky that it was not really bad weather when it happened.

'In 2005, after a terrible long period of storms in which we had no CalMac boats, Colin took *Wave* to Arisaig in a weather window to take friends back to the mainland after a new year party. He was going south, so he left *Wave* in Arisaig. Thankfully, Ronnie Dyer knew there was a really bad storm coming and cleverly fixed her to two moorings; due to this he saved her from possible disaster. It was the same terrible storm that caused the loss of a family on the causeway in Benbecula. The seas here were so high that they removed half the slates off the waiting room at Muck. This was the worst storm that *Wave* has weathered – there may well be worse to come.'

'In the early days, the Glenlight Shipping company owned most of the Clyde puffers that brought coal out to the islands. As time moved on, there was much economy of scale and it was the smallest puffers that were likely to be replaced. We had Tribal class puffers. I remember one was called the *Kaffir*, another *Spartan*, and another *Alaska*. Father had a puffer agent in Glasgow and he would put in an order for the coal. We relied heavily on the puffers and they brought all sorts of goods, including the first tractor that came to the island. Later tractors came on *Wave*. The red Fergie 35X that I still use today came on *Wave*. We bought it new from Fife in March 1964 and it cost £750. It has had a change of engines. The final tractor to come on her was a Ford 4000 in 1975. When she was slung on board, the captain of the *Loch Arkaig* saw us in Mallaig and offered us life jackets because he was so worried that we would never reach Muck with our precarious load. We had to fill the cargo hold with 44-gallon drums to support two planks that we put across. One end of each plank went over the side, so the tractor's front wheels were also over the gunwale. The other ends of the planks were below the gunwale and the rear wheels were against it. The vehicle was placed on this with a crane in Mallaig. Once we were back home in Muck, as soon as the tide was absolutely right we could just drive it on the planks onto the pier. We eventually stopped bringing vehicles; this was because it did look rather hair-raising and I worried someone would complain about the safety aspect.

'Incidentally, that was the tractor that had a dip in the sea in October 2003. I was taking gas cylinders down to Port and I parked it on the newly opened pier. Unfortunately, I didn't put the brake on and the transport box, heavy with all the cylinders, held her stable until I took them out, then the wheel turned and off she rolled into the sea! I do not usually swear, but I am afraid I said "bugger" as she went right in! Next day Jamie Robinson from Knoydart came and dived down to attach ropes to the tractor and we were able to lift it out with the landing craft *Spanish John*. We had quite a carry-on, and I must admit I had to take an awful lot of stick about it, particularly from Colin. The electrics were all knackered and, though John Morris managed to get it going, I am afraid it has never been quite the same since.'

There is much giggling at this point. I also hear some of the other family members grumbling about Lawrence's absent-mindedness and his inability to shut gates, too, with annoying repercussions, particularly when bulls take full advantage and head for the heifers.

'Usually it took lots of us all day to unload puffer cargos. Coal was measured into a five-hundredweight bucket and then tipped into carts or trailers. The council owns the road on Muck unlike the ones on Canna and Rum. When it was finally tarred in 1974, it was puffers that brought all the materials. There were at least eight loads of chippings alone and they also brought a steamroller and tar machine. Soon after there was a big hike in the price of oil, so we were lucky to have had the road done before that.

'In 1974, the start of the building of Port Mor House Hotel, plus a new house for Bruce and Sandra Mathers, who were returning to Muck, was one of several massive projects taken on by my brother Ewen and this necessitated the delivery of 200 tonnes of blocks. It was a very important puffer event. The blocks arrived on two ex-Glenlight puffers, *Eldessa* and *Marsa*. Hugh Carmichael of Craignure on Mull had bought them and was still running them. One was on regular contract, carrying logs to the pulp mill at Corpach, but the other was for charter and brought many loads of materials to Muck.

'It was a terrible summer and due to this we had struggled with haymaking and made silage instead; nothing seemed to be going right. The blocks appeared from Torlundy lime quarry, delivered to the quayside at Corpach by tipper lorries, and from there had to be stacked by a party of islanders including Ewen onto pallets. They were then lowered into the hold, with the ship's derrick swinging wildly. Once in the hold, Bruce Mathers, who was still a tax inspector at that time, and journalist George Hume and me had to restack them. I think this was the hardest day's work I ever did, particularly as both my assistants could not have been said to be in the peak of physical fitness. Luckily, there was a day's grace before the blocks arrived in Muck. Then the process had to be reversed, and even with far more help it still took a day. One load didn't make it, as the puffer grounded. When the tide retreated, we took the tractors and trailers onto the beach and unloaded part of the cargo, thereby lightening the ship so we could get alongside when the tide rose again.

'In 1981, Hugh Carmichael offered me a bargain. During the Second

World War, a freighter carrying Welsh steam coal had run aground in the Sound of Mull and to lighten the load they had dumped it over the side. Divers guided Hugh to the right spot and he was able to lift much of it using a grab. The problem once it was lifted was selling it; I agreed to buy it at a good price and he delivered 50 tonnes to us. It had about 1 per cent limpet shells in it, but it burned with no smoke and it was very good. We took a load two years running.

'Once there were no further incentives from the Scottish Office for puffers, it really marked the end. They had served us so well and the last one, the *Eilean Easdale*, came in 1993 with a load of coal. They were largely replaced with landing craft, a retrograde step, as you could no longer buy in bulk, making everything relatively far more expensive.

'During my childhood, David MacBrayne's *Loch Mor* called at Eigg but did not come here, so we were totally reliant on our first boat and always had boatmen, as we continued to do until relatively recently. *Loch Mor* was built in 1935 probably as part of a scheme to get us out of the Depression of the '30s. She ran from Mallaig on a Monday via Eigg, Rum and Canna, and then went on to Lochboisdale in South Uist, where she connected with the *Loch Earn*, which had sailed out of Oban. At that point, our mail was still being taken and collected from Eigg. Our postal address was *Isle of Muck*, followed by *Isle of Eigg*. On 12 April 1965, we got our first mail delivery direct to the island brought by the *Loch Arkaig*, so our address thereafter just read *Isle of Muck* and our local post office was Mallaig instead. Previously the boatman going to Eigg would have had to walk about two miles to collect the post unless they'd got a lift. Charlie, our boatman, met his wife Katie on Eigg, where she was the postmistress. She had come from North Uist. A native Gaelic speaker, when she married Charlie she became very much a part of Muck life.

'We always had a house cow for milk; I could milk a cow from the age of nine. So if Father bought a dairy heifer from the sales in Oban, she would be delivered by Thomas Corson, the auctioneers, to the pier and put in a horsebox, then she would be taken to the *Loch Earn* sailing up to Lochboisdale. Though there was a specific Caledonian MacBrayne boat, the *Loch Broom*, geared up for livestock, it was not worth it for just a single animal. Our new cow in her horsebox would then be transferred at Lochboisdale by derrick onto the *Loch Mor* and then finally by this circuitous route she arriveed at Eigg, where we met her and transferred her to *Wave*.

'Sometimes rather than using our own boat for the whole journey to the mainland or elsewhere we would meet the *Loch Mor* at Eigg and the thing I remember best about her was that she had a very nice cafeteria; it was 7/6 for a good breakfast and they had white table-cloths. *Loch Mor* went on until 1965. The *Loch Arkaig*, a converted minesweeper, then replaced her.

'Soon after, the *Loch Arkaig* started coming to Muck on Wednesdays. I think my father had been putting pressure on Caledonian MacBrayne, as we really did need a boat. I was still in Australia at this point. *Loch Arkaig* was a bad timekeeper because she also carried out the service to Raasay and then came down the Sound of Sleat to Mallaig with ample opportunity for loss of time. She was also a bad boat to meet because she had big belting around her and this could damage *Wave* as she went alongside to ferry off either the cargo or passengers. We also often had to wait for ages in *Wave* because the *Loch Arkaig* was running so late, so it was a real timewaster. Remember we still had no steamer pier at this point.

'She wasn't very comfortable to travel on either. She was metal on top with wood below and she rolled pretty badly in any sea at all. I remember the nightmare of loading eight tonnes of fertiliser onto *Wave* from her. Almost all the bulk cargo in quantities too small to warrant using a puffer was usually brought directly by us from Arisaig or Mallaig in *Wave* at that period. There was not as much coming unless we had a particular building project. Some years we could do approximately 50 trips to the mainland. Colin still has to go quite often; he is really good on the boat, but really, compared to the past, *Wave* now does very little. Then the *Loch Arkaig* hit an underwater obstacle in Mallaig in 1979 during an exceptionally low tide and sank right alongside the pier. The second *Loch Mor* then replaced her.

'There was a big argument with Keith Schellenberg, the highly controversial owner of Eigg, who wanted to take over the boat service. Due to his track record and all his many problems on the island, no one else wanted him to do this. At one meeting about the future of boats for the Small Isles, I was quoted in the paper as saying, "The problem is MacBrayne's is eternal but Mr Schellenberg is temporal." I was not in the least bit embarrassed about it because it was true, and what a relief that this did not happen. Really, despite everything, MacBrayne's have done a good job. John Lorne Campbell, the owner of Canna, always wanted a large boat to go there. As he was a dreadful sailor and had built a really good pier, I think he felt that the least MacBrayne's could do was to send a good boat. He certainly was not in favour of Mr Schellenberg running a service. Campbell eventually persuaded MacBrayne's to allocate him a cabin when he sailed with them, as he really was very frightened of the sea; apparently he used to get on board the *Loch Mor* and just shut himself away in misery. It must have been rather difficult for him living there.

'*The Columba*, a boat that has since been totally refurbished and is now the exclusive *Hebridean Princess*, used to go to Canna to collect cattle; they had the ability to put pens aboard on the car deck. Bryan Walters was our boatman at that point and he was really excellent. We had a far more reliable service then than now because Bryan met the steamer in the open sea. Due to all the health-and-safety rules of today, the CalMac service on the *Loch Nevis* is often cancelled on dubious days with too much wind and swell to come into the harbour at Port. It still remains at the captain's discretion as to whether she will sail or not. By the time the *Loch Nevis* came on this run, Bryan was probably having to meet the boat five days a week; it was very time consuming and he had to time his lobster, prawn and crab fishing around the island with boat arrivals. We had a system whereby he met the CalMac boat, while I did most of the mainland runs. I did most of the livestock runs, too. At that time we also had another boatman, Simon Graves, the teacher's husband, who learned a great deal from Bryan. He also helped on the farm. He took over as boatman when there was another really terrible tragedy and we lost Bryan.'

Bryan Walters

Lawrence had advertised for a boatman for Muck and went to Iona to meet Bryan, who had applied for the job. It was a terrible day in February 1973, with snow and a gale, and he drove to Fionnphort on Mull in his Hillman Husky, intending to cross over to Iona.

'All the boats were off and the snow was quite deep, so I had to find somewhere to stay – almost impossible because most B&Bs were shut for the winter. I finally did find one, but it was so cold that I had to put all my clothes on to wear in bed, as the place was baltic. Next morning there was still no boat, so I hung around and waited and looked at the scenery. Then eventually in the afternoon a little red CalMac ferryboat appeared loaded up with cattle from Iona. Once they were off I leapt on and asked if they were going to Iona only to be told I had to wait for the next boat. Eventually, I got there. At that time Bryan's father owned the Columba and the Argyll hotels on Iona. They appeared to have had a pretty wild life there, though he did not really seem the wild type; anyway I liked him instantly. However, I did say I wanted him to be married before he came to Muck for the job. I suppose I thought this would help with the island's stability, but I am really not sure why I insisted on this. Bryan apparently rang up his girlfriend Clare, who was abroad at the time, and asked her if she would marry him! Bryan was quite phlegmatic and he didn't demand too much of life, and he was very versatile. Clare was a really great help to Jenny, and she also did lots of sheep work; though she didn't have dogs of trial-winning calibre, it all worked out very well indeed. They were both a huge asset to Muck and became very much a part of everything, with their two daughters, Emma and Ishy, and son, Marcus, until yet another cruel blow hit the island.'

The Walters family were on Muck for 30 years. During an interview with Tom Weir for his excellent television series *Weir's Way*, Bryan talked of his first meeting with Lawrence and of how he had rung up Clare to propose to her. Questioned about the dangers of fishing alone in such treacherous waters, he explained the vital importance of correctly assessing the conditions and never taking any risks. Lawrence, who is often reputed to be quite gung-ho with boats and weather conditions, says that Bryan was an excellent and safe seaman. The interview with Tom seems now all the more devastating.

On 18 September 2003, Donnie MacKinnon, shepherd Archie MacKinnon's son, was out trawling when he saw Bryan's own boat going round and round in circles just east of Muck. He rushed over and found that the engine was in gear but there was no sign of Bryan. There was a massive search. Lawrence was away at a sale in Fort William but got the terrible news and, weighed down heavily with dreadful, ominous fears, rushed home as soon as he could. By then the search included the lifeboat, a helicopter, any fishing boats that were in the area and some of the family on *Wave*. Bryan's body was never found. It was another savage blow for the tiny community and everyone struggled to come to terms with their loss.

On 3 December of the same year, on a beautiful clear winter's day, when the light in the Hebrides is like nowhere else on earth, there was a memorial service for Bryan. More than 100 people came to Muck, and the Small Isles Marquee was erected adjacent to Port Mor House, where they held a special service. *Sheerwater* took a large group out to the scene of the accident and in a moving ceremony beautiful floral wreaths were cast into the sea.

Clare and her family finally left Muck soon after but retain a part of Gallanach Cottage on the cliff top, where they return as often as they can, and all have remained very close to the MacEwens and Muck.

Tex Geddes

On 31 January 1967, just six months after he had returned from his travels in the southern hemisphere, Lawrence was shattered by the sudden death of his father. Charlie and Alick MacDonald, and Peter MacRae, their nephew, dug a grave on Lamb Island in the MacEwen graveyard next to the Bronze Age burial circle on a magnificent windswept headland overlooking Horse Island and Rum. Alasdair and Lawrence went over to Eigg to fetch a coffin. They met Eigg's new manager, Graham Murray, who Lawrence took to instantly, remembering how kind he was to them in their distraught state. The minister, family and various friends came over for the funeral on the *Western Isles*, chartered from Mallaig but, due to the atrocious gale-force winds, Ewen only managed to ferry the minister, lawyer and one other passenger ashore at Gallanach in the dinghy. It was too dangerous to risk rowing more; the rest of the passengers had to return on the boat. Commander MacEwen's death marked the start of a new era for Muck.

The year continued with Lawrence taking up lobster fishing around the island; Arthur, their bull, developed Red Water Fever, a tick-borne disease, the one and only time it has occurred on Muck; the coal puffer came in as usual with 50 tonnes of coal; and at Lochaber Show, farm workers Alick and Charlie received 40-Year Long Service medals from Donald Cameron of Locheil. The telephone finally reached Gallanach, even though the cable was meant to have been buried and still wasn't. Ewen was 21; and Alasdair, aged 28, was largely running the island. By the end of that year, foot-and-mouth disease was rife in the rest of the country, with over 1,000 cases in Scotland. It was also the year when Lawrence's auspicious chance meeting with Tex Geddes would eventually lead him to a life-changing event.

Lawrence and Alasdair often had to go to Mallaig in *Wave* to collect animal feed. Even at the end of the 1960s it was still a bustling herring port crammed with boats, and arrival in the morning made it hard to find a berth in the crowded harbour. 'It was always difficult, so we sometimes went in the night before, and got alongside. In the night, the boats returned and they often hemmed us in, but usually they were quite good at letting us out again. On this particular occasion, though neither of us were heavy drinkers we took off to the Marine Bar. At that time the bars all closed at ten and, just as we came out, we bumped into Tex Geddes from Soay, who had been in the Central Bar. We had not met him before, but we had heard so much about him, though none of it was very good. He was always portrayed as a real baddy, full of the devil. Well, we got chatting and eventually asked him to come back to the boat with us for a dram or two. It turned into a priceless night; he stayed with us for hours, regaling us with the gospel according to Tex. As we soon discovered, he was a great storyteller and his tales, true or otherwise, were hilarious. We both really liked him, as the craic was so good and he was such a character. Not much sleep was had by any of us – anyway, the tiny, short cots on *Wave* were very uncomfortable. We were certainly pretty hung-over when day broke. Tex had consumed at least a bottle of whisky on top of what he had imbibed in the Central Bar, and I'd certainly had far more than usual.

'Tex had met Gavin Maxwell during the war when they had been with Special Forces in Meoble at Loch Morar. There was a great story that only officers could get spirits during the war, but Tex told us that Maxwell would pass out drams to the other ranks around the door. They had built up an unsuccessful shark fishery on Soay together after the war but had finally been forced to pack it in. Now largely retired on Soay, Tex and his wife Jeanne kept a few sheep and cattle on the island. Tex also told us that his boat – also named *Shearwater* but spelled differently to the one that now serves the islands – was not much use for transporting livestock to and from Soay, so somewhere during the small hours in a haze of alcohol we agreed to help him. As far as I was concerned, it was a chance for another adventure.

'From when I first met Tex up until 1975 when he acquired a boat called *Petros* that could transport cattle, he was very dependent on us with *Wave* to take animals on and off the island. On one occasion, I remember transporting a load of calves back to Muck; a storm blew up, so we had to go into shelter on Rum. We had to leave the calves on the boat while we holed up in a bothy for two days. By the time we finally reached Muck, *Wave* required a serious amount of cleaning.'

In his obituary of Tex Geddes, Charles MacLean describes him as 'a character of near-heroic stature on the west coast of Scotland'. He was a sergeant in the Seaforth Highlanders, specialising in amphibious warfare, and even by the time he met Maxwell, when he was just 24, his reputation inspired awe. MacLean writes: 'He was an accomplished knife-thrower and bayonet fencer, a boxer, a former rum-runner in Newfoundland, an orphaned lumberjack "tree monkey" whose father had been blown up while dynamiting a log jam and who had been expelled from school at the age of 12 as "unmanageable".' Controversy surrounded this man who seemed to have left his mark wherever he went. When the shark fishery on Soay failed, he and Jeanne bought the island from the receiver. However, the remaining islanders had requested evacuation and Tex and Jeanne became embroiled in a lengthy legal battle over the abandoned assets and any improvements made to the island crofts. They eventually had to sell off part of the island to fund this and it had been many years before they were able to buy it back. Amusingly, when the local authorities threatened to stop all postal and telephone services to Soay, in order to put pressure on them Tex asked his friends to keep sending registered mail and parcels, the latter often only containing stones. He was certainly not going to lose the mail boats without a fight, and he succeeded. Historian Margaret Fay Shaw of neighbouring Canna, herself a colourful character with a passion for the Hebrides, knew him for much of her life and said, 'Tex was a great storyteller and important as such. He was also immensely kind, and had that hunger for life and fun that is essential if you are to make a go of living in these islands. The Hebrides needs more people like Tex Geddes. So does the world.' Small wonder then that he made such an impression on the young Lawrence and went on to become a friend for the rest of his life.

Six months after he had first encountered Tex in Mallaig, Lawrence finally went to Soay to take a bull. He met Tex's wife Jeanne for the first time. She had been educated at Cheltenham Ladies College and had grown up in the south of England. Bleak Soay must have been a far cry from the life she was used to. And there was another person in the party squashed up against Tex, who had an eye for the ladies; Lawrence says he was instantly 'dazzled' by her. This was Jenny Davies, another girl from the deep south, but someone who would end up fitting into Muck as if she was born to it.

Jenny's Story

'I was born in Cheshire. My father was a civil engineer. I think it's fair to say that he was a very autocratic person and my mother, who was a sweet, loving soul, was quite frightened of him. When I was very young, we moved to Ghana, where he became Director of Public Works when they were building a huge dam and a harbour at Takoradi. They were still using flit boats to get goods ashore, so the new harbour was very important. I was the middle of three girls and have a younger brother, and had a younger sister. I frequently had to look after my younger siblings, but as I have always adored babies and children I was quite happy about this. I was often asked to babysit. I was brought up to always believe that my parents were right whatever; this was to have repercussions in the future. While my sisters were regarded as bright, somehow my father appeared to think that I was less so and that my schooling was not worth the effort. In Ghana, getting us there was also difficult and we needed a driver, so usually I just did not go. During my time in Sussex, I used to go to a riding school and adored Rosemary Marquand and her daughter, who ran it, and we became extremely close. When my father eventually announced we were moving on to South Africa, Rosemary said to my parents that if they wanted I could remain with her instead. Had I only known this then, I would definitely have agreed to stay. I would have loved it. I was I suppose a bit of a loner out on a limb and I always did exactly what my father told me.

'The family moved to Mafeking in Cape Province, where Father was very occupied building the new capital of Botswana, Gaborone. We lived in a very grand area called the Imperial Reserve, a British enclave inside South Africa, consisting of office buildings and houses. There was no apartheid inside the Reserve, so things were very different. Eventually, I went to Johannesburg to college to do a secretarial course and got a job with the government for three years with the Attorney General in Mafeking and also worked with Seretse Khama, who was high up in the government there and eventually became Botswana's first president. In the meantime, the most extraordinary thing had happened. Father had seen an advertisement in *The Times* for a croft on the Hebridean island of Soay. On his way to New

York for a meeting with the World Monetary Fund to try and secure
finances for Gaborone, he had taken a detour to Soay and bought the
croft from the Arthurs. Soay, as it still remains today, had no roads,
little or no communications and no regular boat service. It was bleak,
barren and still very primitive.

'Now, of course, he needed someone to look after his new acquisition. Things were becoming hard in South Africa and there were
considerable issues with apartheid, so it was not ideal for me to stay
anyway. Despite the fact that he appeared to think little of me, he
decided that I should go and look after the croft.

'I was 20 when I arrived on Soay and to begin with I stayed with
Tex and Jeanne. They were both incredibly kind to me, and Jeanne
in particular took me under her wing. Tex was a likeable rogue and
had an incredible twinkle in his eye. They both had a great sense of
humour; she clearly adored him. We had so much fun together. Their
son Duncan, aged 14, was at Portree School.

'Soay had been evacuated in 1952. There was a primitive water
system, but this was extremely spasmodic. It was supposed to be
pumped up to the house with a hydram that often failed, and we had
to pump it with a petrol pump for much of the time. We used to go
out fishing together, with Tex at the helm of the boat, while Jeanne
hauled and I baited the creels. We cut peats and we gathered whelks,
and we also had livestock on the common grazing land. The shore on
Soay is very rocky and tricky, with only the odd patch of sand visible
during very low tides. We collected copious amounts of driftwood
from the shore for the fire. The mail boat, the *Ruby*, came in once a
month and also brought us provisions, so I suppose we were pretty
isolated. The Geddes had a couple of ponies and the idea was to get
them to work, bringing seaweed up off the shore and helping with
the heavy jobs, but they did not do much. We made hay and grew
potatoes and vegetables, and I made more lazy beds. At point
the island leant towards farming; fishing was an activity we did to

supplement this. By the time I left for the second time, the fishing had taken over.

'Tex had some wild Shetland sheep, but he was already getting some tups from Lawrence on Muck in a bid to try to improve the stock. We also had a few Shetland cattle on the island that had come from Jimmy Dean at the Department of Agriculture at Knocknagael in Inverness. There was no proper pier on Soay and only a rock that was used to offload goods or livestock. I loved it from the outset.'

Jenny's father even sent a tank of rainbow trout for a distant hill loch where red-throated divers nested. The logistics of carrying these must have been a nightmare. He also sent Sitka spruce, all of which needed to be planted. At one point a batch of white turkeys also appeared. Jenny just obeyed orders. Soay and all it embraced was as far removed from life as a PA in the future government of Botswana as it was possible to imagine.

'Rum had a dairy at that time; I got a calf from there and called her Violet. She had a rough coat – I think she was a dairy Shorthorn cross – and we eventually milked her. Jeanne had both Saanen and Toggenberg goats, and we milked them too. We had them tethered and also used their milk for rearing pet lambs. Tex, who had set up the failed basking shark fishery with Gavin Maxwell on Soay just after the war, now worked fishing for lobsters and crabs. I had taken a wonderful cairn terrier, Katie, with me. The runt of the litter, she turned into a faithful and loving little companion. I also acquired a collie from Glenbrittle on Skye. I was quite happy on Soay and just got on with the job in hand, which was to run my father's croft.'

Little did Jenny know that Tex Geddes, full of the devil, probably had it in his mind all along that she would perhaps be the perfect companion and wife for Lawrence MacEwen, the young laird of Muck. Perhaps he hoped that things would take off when Lawrence appeared with stock for the island. However nothing to do with Lawrence was ever going to be that straightforward. And the young laird was certainly not as forward with women as Tex was. On one occasion when a tenacious and amorous young woman was chasing him, he is reputed to have taken to the sea to avoid her.

'The first time I met Lawrence he was clean-shaven. He had a lot of ginger hair and had startling blue eyes, and he was obviously very shy, not very good with women. He didn't seem to pay me much attention. He came quite often to collect calves and we spent a bit of time together and really got on, but I didn't even think he fancied me. He always seemed more passionate about farming. Then I had a set-to with my father; he kept saying he was coming back to run the croft himself. I am not really sure what happened to this day, but we had an awful row and in the end he said I should leave. He was very dominating. It was complicated, really sad, and so I left and got a job in Inverness looking after a family, who I was with for some time. Once the children no longer needed me, I looked after other children in the area and then a man called David Maitland, who had lost his wife in a car crash, advertised for help and I went to look after his children.

'He had twin boys and a younger son, and one thing led to another. I was very naive and after some time he said he could not live without me and asked me to marry him. So I took on his boys, whom I loved dearly by now, and soon was expecting my daughter, Sarah. But it all proved to be impossible. There were many things, but in the end it was the fact that he did not pay his bills, though he was well able to, and I could not bear it. By this stage my parents were leaving Soay, so I returned. I took Sarah, and David's sons came with me too. I was not thinking of leaving permanently, I just wanted to give him a chance to sort things out. I really couldn't leave the boys; I wanted them to have a good education and at that point Portree School was excellent. The worst thing was that he insisted soon after that because Sarah was so young Soay was not a good place for her and demanded she return to stay with him. I was devastated. She was with him for a few months. This was a terrible period for me, especially as I still had the boys, which was so crazy. Eventually, she came back after she had been sent to a convent and the nuns recommended she needed to be with her mother. It was wonderful and I taught her for a year myself and then finally Highland Council did up the school on Soay and we ended up with a young teacher when Donita Copeland from Orkney came to teach Sarah and Tex Geddes' two grandchildren. I suppose I blazed the trail and got the school open again, so there were three of them. The first year Donita taught in one of the old outbuildings that Father had done up till the schoolroom was finally completed. I think Highland Council wanted to ensure I was not going to just go off.

'We did have a very happy time in Soay, but I was terribly short of money. As David did not sort things out, I filed for a divorce. Then there was a dreadful tragedy when my younger sister Karen, aged 20, was killed in a car accident in Sussex. My brother Oliver was driving and was seriously hurt and badly traumatised. We were all totally devastated, particularly my poor mother. Afterwards Oliver just wanted to return to the tranquillity of Soay. Eventually, he began to fish with Tex and he has been on Soay ever since.

'In the end, the boys returned to their father, but we have remained very close. They recently came to Muck to celebrate my daughter Sarah and her husband Willie MacRae's 20th Wedding Anniversary. The twins appreciated the problems, but his youngest son had a lot of pressure put on him – blood is thicker than water, so totally understandably he went with his father. When David Maitland eventually died, we all moved on.'

Soon after, Lawrence began to appear on a regular basis. As long as the weather was half decent, he sailed to Soay on *Wave* with firewood and provisions for Jenny and she found herself looking forward more and more to his arrival, though she never knew quite when this might be. Red-blond hair, brilliant blue eyes, weather-beaten and fit, as he sailed across the sea to Soay he must have appeared even more like a Viking at this stage. They often used to use a dinghy to go to visit other neighbours on the island and during one of these forays Lawrence apparently recited 'Lord Ullin's Daughter', a tragic romantic Victorian poem written by Thomas Campbell and set on Mull.

'Your experiences make you the person you are. If I had got together with Lawrence the first time around, then maybe I would not have been able to cope with all the things that I have had to subsequently deal with on Muck. Lawrence was light relief. Sarah was now eight, she really liked him and they have always been great pals; she has treated him totally as a father and vice versa.'

Jenny's divorce was a slow process. She says that the prospect of marriage to Lawrence was never discussed. 'Why?' I ask her.

'Well, he didn't really ever ask me. I didn't know much about Muck, though he talked about it a lot, but I certainly knew how much he truly loved the island. I mean, he really has been in his element here, hasn't he? It is a way of life and not a job. I was a bit worried about how I would fit in. I had the most frightful inferiority complex, due to Father. The MacEwens as a family had largely run Muck and I was just full of anticipation about it all.

'My divorce was still not through, but despite this Lawrence kept making the three and a quarter-hour sea journey from Muck. I had fallen for him by this stage, but he still had not asked me to marry him. He was charming, but shy and not very demonstrative, so I was never quite sure what he was thinking.'

The Wedding

'I suppose it did all begin with Tex Geddes. I took a bull over to Soay and will always remember meeting Jenny. Tex had her pushed into the corner next to him at the kitchen table. Here was Jenny Davies, a girl from the south. I was totally dazzled by her. However, I was in no hurry to get married and so I suppose I was rather slow off the mark, and very shy, and anyway Mother was still at home and so perhaps I did not yet really need a wife.' He laughs, and that familiar gesture automatically applied when things are slightly uncomfortable comes to the fore, as he brings his huge hand up alongside his face and casts his eyes down. The truth of the matter is he had probably not had much practice in wooing women; as well as 'dazzled', a word he always uses when describing the meeting that was to change his life, he was probably overawed.

'I saw Jenny on numerous trips to Soay, and I think she probably did consider me, but I was far too slow off the mark – my brother Ewen was always far quicker at that side of things. However, I did keep thinking of excuses for going over there. When Jenny's father came back and took over Soay, she was pushed out and she goes off and becomes a childminder in Inverness. I went to see her there; I drove north from a calf sale in Stirling in my Hillman Husky. It was a freezing cold winter night and I had nowhere to sleep, so dozed in the car, but because it was so cold I had to keep driving again a bit further to get the car warmed up and then have another little sleep. Yes, I am sure she considered me then. But soon she got a job looking after the children of a man who had just been widowed. He was simply not coping at all and, as you know, Jenny has always been highly competent at child minding. Then he asked her to marry him and she did, as she could see he was struggling and she loved his boys. I was really shocked and upset when I heard about it. In fact, I was devastated.'

Lawrence had missed the boat. However, to cover up what he refers to as his stupidity, he counters it by saying he had other possibilities. Fate clearly played a part in his love affair with the 'dazzling' Jenny and, when things failed with her husband, Lawrence was certainly quick to ensure that he was not going to miss his chance a second time when distraught she returned to Soay.

Lawrence's mother Edith had died in 1977 and, by way of an excuse, he says that the pressure was now on to get married. Even now things were far from straightforward, as Jenny was still not divorced. More patience was needed and the forays across the sea from Muck to Soay continued, despite horrendous weather at times.

'I used to look for excuses to go over to Soay to see her. As if I did not have more than enough work to do with our own flock of sheep, I used to go and help with the ones on Soay. They had some very wild moorit-coloured Shetlands, and the ground was very boggy with scrub and a lot of deep heather, so it was very hard to gather and anyway the sheep took little notice of dogs. Some swam out to sea, while others got stuck in the bogs. We wanted to introduce some Cheviot blood to them to improve them. I wanted to get all the males out, but it was very hard going because on the east end the terrain was impossible. Perhaps at the west end it was ever so slightly easier because the sheep were concentrated around the cliff tops where the grass was greener due to the guano. We went in a line and tended to have a person furthest inland slightly ahead to stop the sheep breaking back into the centre of the island. Soay is like an hourglass. Finally, we would arrive at the fank in an old house where a temporary fence down the shore stopped them going any further. On one occasion, while I was helping Tex, we finally did manage to catch all the old tups. We just had to slaughter them there and then, and dig a hole for them, and then had to castrate the young ones to stop them spreading their genes; any ewes amongst them were shorn at the same time. We never achieved a 100 per cent gather, but we did pretty well, considering the obstacles. Later on in the summer we did the same again and had to tie the legs of the lambs to transport them out to *Wave* in the dinghy and on to Muck and eventual sale. In the autumn we provided Soay with Cheviot tups in a bid to improve the stock and make them a little more domesticated. We tried to do the same thing at the end of the island where Jenny lived, but these beasts were so wild it was impossible to get them to flock and we ended up having to run them down individually.

'Going to Soay was a big adventure. Jenny was always providing cups of tea and cake, and manpower by way of the children: the boys Neil, Lewis and Angus, and Sarah too, all helped.'

Meanwhile, during all these ovine excursions, Lawrence was still patiently waiting for Jenny to be a free woman once again. Finally when he was able to ask her to marry him they set a date for the end of September. Suspicious, I ask if this was to coincide with events in the farming calendar. He laughs.

'No, Polly, this was nothing to do with the farming calendar, it was because she was still married! We planned the wedding for 25 September. It was all going to be very quiet, but unfortunately Jeanne Geddes had spilt the beans to a pet reporter, someone she knew who worked in the business.'

Lawrence, who is a very modest and paradoxically shy man, is certainly not going to explain that his wedding and indeed many of his other activities on Muck were frequently of considerable interest to the press, mainly for the reason that the 'Laird of Muck' makes a good newspaper-selling headline, something that has often rankled. Muck being in the ownership of one family, and well run for so long, is another unique aspect. Throughout his life Lawrence has dealt well with the many journalists and television reporters who have come flocking to the island, but other family members have understand-ably found it a great deal harder.

'He probably made masses of money selling the story to the vari-ous newspapers. There must have been some good headlines: "The Laird of Muck Sails for his Bride" or "Lady Muck Comes Home" and other similar things. As the date neared, the weather deteriorated. Nothing was going to be straightforward. However, Jenny had made all this amazing food for the party afterwards and so we did not have much leeway. If we postponed things for more than a day, all the food would have been wasted, as there was nothing like refrigeration on Soay and you know how wonderfully she caters. So we postponed the wedding for a day –in fact, the *Daily Mail* even offered to fly Ewen, my best man, and I out by helicopter. I did not want to do that, as other people were coming.

'It was also going to be Ian Forbes the minister's last official event, as he was retiring on 1 October. He was such a nice man, and I was worried he would not get there.

'Another problem now occurred, as the coal puffer was due in Muck the day of the rescheduled wedding and this meant that all the men would have to stay on the island to unload it. So Ewen and I set sail for Soay with a handful of female passengers. Meanwhile my sister Catriona and her husband David White and the minister came out on the *Western Isles* from Mallaig with Jenny's close friend Brenda Watt from the Mallaig post office, plus a few others. Anyway, they finally reached Soay, but there were hardly any people from Muck, as many of the women were bad sailors. The weather was so uncertain they had stayed behind frightened of becoming really seasick. When the minister, who had small feet, arrived, he had forgotten his shoes. Jenny's father, William Davies, who had huge feet by comparison, lent him a pair of his and Jenny always remembers how these big shoes stuck out underneath his robes, it was very funny. But the funniest thing was that Ewen, all dressed up in his formal kilt outfit, had forgotten his shoes too, so he was to be seen at the wedding wearing a pair of green wellies.

'Jenny and I were both very daunted when we saw that there were six helicopters that had brought all the press. There is no church on Soay and the service was in a very rudimentary outhouse, with everyone squashed in. The press all stood in a line at the back. The weather was not too bad then, but a storm was coming in from the west. After the wedding, we trooped down to the headland and had photographs taken, and once this was done the helicopters all took off again. It was indeed daunting and it was the last thing we wanted. Jenny certainly did not want it at all; we wanted a nice, quiet wedding, particularly as she had been married before. Very appropriately, she wore navy blue. Then we had a lovely reception.

'Jenny had packed everything up ready to leave, but in the meantime Ewen had disappeared. He had clearly been taken hostage by Tex and his whisky. The weather was now changing again and it was high time we left; the light was beginning to go and we had no wheelhouse or lights on *Wave* at that time. Ewen was meant to bring the boat round from the next bay to collect us, but there was no sign of him whatsoever. So we stood about like idiots for what seemed ages and still there was not a sign, and the wind was building up more and more. In the end Catriona and David nobly brought *Wave* round to the side of the island in front of Jenny's house. The bay there was very dodgy, with lots of rocks, many of which lurked underwater; it was far from easy. Then we had to load up all Jenny's belongings.

'Finally, someone went off to extricate Ewen, who had been totally led astray by Tex and who was now blazing drunk. Of course he was no help whatsoever and, needless to say, Tex was unrepentant. Ewen is a big chap, but we somehow managed to drag him into the dinghy and got him onto *Wave*. We had a big green tarpaulin over the hold and we literally shoved him underneath it. We were taking Nessie Jones back to Muck too, and she was also well oiled. She hated the sea and was in a poor state, so we shoved her under the tarpaulin too. Poor Jenny had to look after Nessie's two children, as they were being so dreadfully seasick. In fact, nearly everyone was being sick because it really was exceedingly rough.

'Halfway across we saw a helicopter and thought perhaps someone had sent out a search party for us, but luckily that was not the case, it must have been heading elsewhere. It was some journey back home. Once we passed Rum, it got very squally indeed, with waves coming over us, so I kept tapping David White's shoulder as I peered out through the gloom and he would then throttle back to avoid the sea coming right over the bow and inundating us. Ewen didn't stir till we finally reached Gallanach, where we could see a light on in Gallanach Cottage on the headland. We were meant to go into Port, but that was out of the question due to the harbour being so tricky in darkness. Meanwhile the islanders were waiting for us at Port and had tied all sorts of tin cans and paraphernalia to the back of a tractor and trailer ready to transport us to Gallanach by road. However, this was not to be. It was amazing that we somehow managed to get ourselves ashore in one piece. By now Ewen had sobered up a bit – well, I remember he was able to at least move unaided.

'When we got into the house, the fire had been lit by Clare Walters and she had made it all welcoming for us. She had also made us a wonderful card – it is very beautiful and I was very struck by it; we still have it. We were meant to have a day off between the wedding and a party on Muck, but that was also not to be due to us postponing the wedding. Next evening the ceilidh commenced in the shed at Gallanach and people came from all over the place, including Eigg, and there was also a party from Rum, who we had invited at the last minute. I was totally worn out by now, but Ewen redeemed himself by stepping in and doing a superb job as master of ceremonies, ensuring that all went well. We had music and dancing and copious amounts of food until the small hours.'

Clare Walters remembers it well and her description of this celebratory ceilidh, and indeed many others on Muck, is typical of so many of these unique Western Isles events – and like so many I myself clearly remember in Ardnamurchan. Impressive amounts of superb home-made food beautifully laid out on long tables as the band strikes up, yet for a time people are too shy to dance. Men lurking gingerly outside, around byre doors in huddled groups, boosting their courage and testosterone levels with swigs from omnipresent bottles in readiness for their debut on the dance floor. Dark shadows lurking against walls as someone has a pee while perhaps also participating of a fly cigarette. Inside, exhausted babes and children have run themselves into the ground with excitement and finally collapse in slumber. They lie in prams or peaceful corners, often curled up on grubby bedding, totally oblivious to the noise and the music. The wild dancing that often left bruises on arms and legs as men flung the unwary madly across the floor. And always the obligatory handful of drunks, lurching about like sailors in a storm-force sea, making amorous proposals and causing amusement to begin with but diminishing to annoyance, followed by a comatose state.

Clare too clearly remembers their fears for the wedding party as they sailed home from Soay in dreadful, dangerous weather conditions: 'By the end of that wedding party and the events that led up to it, we were all totally shattered. Jenny was thrown right in at the deep end and shortly after this accompanied me to one of the cattle sales in Oban.'

Lawrence's mentor and dear friend Haig Douglas sent them an amusing telegram that simply read:

To the Laird and Lairdess of Muck,
Congratulations on making it. Apologies for absence. May you have many doglets to round up the Soay sheep.
Haig, Hillslap Castle

'I have been fortunate as, though I had plenty of other possibilities, no one could have done more for this island than Jenny, and Colin has done so well with Ruth, too. It's amazing; we really could not have done better. Ruth was simply made for Muck. Mary is so very lucky with Toby as well. These are the big things.'

And Lawrence's hand comes up to his face again as he looks down, thinking about it all, clearly emotional, though he could never put it into words.

Arable Matters

'In the early days we followed a seven-year rotation, which was fairly standard on Scottish farms at that time. Four years grass, followed by lea oats, followed by roots, then oats under-sown with grass. This usually meant we had one field of roots, mainly swedes, for feeding to the housed cattle. But we always grew about two acres of potatoes for sale in Mallaig, where we had an agent called Donald Morrison who supplied many of the fishing boats. The fishermen wanted either Kerr's Pinks or Golden Wonders, but both had their problems. Whilst the Kerr's Pinks had a good yield, they were susceptible to blight, and the Golden Wonders, though much more disease resistant, needed an exceptional year to yield a decent crop. However, Donald paid us a premium for these types of tatties. The swedes were grown on ridges and, together with the tatties, received all the dung from the housed cattle. For most of my life, we have used a precision seeder that sowed a single seed at a time at varying distances. But we still hand-hoed the crop in July not only to space it properly but also to get rid of the weeds and give it a good start. The main issue with swedes was the increasing problem of geese, as numbers on the island started to escalate, and this sadly finally forced us to give them up altogether.

'The oats were cut with a binder and for years we had a Danish JF machine that was able to handle the common problem of tangled crops. It needed two operators, one of whom always sat on the binder. Each sheaf was bound with twine and made into stooks by hand, four to each one. Due to the strong wind here, we also had to tie the tops with a band of straw. Providing that there were no thistles in the sheaves, stooking was a very pleasant job and less physically challenging than making hayricks. If the weather was reasonable, the stooks remained out for about ten days, but it was often far longer. Then they were forked into trailers with one skilled person on top building the load with the butts of the sheaves out. Then the trailer was reversed into the barn and the load forked onto a "dash" or one separate section of sheaves. To build safely, the centre of the dash had to be kept really solid and heavier people were at a premium. My mother, who was a little overweight, was usually roped in to do the building. If the weather was poor, we had yet another process to undertake, hutting. The huts were built by hand with a tripod in the centre and the sheaves were placed again with the butts out and on a slope, so that the rain ran off. This also helped to protect the grain from crows and seagulls. The hut was finished with a single stook on top of the tripod and then secured with ropes.

'During the winter we threshed every week, and this needed three people. The thresher was on wheels, so it could be moved to the best position in the barn. One person forked the sheaves to the "table" on the thresher, one fed them into the drum, whilst a third removed the bags of grain and the straw. Growing corn this way was very labour-intensive, and when the opportunity arose to get a combine harvester I thought it was worth a try.

'Where there are farmers, there are farm suppliers, and over my lifetime there have been a number of individuals who have realised that farming on Muck is not just like farming down the road, and these people have bent over backwards to help us. People such as Donald Forbes of Foyers Services, Bob MacWalter of Harbro, Hugh MacLean of Hamilton Bros, Derek Sutherland of the Agricultural Training Board and Sandy Russell of Farm Services, Elgin (now Ravenhill). When we decided to try a combine, it was to Sandy Russell we turned. He found us one on a farm near Inverness, an ageing Massey Ferguson 788. It was in good working order, but as we shall see later the brakes were less than perfect. He got it loaded on a transporter on the chosen day in July and set off for Corpach, where there was a loading bank at the old Auction Mart. The railway bridges between Corpach and Arisaig are 12 ft 6 in., so there was nothing for it but to take it off the low loader and drive it. Knowing this, I had set out from Muck with David Jones, who was to take the wheel, with Bruce Mathers to assist. Because the combine table was 10 feet and much of the road was then still single track, we had a police escort too. Everything went fine until we reached the steep hill above Loch nan Uadh. The road was wider here, but the police car stopped on the inside of the wooded bend. When the car came in sight, Davy slammed on the brakes, but he could not stop in time without ramming the bank opposite. The police car survived.

'Once in Arisaig, we had another close shave. A friend of Murdo Grant had purchased a very small landing craft onto which Davy reversed the combine. It fitted, but only just, as the "table" had only an inch to spare on either side of the ramp. Once on Muck, we grounded on the beach with a rising tide and Davy drove our new elderly combine across the sand and into the barn. Later Sandy Russell came out to give us instruction and Davy did a fantastic job keeping the machine going, though our results were very mixed. The oat crop had to be much riper than if it had been cut with the binder, so it was later in the autumn before we could set to work. We stored the grain in a bulk bin treated with Propcorn, an acid preservative. Sometimes a lot of the crop was flat on the ground before it was ripe, and though the combine could still cut it the birds were as much of a problem as in the days of stooks. When we lost David Jones, I decided to call it a day. Bruised oats mixed with high protein nuts ceased to be on the menu of the Muck sheep and cattle.

'However, Jenny was very enthusiastic about growing corn and after a few years she insisted we try again, just in a very small way. She actually strimmed all the grain herself and then we did all the binding by hand, then bought another binder from a man in Acharacle and we did more and more each year. Then we started to cut it with the hay mower and used a baler. We still have a small square baler, and if Colin is persuaded to make a bit of hay then we use that.

'Gradually, we cut down on haymaking and made pit silage using a side-mounted forage harvester and blew the grass into trailers in the old method. By then, everyone else had gone over to big bale silage, though I was very reluctant to change due to the financial outlay. Eventually, I thought that we ought to as well, especially as the first year we used a lot of plastic bags and it was not entirely successful. So I called in Hughie MacLean, who until recently was the main salesman for Hamilton Brothers, leading suppliers of agricultural and construction machinery in the west. He has travelled the length and breadth of the Western Isles and knows everyone. He is a marvellous man and is a hugely popular character with a great deal to say. No one could have been more helpful or enthusiastic over the years; he still comes over from time to time to our Open Day and has become a very good friend. We bought a smart red Welgar baler and he brought it over on the landing craft *Spanish John* and showed Barnaby Jackson, one of the islanders who has been here now for some time, how to operate it. Soon after we got the Parmiter bale wrapper and once again Hughie came over. Now we have the whole caboodle and find it all much easier than hay, given the erratic weather. Silage-making suits us much better, though of course it's not so much fun to make.

Catriona's Wedding

'Catriona went to Girton College, Cambridge. She was following in mother's footsteps, studying biology, and like her, too, she is a real farmer at heart. It was during her time there that she met David White, a computer programmer. Her first job was as a biologist working with the Lea Valley Conservancy in East London, and I think she became very concerned about the effect of water pollution on fauna and flora at that time.

'When I came home after a long stint in the southern hemisphere, I thought Catriona would be thrilled to see me after a year away and I hoped we would have time to do things together. However, she had other things on her mind and had brought David to Muck for the first time. I had not met him before and did not even know much about his existence, so my nose was put out of joint.

'They soon announced they were to be married, and on 21 June 1968 their wedding took place at home. It was another of the early catering events we undertook here. I remember that Catriona's friends had made amazing papier-mâché lobsters and lots of lovely mobiles of cut out birds to hang around the barn. Alick MacDonald, who had been left a legacy by Father, had just moved to Tobermory and we had agreed to take his furniture over there for him on *Wave*. So we combined the furniture removal with a voyage to Luing to fetch a wooden floor that we laid in the barn to dance on. After we had offloaded the furniture, Alick treated us to a posh lunch at the Mishnish Hotel – not that the Mishnish ever did a posh lunch. The floor we got on Luing was very good and we used it for many years until we finally made our own sectional floor that we still often use for dances and ceilidhs when we are using the farm sheds.

'The reception was in the byre and we filled in the gutters with sleepers so people didn't fall in and hurt themselves, especially after they'd had a few drams. The *Daily Record* came out to cover the event, but luckily they were the only members of the press, unlike at our wedding, when there was so much interest. The only sadness for us all was that Father was not present.

'At 4 a.m. as the dance finished the idea was for Catriona and David to sneak away in secret for their honeymoon. They were to take my 12-foot dinghy over to Arisaig, but they could not get the Seagull outboard started and had to mess around for ages. Some of the guests strolled out of the barn to clear their heads on the beach and spotted them, so the game was given away. Eventually, they managed to get the engine started and set off for the mainland. It was not very calm, but the weather was coming from behind them so they were quite safe, though it still took some time to cross 12 miles of open water.'

The Great Rum Fire

In 1969, the future of Muck was under serious discussion, as Catriona had just got married and Alasdair was leaving to go to Hardiston Farm. Tex and Jeanne Geddes' son Duncan from Soay had come to help on the farm as a student. Many similar young people came to the island but were only paid pocket money. Lawrence told me that Duncan used to supplement this by borrowing his little boat and lobster creels. He often stayed out very late, causing Lawrence's mother much worry. Lawrence recalls that Duncan was a 'super chap'. With red hair, he was 'quite fiery but was another great worker. He was very good with the hayfork.' This comment makes me giggle because it is a statement I have heard Lawrence make about several islanders past and present. It is clearly a way he judges whether someone is to be taken seriously or not.

That year they'd had a very dry winter. Little did they know that it was to have serious repercussions. The Nature Conservancy Council – now Scottish Natural Heritage – owned the island of Rum during this period. It had planted 250,000 trees on the island in the north-east sector and because the island had been six weeks without rain instructions came from Edinburgh to burn a firebreak between the inhabited area and the hill for protection. Lawrence takes up the story.

'There had been no burning on Rum for at least 12 years. Most of the hill pasture consisted of purple moor grass, molinia and nardus grasses that, by the end of the winter, were all dead and dry. The peat had dried out as well, so when they tried to burn the firebreak their fire got right into the peat and smouldered and was impossible to extinguish. During the night, it spread to the open hill. Next day we were amazed to see this vast mushroom cloud rising over the east end of Rum. It was how I imagine a nuclear cloud might look. The fire was heating the air so dramatically that, even though it was a calm day, as it rose it was sucking in cooler air from the surrounding area and by evening the air current had reached gale force and was helping the fire run amok. We rang Rum to get an update and to see what we could do to help. It really did look dramatic. By now, it was evening. We had been lifting turnips all day and had seen it getting worse. The wardens George MacNaughton and Peter Wormall must have been very worried indeed. Next day a party of eight of us, including some visitors and Duncan Geddes, set off in *Wave* and arrived there by 10 a.m. George met us at the pier and took us up through the glen in his Land Rover, then we had to walk half a mile across the charred, smoking landscape. We were each given fire beaters. When we reached the front, we started at sea level and worked up the hill, leapfrogging as we climbed the hill. We beat the fire up the hill as hard as we could. We got on very well, considering the heat was so intense, but really it was probably pointless. The flames were leaping very high and every now and again I could see this orange ball of the sun through the dense smoke. Most of the time we could not even see the sky, with the dark smoke right overhead totally engulfing us. There were skeletons of trees everywhere. It was not, in fact, the trees that were the problem, as they were very small at this point; the fuel for the fire was the dry moorland grasses. I will always remember a crew appearing from Eigg in mid-afternoon armed with knapsack sprayers filled with water: frankly, we might as well have peed on the fire, for all the good that was going to do. It was quite funny.

'It was absolutely exhausting work, the hottest thing I ever remember, and we were all totally parched. We did not even have any water to drink. We should have drunk the water in the knapsack sprayers. And we had been beating the fire hard for hours on end. George eventually appeared through the smoke and told us to stop because the fire was burning from the Kilmory end and the two areas were about to meet up. Wearily, we made our way down the hill to George's house, where he dished us out some beers. I have never ever had a better can of beer in my life.

'I think in the end it was the lochs and rivers that stopped the fire spreading to the whole island. I think about a quarter of the island must have burned – say about 10,000 acres. Despite being burned, some of the trees survived. The pines were all killed, but the alders and some other hardwoods sprouted from the bottom again.

'An interesting sequel to all this was that the island wanted to give us something for our efforts and they eventually gave us a Rum pony – Rum Beauty – a grey mare from their famous stud. She was in foal and we went across to fetch her in *Wave*. She was a middle-aged brood mare and had some foals and we kept her for a while. Eventually, we sold her on to Willie MacPherson on Skye. We took her in *Wave* to Loch Eynort and, as there is no pier there, we managed to push her up the ramp and into the sea and swam her ashore. This was the only time we ever pushed a pony into the sea. Though she was a nice beast, she was rather a heavy type, unlike Guamag, another of our mares. But of course I really must not look a gift horse in the mouth!'

Ponies

'Ponies eat a lot of grass and it can be at times a little bit of a struggle to turn them into cash. I think our Highland ponies are a great interest, and I know Ruth likes them, but Colin isn't so keen because of their grass consumption; I am sure they might disappear when our stallion, Strathmashie Seumas Mhor, finally turns up his toes. We do have some lovely ponies, though; however, some of them do really well once they reach the mainland. We sold a stallion, Charlie of Muck, to a Mrs Osborne for peanuts and he and his progeny have been winning prizes all over Scotland.

'In 1963, we were at Lochaber show. While we were there, we were looking at the ponies and Father had this idea that a pony would be a good thing for Alasdair to use for going around the sheep. There were no quad bikes or anything like that then. We were particularly attracted to this little Calgary-type Highland mare, Guamag, who belonged to Alison MacAlpine-Downie from Appin. The pony was being shown by one of her farm men and had actually been sold to the great Highland pony breeder Cameron Ormiston. Despite the fact she was quite small, we really did like her. She was a lovely mouse dun, with light bone, a true west Highland type of pony. Eventually, after a long conversation, the man said he was sure Alison would let her come to Muck and that Cameron, who had dozens and dozens of ponies, probably would not even notice if she did not arrive, providing he had not had to pay for her. She cost us £200 and we had to make arrangements to get her home.

'Finally, we got her back in *Wave*. Cameron probably would have had the last laugh, as she turned out to be very self-willed and stubborn. If you were going to Port on her, as you were going along the beach at Gallanach she would suddenly refuse to budge and whoever was riding her had to beat her to make her move at all. Sometimes she would suddenly whip around, catching the rider unawares, and then gallop straight back home again. In the end Alasdair did not use her very much, as she was so nappy, but it was a nice idea, I suppose . . . another of our hair-brained schemes.

'Eventually, we decided to put her in foal. We took her to Rum in July and after the initial time we pushed the foal into the boat first and then she leapt in after it. The first time we took her I had never seen ponies having sex before and I must admit I was quite impressed. I did not know much about pony breeding at that stage, as we had only had workhorses and never had any foals. Guamag would stay on Rum for a while and then we would go back to collect her. The Rum ponies, though bigger, were very much of a similar type.

'So we went on breeding foals and we also used Beauty, the pony, we got as a thank you for helping with the Rum fire. Guamag had very nice foals. We did manage to sell a few of them, but they never made enough money. The children rode some of Guamag's progeny, but they were so strong – and usually the problem was trying to stop them eating while the children were on board.

'Our good friend Tex Geddes in his latter years got fed up with fishing on Soay; instead, he took a great interest in ponies. He went over to Rum and eventually managed to persuade them to sell him a mare. The Rum ponies are very unique, and one particular line have lovely silver manes and tails. Tex also visited various studs on the mainland, including Cameron Ormiston's at Newtonmore, and after a good few drams he managed to persuade Cameron to sell him the stallion, Seumus, on condition that he was not sold on.

'Tex built up a nice little herd of ponies. I think it is fair to say that his ponies did not do very well on Soay; several good foals were lost in the bogs there. Tex really loved them, though, and was always trying to get them to work the croft, albeit rather unsuccessfully.

'Tex died in 1998. Due to Jenny's involvement with his father and mother, and my close friendship over the years with Tex, Duncan thought it would be a nice gesture to give us all his remaining ponies. So this involved two separate trips in *Wave* to get them home. They were, in fact, very quiet, but we put gates along the sides of the boat to make it safer. It was a problem to get the first ones on each time, but once we had done so the rest just followed on and we got them back to Muck.'

Colin has a very different take on fetching the ponies from Soay. He raises his eyebrows very high when I ask if the ponies were easy to move. 'They were as wild as the wind! They had not been handled much at all and they led us a merry dance. We had several mad trips back home with them; it was just another of my father's crazy sea journeys with livestock.' He smiles broadly: 'And so often we used to go in such difficult weather, too. I think I am much more cautious.'

'In 2000, the BBC were about to film *Castaway 2000*, the reality TV series set on the Hebridean island of Taransay off Harris. They wanted a Highland pony for the so-called 'castaways' to plough the croft and had heard about our ponies. Eventually, a ridiculous deal was struck up, where we agreed to lease them Eilidh for the duration of the programme. From Muck to Arisaig, she was accompanied on her circuitous journey by Colin and Ishy Walters, Clare and Bryan Walters' daughter; she was then collected by Ian MacNaughton from Mallaig, who transported her to the ferry from Harris to Taransay. We had agreed to lend her to them for a year for the sum of £500. The weather was fine for the Arisaig trip, but by the time they took her north it had deteriorated so much that the Skye Bridge was shut; the *Hebridean Isles* would not take her, so she had to stay in Skye that night. Next day it was a little better and she was finally handed over to the owner of Taransay and taken to the island by landing craft.

'We had broken her to carry panniers and to drag tyres, but the plough proved to be far too big for her; they really needed two decent-sized garrons instead.

'Due to the fact that we did not know the whole history of this pony, and she had come from Soay, we had warned Lion TV that there was a small possibility that she could be in foal. Needless to say the next issue was that she produced a colt foal (which they named Arnie). This then meant that she was unable to be used for working the land, so all the Taransay castaways were far less enthusiastic about her and did not want her any more. Then we had the logistical problem of getting her back via Skye. Using a haulier was a very expensive option, so, as I am ever on the lookout for another adventure, in a moment of madness we decided to go and get her ourselves. Incidentally, I thought it was a great idea. It was the middle of July when the situation blew up, and Colin and I set sail all the way up to Harris to fetch her in *Wave*. Experienced yachtsman Ranald Coyne, who used to be the factor at Ardtornish Estate, accompanied us. It was a 12-hour journey. We finally reached Leverburgh, where we walked around a bit after our long sea voyage. I was very struck that it appeared to consist of a very ageing population at that time and there appeared to be little crofting, too.

'Next day, it was fairly windy. We climbed a hill above the town and could see white caps on the waves. We decided we would take a chance and leave for home. Ian MacKay, owner of Taransay, who had a landing craft to service the castaways, brought her across to Leverburgh and we set off back down the Sound of Harris with the mare and foal aboard. We had them haltered and roped to rings in the gunwale, but we were worried they might fall over and then subsequently hang themselves. So Colin and I had to stand with our backs to the seas and hold them, while Ranald did an excellent job throttling back when the need arose. The first four hours were difficult because it was the open Minch and the wind was straight ahead, so we got soaked with spray coming right over the bow. Luckily, it was quite warm. I am happy to say that the ponies survived the ordeal and did manage to stay on their feet for most of the voyage.

'When we eventually reached Neist Point on Skye, we were in the lee of the land and passed Canna and then journeyed uneventfully on across to Muck. It was interesting to hear on the radio that some of the people building the pier back home had set out to try and rescue a yacht in difficulties between Muck and Ardnamurchan. The whole unfolding drama kept us entertained on the journey home. The end of the pony tale was pretty frustrating, as Lion TV, who were producing the series, did not pay one penny towards either the hire of the pony or our rescue mission voyage, even though we had well warned them about the foal possibilities. As ever, we came out of it with nothing at all, except isn't it a great story?'

At this, Lawrence laughs sardonically but seems quite infuriated, then quickly adds by way of a disclaimer, 'It was yet another of our hair-brained schemes that went wrong. I really don't know how we get ourselves into these things.' Colin just raises his eyebrows.

Livestock

'I have always loved cattle. Farming, to me, isn't love, it's passion. When we were children, we had a beef Shorthorn bull, and he used to lie on the beach at Gallanach and I used to climb on his back while he was dozing. He was so quiet, such a nice bull, that he would even allow all three of us to climb on him and did not seem to mind at all. We had an excellent cattleman from Tiree at that point, Lachlan MacLean, and he looked after the byre; it was very similar to how we have it now, with probably about 20 cows housed inside. We had no water and so had to let them out for a drink every day. Like me, Father was very keen on cows and, as well as the ones inside, we had a herd of cross-Highlanders on the hill. We used to buy Highland heifers and then used a Shorthorn bull on them and kept the female calves for breeding purposes. We also had pure Highlands on the farm and had bred bulls for the Department of Agriculture; they even used to deliver them to places such as Soay and Ardnamurchan during the '20s and '30s, when either they had very unsuitable boats or road transport to these remote places was difficult. After the war, they stopped doing this.

'Father had a brief foray into Aberdeen Angus in the 1950s. He bought six in-calf heifers but sadly three of them managed to lose their calves; they had been hopelessly overfed for sale purposes. I think he wanted to breed some good bulls, so he did keep one of their calves:

Katapult of Gallanach, spelled with a 'K' because the breed society allocated a letter for pedigree stock each year and K was for that year. During the '60s, Father bought half a dozen Galloway heifers, but they were a bit of a mistake because these particular animals were fiery and difficult and smashed their way through various wooden cattle crushes.

'When Alasdair took over the farm, he decided to expand the cows because the hill cow subsidy was worked out on a headage basis. It was decided to run two herds, one on the west side of the island and the other on the east, so we required two bulls as well. Much later, on when he had left Muck and moved to Hardiston, Alasdair kept pure Herefords. He sent us a bull once, and though I really liked him we eventually changed to Simmental, a breed that is ideal crossed with the Luing. I went to the well-known cattle breeder Finlay MacGowan to get the first one. I certainly have a soft spot for the Luing and it produces a superb beef calf when put to the Simmental and suits us well.

'By the time I returned from my trip to Australia and New Zealand in 1966, there was really no job for me, as Alasdair was at the helm. Father was concerned about this and, as I previously mentioned, he even looked into buying a farm on Eigg for me. Eventually, it was agreed that though Alasdair was in charge I would be given the job of looking after the cattle. Alasdair had decided to expand the cows, as the subsidy system encouraged this. Over the years, we have had very good cattle, but early on we made a serious mistake when Alasdair, who was very clued up on market prices, told Father and I we were not to spend more than £70 per calving heifer at a sale in Oban. All the best ones we had earmarked went above our budget at £90. We missed our chance. Instead, we bought the tail end; I think it was the stupidest thing we ever did. Father was so fed up that he went into the other ring and bought two nice bulling heifers from Ulva. These were good beasts, but they were quite a lot younger. He got them for

£70, but they were not in calf, so we lost out there. The others we bought were so much smaller and not nearly as good; they just never did so well. We learned our lesson the hard way and ever since have always tried to buy the best stock we can afford.

'During the 1950s CalMac's *Loch Broom* transported the livestock. They actually took the eight cows we had bought that day out to Muck for us. You got a free one-way trip with your animals. In fact, that very last relic of farming concessions still remains today: when you have livestock in a trailer on board CalMac boats, you still get one trip free. This is something that greatly helps crofters in remote places.'

This makes me think back some years ago, before new regulations stopped transportation of livestock in the back of cars; I remember being highly amused by a newspaper headline in a popular red top: 'Sheep Day Return!' This was the tale of crofters in some of the islands taking full advantage of a free shopping trip to mainland metropolises. In order to qualify for the scheme, they were taking ancient pet sheep in their cars with them, leaving them in friends' fields or gardens for the duration and then taking them back home again once their sprees were over. I thought it rather entrepreneurial, though the authorities took a very dim view.

'Before we had a proper pier on Muck, we had to drive cattle across the slippery seaweed and rocks, and then onto a large rock by the new pier called Sgeir nan Ron – seal rock – where we put a ramp across to the boat. It was labour intensive, but we had islanders holding up a roll of netting, stopping them from breaking back. It sometimes did not go according to plan, as the animals often had other ideas, though they were really very quiet, having been handled all winter.

'We always had to rope each beast, and haltered them, and there was much pushing and shoving to get them onto *Wave*, and then it took time to tie each one to a ring at the side in her hold. If they were going in the *Loch Broom*, or later the *Loch Carron*, then they were put into a canvas sling that went under their belly and then had to be tied in safely with a rope to stop the risk of slipping out either backwards or indeed forwards. Each was then individually heaved up by a derrick and lowered into the hold. If we were taking 30-odd animals, it could take at least six hours just to get them onboard, as we used to have to load them a dozen at a time. All the men who worked on MacBrayne's boats tended to be stockmen who had grown up on farms and crofts, and so they knew exactly how to handle beasts. *Wave* would have to go right alongside the bigger boat and we had tyres put along her sides to stop her from getting damaged.'

Sometimes Muck shared CalMac's *Loch Broom* with Coll, but the islanders there refused to load their livestock at low tide, meaning that on occasion the MacEwens had to; this meant that there might be at least one load of livestock taken out on *Wave* when the tide was really low, something they were none too happy about.

Clare Walters, who lived on Muck from 1973 to 2003, has a humorous take on cattle transporting events. As I had imagined, trying to get the beasts onto the boats was a rodeo further fuelled by testosterone, as the island's males eagerly showed off their strength and indeed perhaps their cowboy prowess, when on many occasions animals had to be forcibly manhandled into the right place. The effect of putting cattle into slings and then lifting them onto boats with a derrick in turn had a highly laxative effect on the poor beasts. Clare has a photograph of the unfortunate Colum Beagan, who must have been standing in the wrong place at the wrong time, totally plastered from head to foot in dung. Clearly, his Irish humour had remained intact; his smile was still as broad as ever.

Over the years, it would seem that Lawrence's refusal to be beaten by logistical livestock movement issues has become legendary. His son Colin remembers numerous trips to fetch and carry beasts literally through hell and high water and raises his eyebrows as he smiles broadly. 'Dad is incredibly stubborn and some of the things we did were probably utter madness. I do remember numerous occasions when we hid beneath the tarpaulin on *Wave* as we sailed back with various beasts.'

A friend on holiday at Glenuig many years ago was standing admiring the view at the jetty one bright summer morning when he spied a thick-set Viking-looking man struggling to get a very large pony onboard a very small boat. He remembers the man's hands being of particular note, as they were the largest he had ever seen; he also remembers how in the end the man just tucked his broad shoulders right in behind the pony's backside and hoicked the surprised creature straight aboard. 'I later found out that this was Lawrence MacEwen from the Isle of Muck. When I talked to locals about him, they said that he was ever thus and would never give in when it came to putting animals onboard boats. I was totally amazed and have never forgotten it. Most people would not have dared to do that, but it worked a dream and showed his incredible strength, too. And his attitude really made me laugh.'

A Load of Bull

In 1965, an exciting new development for cattle enthusiasts saw the passing of a Special Act of Parliament when the newest breed, the Luing, was officially recognised in its own right. Specially developed to thrive in exceedingly wet parts of Scotland, the Luing has proved a real success story and is very popular not only in Scotland but also further afield.

The Luing was the brainchild of the highly respected and astute Cadzow brothers: Shane, Denis and Ralph. Three great agriculturists, and unsurpassed stockmen, their careful breeding of this supreme beef cow has been valued worldwide. Each of the three brothers farmed in his own right on productive arable ground on the eastern side of Scotland. They all had the same aims and each had found that it was expensive and unreliable to have to buy cattle in from other farms for fattening.

During the 1800s, Lord Breadalbane had owned Luing. In 1947, the Cadzows jointly purchased part of it, and shortly afterwards acquired much of the rest of the island. They aimed to breed cattle on the west and then send them to their farms on the east, where they would be fattened for the butcher. They wanted to develop a particular type of animal that was acclimatised to the incessant wet and would have inherent resistance to the health problems associated with areas of high rainfall; above all, it would be able to live outside in winter. Breeding replacement cows for their own use was also an important consideration.

They had been buying the highest quality Highland-cross Shorthorn heifers and it was some of these cows that formed the basis for their new herd. The Beef Shorthorn, frequently nicknamed 'the great improver', has tremendous fleshing capabilities. It has been used all over the world and the result of an infusion of its blood in various breeds has done much to improve beef productivity. When crossed with the Highland, with its tremendous hardiness and ability to survive on the roughest of herbage, a highly efficient hill cow is produced. Eventually, the cows were crossed back to one particular Shorthorn bull, Cruggleton Alastair, bred by the renowned cattle breeder Bertie Marshall from Wigtownshire. This bull was not only the old-fashioned 1940s type, but it also had a character that left a very distinctive mark on his offspring. The breeding proved a great success and two sons from this liaison, Luing Mist and Luing Oxo, were kept and used on their half-sisters. Through a combination of the Cadzows' careful monitoring and excellent stockmanship, and their knowledge of inbreeding and line-breeding, a type was eventually fixed with all the qualities that they were looking for. The Luing was to be a commercial breed, bred specifically to be self-replacing; a producer of prime beef.

Despite living in such a remote spot, the MacEwens have always been to the fore in livestock farming developments and were very interested in the Luing. Lawrence remembers being present at the first Open Day on Luing in October 1965, as the new breed was unveiled.

'It was a very exciting event. It was held during the ten-day cattle sales in Oban. During the 1960s, there was just so much stock brought in from all over the Highlands and Islands, and remote parts of Scotland, that they needed all that time to get through it – such a contrast to today. The Luing celebrations were held when there was a break in the sales days. I remember there were hundreds of hard-bitten farmers there from all over the country and the press were out in force. We really liked what we saw and realised that the Cadzows were not only good stockmen but also very good salesmen and excellent promoters of the breed as a whole, working in a way farmers of that era had never seen before. I remember they had barbecues going with Luing steaks on them and it was all very professional. Typically, some farmers were sceptical. However, we waited for some time to see how good the Luing really was before we bought a bull for Muck, which would eventually mean we could breed our own replacements. Subsequently, we have had them as the basis of our herd here up until the present day. They usually have docile, easy temperaments and give us few problems, and they thrive on Muck despite the weather.'

Despite this comment, some of the so-called 'docile' Luing bulls bought for Muck have certainly given Lawrence the runaround throughout the years. The inauguration of the breed on Muck is certainly noteworthy.

In January 1972, Lawrence bought a yellow-coloured bull, Luing Pathfinder, in Oban for £350. Local livestock haulier Ewen Bowman transported the bull to Mallaig, where he met Lawrence ready to put Pathfinder onto *Wave*. Farmhand Peter Macrae had been waiting with the boat, but, as was his want, he had mysteriously vanished into the depths of the Marine Bar. Lawrence anticipated that the next operation of haltering the bull and putting him into the waiting horsebox ready to be lifted onto *Wave* would take only a few minutes. But, as all the best 'five-minute' jobs often turn out, this was not to be.

'It was a fine day and all I had to do was load him into the waiting horsebox that would then be lowered by derrick onto *Wave* with our new purchase safely inside. However, as I went into the horsebox first, leading the bull, Ewen had to open the front door to let me out again. He had already warned me that the bull had been fiery. It was a bit tricky, and I should have tied the bull up, but I didn't. Pathfinder just went straight in and sped out again through the front door; he took off with style and speed up the pier, turning right towards the herring shanty town on the west side. There was absolutely nowhere we could pen him up or corner him, and he was heading off through the middle of the mass of huts, making for the sea. Then suddenly he turned around and came back down the pier. There were some men suspended on boards below the pier doing maintenance work to its structure. They were idly chatting when this great big bull peered over right into their faces and snorted loudly, giving them a really dreadful fright. Then he turned around again and headed off in the direction of the railway line. Ewen was in hot pursuit and was following him with impressive speed. Meanwhile I had hijacked a car and driver and had taken off towards the other end of town. Luckily, I knew what time the trains were running, so I was not worrying about that for the moment. Ewen, who is very good with stock, saw what I was doing and followed as fast as he could, anticipating my plan and following the beast. I was trying to get ahead of the bull, trying to cut him off. However, he had other ideas, and when he saw me he descended into a deep hollow between the railway and the cliff. Meanwhile a stray fisherman had joined Ewen and was also on the bull hunt. They had lifted a large plank of wood and were holding this up to corner Pathfinder. I was praying that he would just suddenly slow down and then stop altogether. So I had descended down the other side with a loop of rope, hoping to drop it over his head. The bull, of course, then decided this was not the place to be. Ewen and his fisherman accomplice held up the plank in front of him to stop him. At that moment, the bull turned around again and then changed his mind, and instead launched straight towards them with great purpose. At this the poor fisherman dropped the plank and fled in terror. The bull then shot past Ewen and started heading off out of town in the direction of Fort William on the railway line. So I followed him. Ewen meanwhile had raced back to the pier to get the lorry and was quickly heading back up to my rescue. Ewen parked the lorry past the bull where the road descends into Morar village. Then he went onto the railway line when Pathfinder saw him, and for some reason turned round and headed back to Mallaig. The bull was now fired up, his nostrils were flared and steaming, and he was foaming at the mouth with his tongue lolling out too, so I know he was getting tired. He was slowing a little and there was a brief chance for me to drop a rope over his head and make him fast to the rails. We then slowly progressed back towards Mallaig; where the railway crosses the Glasnacardoch road, there was an opportunity to remove some wooden railings and we managed to get him off the line and onto the road. By now there was an audience and if they thought they were going to have more entertainment they were unlucky because by sheer luck we got Pathfinder straight onboard Ewen's truck and he was taken smartly back to the pier. Luckily, after all this time, the man who was operating the crane was still there and we got the bull quickly onto *Wave*. By now, it was evening and I had to go and retrieve the wayward Peter from the bar. In his haze of alcohol, he had managed to miss the entire escapade. There was a full moon and we sailed back to Muck with no lights, arriving home very late. Then I had to lead our new bull all the way back up the road to the farm. He was so worn out after all his exploits that he lay down on the road three times on the way. I was relieved to get him safely into a pen for the night. He was a very good bull.'

Ewen Bowman has come a long way since the early days of his livestock transporting business and, together with his family at Duisky on Locheilside, he runs a thriving recycling business, as well as state-of-the-art livestock transportation to and from many far-flung spots. Large and jovial, his memories of working with Lawrence cause peals of laughter as the stories come flooding forth.

'Anytime Lawrence contacted me about moving livestock I always knew that things would not be as expected. Och, I remember that bull story only too well, though I think my tale is a bit different, as I had to look after that young bull for a couple of days and frankly I knew he was a fiery wee bugger. Jesus, he was jumping! I did try to warn Lawrence, but, well, he was having none of it and I just knew that if that wee brute saw daylight through the trailer he would be straight out. It was hilarious.

'I never went to do a single thing with Lawrence without thinking to myself, I wonder what on earth will happen this time. I must add that this was always in the nicest possible way. He created all these adventures and when we met he always had a long tale to tell about the things that had gone wrong and the incredible amount of mishaps. And I would think to myself, how on earth could all this have happened? You know, I have had to deal with one hell of a lot of awkward bastards over the years – in particular those who complained about every last thing, they were just moaning gits – and I always thought, now here's a man fighting a daily battle with the elements and he has to pay more than twice as much to get livestock moved and has every last thing stacked against him, but I have never heard a single complaint. He has a heart of gold. I have always liked him and have tried my utmost to accommodate him, even though I knew it meant hours and hours of hanging about and waiting to see if he could set sail from Muck. He was ever waiting for a break in the weather, so I had to play the devil's advocate. I have often seen him arriving into port really late at night.

'He always used to stay with an old lady at Corpach when he was going to the market and on one occasion he was so late arriving that he felt it was far too late to disturb her and told me he would just sleep in with the sheep in the mart. I insisted he came home with me; he was very reluctant. On some occasions I have even known him to travel in the float with the sheep too.' Ewen laughs heartily. 'He really is some man. And do you know, he has never worn any socks in his wellies, even in the middle of winter. That always used to make me laugh. Sometimes he would come to Glenuig pier with his excellent boatman, Bryan Walters, and a beast would leap off *Wave* and go into the sea. Well, Lawrence always reminded me of one of those collies that loves water. You know the type that is forever diving right in? Either that or perhaps a diving duck. Anyway, he would leap straight in off the boat after the beast and grab a hold of it by the neck and try to guide it ashore. No one else would have tried, but he did. He was not so fast on shore and often got in the wrong place and sometimes I would see him holding up a makeshift post or bit of netting to try and stop a beast from breaking back. I used to think it was like holding a bit of A4 paper up in a Force 10 gale. That man had plenty of opportunities for losing his temper, but, you know, he never did. There is no doubt about it, he is the one who has kept Muck such a successful working island. For years, he has been asking me to go over to see him there, but, I can tell you, there is no way I would ever go in a boat with him. I always used to think that Bryan kept him under control on that front. You should have seen some of the loads he had on that boat and never a life jacket in sight. No, I would never go with him. I reckon he has a great wife in Jenny, and she has certainly kept him right. What a man!' Ewen sits back at his desk and we both laugh and laugh.

Another Luing bull bought from the well-known cattle breeder

Finlay MacGowan in Angus during the 1980s also proved to have a treacherous journey back to his new home. Bulls were far too large to put into slings and for safety reasons Lawrence preferred to put them in the horsebox and then load that onto the boat with a derrick.

'Jenny was away in the USA and I had taken Colin and Mary with me to the market in Oban. I had arranged for Bryan Walters to come over to Mallaig in *Wave* to meet us with our new purchase. As we were trying to load the bull, Mary started crying and screaming because she was scared of him, then it started to snow really badly for the entire journey home. I remember this because it was February and that was the only precipitation we'd had for the whole of that particular month. I had to stay under the bows with the children because they were being sick and that was making Mary cry more. Bryan had to navigate using a compass because the visibility was so terrible.

'On another occasion we picked up a new bull from Glenuig . . . That was also a difficult experience.' Lawrence laughs, and I laugh too, as I imagine this is just another of his glorious understatements: for difficult, read impossible.

'In 1991, I bought Luing North Star at a cost of £940, and later he was delivered to Glenuig for us by livestock haulier Ewen Cameron, who had a very small truck. However, that is a very tricky place to load stock onto a boat. The lorry had to be backed down the narrow jetty and there was literally only a foot on either side of the wheels between the jetty and the sea, so it involved a skilled manoeuvre on the part of Ewen. Then I had to lead the two-year-old bull down onto *Wave*, and that too was awkward because it really was narrow. Once on the boat we tied him up really carefully. Back home at Muck, the new arrival absolutely refused to go up the ramp and out of *Wave*. We did our utmost, but he just dug his toes in – it was impossible to manhandle such a big chap. He just would not budge.

'In the end, I had to employ serious tactics and finally, in sheer desperation, I gave him a great whack on the backside with a fence post. He immediately leapt out like a rocket and swam right over to the other side of the harbour, finally emerging in one piece on the shore.'

Recently, most of Muck's bulls have gone on to work on Eigg after three years and then are eventually moved to the mainland. However, Luing North Star was sold to the Reades at Sgroib-ruadh and taken in *Wave* to Tobermory.

'Not all bull journeys are fraught with hassles and I think Luing North Star had certainly learned his lesson about boats after the incident with the fence post. I do remember we had a very good day for taking him across to Mull and had an easy journey around Ardnamurchan Point for a change. When we got to Tobermory, there was quite a large audience and the bull was led up the harbour steps like a lamb to the waiting trailer. I am sure the audience was very impressed.'

When Lawrence bought another Luing bull from Major Dalrymple at Oxenfoord Mains, Midlothian, the major offered to buy bull calves from Muck on a kilo basis worked out by weighing the lorry transporting them on the weighbridge at Fordel, south of Dalkeith, empty and full. It was a great arrangement and Lawrence says that the major was a very good man, fair and straight to deal with.

The heifer calves usually went to the Oban sale and in the early days were driven down the streets, often passing unfenced gardens, causing mayhem. Latterly, there might have been some compensation to pay. Thomas Corson, the market owners, had plenty of fields around Oban then, and places where the stock could be grazed.

'Tesco and other big stores like that have now built over the old auction mart site; it's totally unrecognisable now compared with how it was when I first sold livestock there. We would stay in the Lorne Hotel or the Lochavullin, and all the prospective buyers and sellers got rather intoxicated. Jenny used to come with me, and it was great fun, with boats coming in from the islands during the previous week and then the rest of the mainland stock arriving on a Tuesday. The sale continued all week, with various days for various different classes of stock: island calves on a Monday, Tuesday for mainland calves, Wednesday was a free day, Thursday was for breeding heifers, Friday was for cast cows, and then the following week Monday was for older forward cattle, Tuesday for pedigree Highlands and Galloways. What a racket there always was because calves had been weaned straight off their mothers!

'When I was ten years old, we had had a very good haymaking and harvest, and Father decided to speculate and buy in some new calves. As we had no car then, we had to go to Oban by public transport. We first took the train from Arisaig to Fort William, then we got a bus to Ballachulish and walked up to the railway and took a train the rest of the way. There were cattle trucks in the siding at Barcaldine already loaded with calves. Once these were coupled, we set off for Oban. During the 1950s, there were four special trains for calves leaving the market and the departure times were all written up on a blackboard in the mart. I really loved these jaunts – they were such an important social event, too.'

The transporting of livestock on and off Muck, and indeed any of the islands, was ever fraught and hampered by the weather. Important annual sales are frequently missed when gales sweep over the Hebrides. And now that there are far fewer sales and the market system has altered, with all the smaller marts closed altogether, it can mean having to keep stock for months until the next suitable event, with the inevitable loss of revenue. There is also the sad loss of important social events that have ever been an integral part of farming and crofting.

On one notable occasion when some Muck calves missed the boat, Lawrence endeavoured to get them off the island to no avail. 'It was late October and we had things all organised to get another batch of calves to Major Dalrymple near Edinburgh. We had Ewen Bowman lined up waiting for us with his lorry at Glenuig. Bryan Walters and I had loaded the calves at the high pier at Port and I clearly remember it was a south-easterly wind and we were heading straight into it, making for Glenuig. Frankly, it was not a very good day. The calves were all safely onboard and we had put a big green cover over the hold of the boat to try and stop the water coming in over them. It's not totally waterproof, but it really helps; it is what we always used for family camping trips on the boat. The weather was rough, so I went under the bow because some of the calves were falling down and I had to keep helping them back up onto their feet. Bryan was at the helm; he was slowing down all the time to avoid the bigger waves coming right over us and had to carefully anticipate each one. It began to get really very squally indeed and after a short time Bryan told me we were making no progress and should turn back. He felt it was a waste of time. So we turned the boat around and then with the wind behind us it was much easier, as she just slid along with the weather. However, when we got near Port, we realised the tide was too low to offload the calves at the pier there, so we decided instead to go around to the Gallanach side. So we got in and made fast to the mooring. But the next issue was trying to get the calves off with no pier. We had a ramp on the boat and we pushed and shoved each one onto it, and then literally had to manhandle them into the sea, so each one was taking a great leap of faith and of course they hated this. At six to eight months old, they were quite big, so it was jolly hard work. We often had to do this when taking stock to the other side at Arisaig before they had a proper pier there. I had this theory that had not been proved that when cattle are in the water they swim into the wind. So I prayed they would swim in towards the beach and get out themselves. But that just didn't happen. The tide was low; some of them swam in the right direction, whilst others headed for the open sea and some uncovered reefs. By now, we had got into the dinghy and were rowing to the ones heading the wrong way. We then had to attach a rope to each head, and one by one guided them ashore safely while rowing like mad. Amazingly, none of them were drowned, but it was all a bit difficult.'

And there is Lawrence's glorious understatement again.

'Poor Ewen Bowman was sitting at Glenuig waiting for us but communications were very difficult at that time and it was at least a week later before we got a calmer day and set forth again.'

Sheep

'Most of my life the aim has been to have about 530 ewes on Muck. We started out with South Country Cheviots – Southies. They were quite common in Skye and some other areas of the Highlands and Islands, too. In the past, even long before my day, my family used to sell rams to the Department of Agriculture; they went to Knocknagael at Inverness and were then hired out to farmers and crofters all over the place, as part of the Livestock Improvement Scheme. In my father's day, the department used to buy most of the rams privately, but there were complaints in parliament that they were showing favouritism to certain breeders and perhaps there was the possibility of corruption, so it then became policy to buy all their rams at auction instead. When this happened, Father wrote to the department. He asked them, as it was very logistically difficult for us to get sheep to the sales, would they consider continuing to buy privately from us? They agreed and gave us special dispensation. Every September someone from the department came out here to pick the sheep they wanted. They also punched holes in the calves' ears to show that subsidy had been paid. They were always very fair to deal with and gave us a good price; it was a very satisfactory arrangement for us.

The North Country Cheviot – or Northie – is a really super sheep, which survives and thrives in areas where even the Blackie won't. They are great sheep and, with considerably more size and longer legs than the Southie, are well suited to Muck. Gradually, farmers on Skye and in Wester Ross decided to change to the Northie and, as we were breeding the Southie, the Department of Agriculture ceased buying them. I immediately followed market trends and also changed to the Northie by crossing our ewes. Though we never sold them to the department after that.

'However, very much earlier, during the 1920s, Father decided to go in for blackfaces and he got some hogs from the market in Perth that came from Braes of Monzie Farm, near Crieff. In those days, getting stock on and off the island was even harder than it is now. We relied heavily on MacBrayne's boats from Oban to Tobermory. On one occasion, apparently the weather was so bad that no one could get to Tobermory from Muck to collect the blackface hogs off the steamer, *Lochinvar*. As there was no telephone on the island, Father would not have even been able to ring up to make other arrangements for them. However, MacBrayne's must have had contingency plans in place with Mull farmers and our hogs were delivered to a farm near Tobermory called Erray. They were there for a while, and some of them got really bad tick, and due to the fact that ticks carry fatal diseases some of them subsequently died. Those that did survive must have been very hardy and immune to the problems caused by these insidious little beasts. Eventually, the hogs were brought over to Muck and put out on the roughest west end of the island.

'Once we had changed over to the Northie during the 1980s, as we were slaughtering some sheep on the island for our own use, I thought it would be good to try curing sheepskins as a sideline rather than just discarding them. So I went to Coll, to Acha Farm, where the island's laird, Kenny Stewart, kept up to 26 rare breeds of sheep. My idea was to buy some Jacob sheep because they have such beautiful-coloured fleeces and we could introduce this into our flock. Their fences were not very good, so I think they also had about another 26 cross-bred sheep, too. I bought six Jacob hogs from him and later I got a tup as well. I used the tup on the Northies and we began to get black lambs and some super coloured fleeces. We soon found that this was a really good, hardy combination.

'During my time, I had quite a menagerie of sheep breeds and had them all over the place, but since Colin took over he has tightened up and rationalised things with the sheep considerably and we now only have one pet blackie left on the entire island.

'When we had the blackface, I decided to try a Lleyn tup on them to produce better fat lambs; Colin, too, is now buying Lleyn tups to use on the cross-bred ewes. It appears to be working very well indeed. We have been getting some excellent prices for our lambs. It is interesting that he has kept some of the Cheviot-Jacob ewes going and still keeps a Jacob tup, so that combination has clearly met with his approval, though there have been other changes.

'David Barnden and his stepdaughter, Vicki Tubb, make wonderful felted rugs with the lovely dark-coloured fleeces and sell them in the Green Shed. They are very popular with the visitors; they undertake commissions, too, with favourite animals designed on them. Actually, they are usually bought as wall hangings, as they are far too nice to walk on, and I am very pleased that our fleeces can be made into a real Muck-produced craft.

'I think Colin is streets ahead of me on the technical side of farming, but perhaps less so on the stock side. However, he recently got a very nice Luing bull from the island of Luing. Though he is a less fashionable colour, being roan not red. Red is the popular colour for the Luing at the moment. Fashions play such a part in livestock farming.'

We go out to the field close to the farm buildings at Gallanach and find their two current bulls, a Luing, and a Simmental, dozing in the late afternoon sunshine. The two lads put their heads up when they see Lawrence approaching. He wanders over to them and begins to rub the neck of the Luing, who puts his head back down and shuts his eyes in raptures.

'I like to make sure that the stock is all like this if I can – it makes life so much easier. I spend a lot of time in the field just scratching the bulls and chatting to them. Both these boys are all right, though the Luing may be a little more unreliable; but he likes being scratched too.'

He walks slowly over to the other bull and he too goes into a brief blissful trance as Lawrence scratches his neck and tail head. Many of Lawrence's cows, all named, are much the same, and I am reminded of the fact that to my mind good stockmen are born and not made, and really know their animals; a really fine stockman will notice an animal is sick the day before it is, an accolade justly deserved by Lawrence, and Colin as well.

'In the '20s, Father used to sell Highland bulls to the Department of Agriculture and often had to deliver them to their destinations, too. For example, he supplied bulls for the crofters on Soay and to Sanna in Ardnamurchan. As you will know, Sanna, though it has its very fine beach, is a very tricky place to land, but we still go there from time to time because it's one of the shortest routes for us to get to the mainland. If the swell is bad there, the narrow entrance into the bay can be a bit scary, though. We used to take bad sailors who were prone to seasickness back to the mainland that way to avoid a long sea crossing, but then of course there was that really terrible single track road all the way back up the peninsula to contend with instead, though it's vastly improved now. Maybe they got car-sick instead of seasick.'

This jogs my memory to a time at the beginning of the 1970s when my mother and stepfather had the Kilchoan Hotel in Ardnamurchan. An English couple came for a week's stay with us. On arrival she was in such an acute state of nerves that she vowed never to leave again, so petrified had she been by her husband's driving on the single-track road, with its vertiginous drops into the sea, and its sharp bends, switchbacks and peat bogs waiting to trap anyone who was not adept at reversing. My kind stepfather could see that their week was to be ruined by the neurotic woman's fretting and consoled her not only with the sort of sized dram that makes women into men but also by offering to escort her and her husband back to Fort William in his smart new boat, the *Penny Red*, and to arrange for someone to drive their car there to meet them. With visible relief, she duly agreed. A week later departure day dawned and the couple were taken to the pier at Mingary. My cheery stepfather, dressed in heavy three-piece tweed plus-four suit, and his Norwegian skipper, looking suitably more nautical, greeted them. As usual the weather was not obliging, deteriorating fast and giving a fine excuse for the fragile passenger to have another fit of nerves due to the boiling condition of the sea. However, the couple stepped aboard and my stepfather gave them a swig from his hip flask. Just as they were relaxing a little, he fended off with aplomb. There was an exceedingly loud splash. He had forgotten to let go and was floundering like a fat tup in a sheep dipper between the pier and the boat weighed down by tweed. This nearly finished the poor woman off and she became apoplectic. My mother quickly reassured her, saying grandly, 'Don't worry, my husband frequently takes a cold dip before breakfast.' I digress, but it shows how roads and sea during the period of Lawrence's youth were particularly hazardous and the subject of many colourful tales.

Sheep have long been a vital part of Muck's farming enterprise, however methods of sheep husbandry have altered dramatically, as in all other walks of life. When Duncan MacLeod was shepherd during the '50s, and right up until sheep dips containing arsenic and PCBs were banned, having been found to cause many human health concerns, as well as polluting water courses, dipping was a twice-a-year event. 'Filling the dipper prior to having water at the steading was

Landing feeding stores from the puffer in Commander MacEwen's launch, 1931

Unloading coal in the 1940s

Right. Putting a cow in a sling from the flit boat for the Caledonian MacBrayne steamer, c. 1950

Below. Loading sheep onto the estate boat, 1940s

Left. Commander MacEwen

Below. Alasdair, Lawrence, Ewen and Catriona

Above. The Commander, Mrs MacEwen, Alasdair, Lawrence, Catriona and Ewen

Right. Lawrence c. 1960

Shepherd Archie MacKinnon with Alasdair, 1960s

Lawrence and Jenny's wedding, Soay

Rainbows over Gallanach cottage

Camus Mor

another laborious process. Alick used to fetch it using a bucket from the burn to fill up old whisky casks that he then transported on a sledge pulled by our Clydesdale Dan. Once he got them to the dipper, we just knocked out the bung and it made a dramatic glug, glug, glug sound. The dipper was very large, so it took ages. Duncan or another farmhand stood in a hole right beside the bath at stomach level as the sheep were dragged in feet first. Sometimes I would stand there in my shorts and help to push their heads under with my feet so that the dip had maximum efficacy. Unlike me, Duncan had been brought up in the arsenic age of sheep dips and was therefore sensibly better protected; he wore a large coat on back to front and had sheepskins on his legs to protect them from abrasion on the sides of the dipper. It was gruelling work.'

Much later on, before dipping laws finally changed, Lawrence's battered waterproof trousers, with more holes than material, and worn while dipping, were the subject of much amusement, for they offered no protection whatsoever. Equally controversial was the fact that on some occasions either Colin or Mary was seen to literally suck on the draining pipe to start the flow of water when it was time to empty the dipper again.

'The clipping was, of course, all done by hand. Charlie, Peter and Duncan sat on stools and used a backhanded cut for one side. Alick and I used to clip with a sheep sitting on its bottom instead, rather more like today's conventional method. By 1970, we had a 4.5-kilowatt generator at the farm, and some of the island had been wired up, so we began to use electric shears. We always had several generators, as they gave trouble and often broke down.

'Before clipping time, Alick slaughtered a sheep and my mother would make a huge stew from it, ready to feed about a dozen hungry workers at lunch time. It was ridiculous really, as it was a lot of work for her, but it was the tradition. We usually had a two-course meal followed by tea and scones, and then it would be straight back out to the shed again to get on with the hard labour. We traditionally killed approximately ten sheep annually for our own use and also used to slaughter a cattle beast or two, perhaps using one that had broken a leg or met with some accident. The sheep were hung for up to five days, the cattle for up to three weeks, depending on the weather, but when we slaughtered pigs we used them right away; they are not hung at all. As there are no deer on Muck, we get venison from Rum or other mainland estates and really enjoy that. It does not need to be hung for as long as cattle, just about a week is plenty.'

The MacKinnon family came to Muck in March 1963, when Archie MacKinnon took on the job as shepherd. He and his wife Agnes had previously been in Eigg. They and their family were all native Gaelic speakers and quickly became an important part of life on the island. Archie was shepherd for ten years and got on really well with Alasdair, who was particularly keen on sheep. They both enjoyed showing and it was during this era that, weather permitting, Muck often took a few sheep to the local shows. Archie was on the island when the MacEwen's tup-breeding business was at its peak.

'Archie and Agnes had four boys – Alasdair, Donald, Archie and then later, just a few months before his father died of cancer, Charlie. Young Archie was only nine at the time and I will never ever forget that following his father's death, when we had no shepherd to help with the lambing, young Archie and I did it together. The most amazing thing was that he had his father's dogs, Jet and Floss, and moreover he was in total command of them. He was absolutely fantastic; he knew exactly when a ewe was about to lamb. He knew such a lot about sheep for someone so young. In fact, I would have really struggled without him. Luckily, all this largely coincided with the school holidays.

'We missed Agnes and the boys when they finally left Muck. We were so keen for her to stay that we hoped the weather would stay bad so that she could not get off the island. It did stay bad for a long time, but eventually she had to go. We have kept in close touch ever since, and Archie has become a well-respected sheep man, working for Lord Cadogan in Glen Quaich in Perthshire. He totally lives and breathes sheep.'

Donald John MacDonald, an agricultural student who came from Braes on Skye, also made his ovine mark on Muck. 'While working in the fank one day, he claimed that once he had seen a ewe he would never forget her and would always be able to recognise her. I took this with a pinch of salt, though I know there are people like that. After he had left Muck, he returned again for Charlie MacDonald's 50 years long-service skite. It was midsummer and we had a typically good Muck party, with an excellent band and an influx of visitors, including a group from Eigg. Once it was all over and Donald John had consumed plenty of liquid refreshment, he set forth up the hill with my dog at 4 a.m. to gather sheep into the fank so that he could pick out the best ewes and lambs for Lochaber Show. We were all amazed that the sheep Donald John picked went on to get lots of red tickets. I think he proved his point, and I must admit I was very impressed indeed.'

Like the cattle, sheep manoeuvres too were the cause of many near catastrophic boat journeys. 'On one memorable occasion we were heading to Arisaig in the rotork, a lightweight landing craft belonging to Keith Schellenburg, the owner of Eigg at that time. We had a cargo of draft ewes aboard and had failed to push them far enough back into the boat's hold. Had we done so, then the bow would have been higher and less prone to hit a wave. The day was not windy, but there was a heavy swell running. All went well until an extra large wave reared up in front of us and our bow ploughed into it. Tons of water poured aboard and it rapidly washed aft, swamping the engines, and the boat stopped. We soon found that the deck was now covered by a foot of water and, though we tried to push the ewes further back out of danger, we had no gate to hold them there. It was impossible because we simply had no idea how we would get the engines started again. Schellenburg's boatman, Ian Munro, was very good because he did not panic – but both of us honestly thought that we would have to literally ditch the ewes to save ourselves. At one point we were all standing about, looking like idiots, with all this water sloshing about, so something had to be done. We had two female medical students with us, Caroline Hampton and her friend Jane Dunbar, and I told them to get their wellie boots off quick and start baling. Needless to say, it did not make any difference, but at least they thought they were doing something to help. However, we were so lucky, as the weather improved and somehow Ian managed to get one of the flooded engines going again. That boat had self-draining scuppers that closed when you were stationary but opened as the boat was moving forward. Anyway, miraculously we made it, but it really was touch and go.' And if Lawrence says that, then it must have been a death-defying experience.

Doctors and Vets

'Before we had a telephone, getting the doctor entailed a boat trip to Eigg to either go to see him or bring him back. We were very lucky because really we were a pretty healthy lot. I do remember when we had scarlet fever and the doctor was sent for; we were still romping about and quickly had to get into bed in readiness for his imminent arrival. It was ridiculous because we did not feel ill. My mother got on very well with the doctors, but they were always treated rather like royalty: when they came here, people seemed keener to look after them than to get them to look after their patients.

'Before he went to Eigg, Dr Hector MacLean had been at El Alamein in the casualty department. He was a major there, but he never used his title and seldom mentioned it either. He came from

Argyllshire and he was a tremendous character; he always wore the kilt and he always carried a wee rucksack for his medical stuff. His wife, Helen, really kept him up to the mark and he depended on her a lot.

'He always liked to ensure that pregnant women were safely taken off to the mainland to have their babies. He used to stride across the island when he came to see people; he seemed to look exactly the same all my life. He always had an opinion on the weather and was an excellent source of gossip, though obviously nothing was ever revealed about his patients. Then Helen tragically took her own life. She was such an excellent person, and that was another awful shock for everyone. After she went, it was all rather sad, but he was a very good doctor. He was on Eigg for almost 40 years.'

Dr MacLean clung on until he was 77 because he was not happy about leaving his practice until the local health board had installed a replacement – and he was certainly unhappy about the threat of having part-time doctors instead. He was quoted as saying, 'Replace me and I will retire, but it is a catch-22 situation; I am determined to continue until the board commits itself to putting another doctor here on Eigg. An old doctor is better than no doctor.' He started in 1951 and during his time acted as unofficial dentist and on numerous occasions vet as well. 'It is frontier medicine . . . the medical equivalent of the Falklands,' he said. Small wonder that he was held in such high esteem.

'When he finally retired, Dr Christopher Tiarks took over as doctor for the Small Isles. It was largely due to his love of wildlife that he'd ended up on Eigg in the first place. He really valued being on the island and once said, "How many doctors are regularly accompanied by whales and dolphins while making house calls?" This referred to the numerous trips the doctor had to make by boat. Dr Tiarks was very politically minded. He had fought a by-election in the Vale of Glamorgan against the Conservatives and really knew the ins and outs of the health service. He was a diligent man and when he moved south we all missed him. We then had a Dutch doctor, Dr Weldon. She too was very good indeed and was often transported from island to island by her husband, Eric, accompanied by their collie, Laurie. Devastatingly, after 22 years of loyal service, she also took her own life in 2012. Everyone was shattered by the news.

'Now we are really struggling with doctors and just have locums. There are talks about joining various practices together, but it's quite worrying for us: though we all seem thankfully very healthy, we never know when things might change, and both doctors and teachers seem to be in very short supply for remote places such as this. In emergencies, people are flown off by helicopter, but even that can take precious time.

'When Mary was away at St Leonard's School in St Andrews, a place that did not seem to suit her at all, she brought some school friends home during the holidays. They biked over to Port at night for a party and came home in the dark. One of the girls managed to crash into a gate across the road and knocked out three teeth. Next day Barnaby found the teeth lying on the road and took them back to her. At that time, there was an eye surgeon called Sarah Caswell staying in one of the cottages. We had to find out if the Lignocaine bought for anaesthetising the area around calves horns when they were being disbudded was also suitable for use on humans. After numerous calls, it was ascertained that this was indeed the case, so Sarah cleverly stuck the teeth back in. I think, due to her work, they were saved.'

Lawrence has always been very keen to run as many teaching enter-prises as possible through excellent free training schemes given by the Agricultural Training Board. Despite the remote location, he has often managed to gather enough souls together to make it worthwhile for them to run their courses. When they first started to use electric clippers in 1970, he gathered together enough people from Eigg and

Canna, and Derek Sutherland from Elgin came to teach them. 'Being left-handed, I struggled a bit and had to copy what was going on, but Derek was excellent. He used to say, "It takes a year to grow it and only a minute to spoil it," as we hacked away into the fleeces.

'During a lambing course, the well-known television vet George Rafferty came out to instruct. He was a real character. He brought a lambing simulator and was a good teacher, but amusingly totally contradicted the previous instructor who had been the year before. I often have to get Jenny to help me with bad lambings, as I have such vast hands, so it is hopeless for me to sort out problems. Anyway, one of the islanders on the course had an accident on his bike and needed stitches and of course there was no doctor here. So George stepped in and just stitched him up instead.'

Lawrence as Film Star

'It was the end of June 2002 and we had gone to Tobermory to our favourite coal merchant, Fergus Whyte, to collect supplies. We used to carry the heavy hundredweight bags down the slippery steps to *Wave*. I was still pretty strong then. Nowadays, one of the Reades from Sgriob-ruadh, the dairy farm on Mull, comes with a tele-handler and just loads us up.

'The Reades are probably my closest friends. I love any opportunity to work with them and help them on their farm. They run a very efficient business – in fact several businesses, including the Isle of Mull Cheese Company.

'Anyway, we had just finished the work and I was waiting for the others to finish their shopping when this girl appears and asks if she can take my picture. I was a bit taken aback, so I asked her why. She was a researcher who had been sent to find some likely local candidates to appear in a film and she must have thought that I looked highly suitable. Finally I agreed, and she got me to go up on the pier with a pair of binoculars to pretend to look out to sea. I had to look this way and that while she took all these pictures. It seemed a bit odd – and then she said she wanted me to play a part in a short advertising film for Peugeot cars. Despite her enthusiasm, I took no notice and thought no more about it, and finally we set sail for Muck. A few days later Jenny got a call to say they wanted me to come over to Tobermory to feature in the film. Well, I know the BBC don't pay much, but sometimes these commercial things can be quite lucrative, and I was really surprised. The next thing I had to get Bryan to take me over to Ardnamurchan, to Sanna, where he dropped me off. A taxi then took me took over to Kilchoan, to Mingary Pier, so I could get the ferry across to Tobermory to join the film crew. I found it all a bit unbelievable. It was great because I had arranged to stay with the Reades and this meant each morning, as I always did when I was staying with them, I could help with the milking at 4 a.m. before I was needed for the filming.

'The film crew was enormous. They had some buses parked down on the other side of town by MacGochan's pub. One of these was a catering bus and there was also a minibus where you could drink endless cups of tea and have a snooze when you were not needed. On arrival *on location*' – Lawrence giggles at the technical film-speak – 'they taught me how I should stand and walk – they clearly did not want me all bent over as I usually am. Quite funny really, though I admit I was scared stiff about the whole thing.

'Basically, the story was that they wanted all these people to be filmed going about their day-to-day lives. This included me sitting in a dentist's chair with my mouth wide open, then leaping out of it so many times I lost count. In another clip – and it was only a clip and all this fuss – a flare was sent up and you saw this boat in trouble. The lifeboat was called out, so we were clearly meant to be the crew doing our daily tasks. So we had a filming session on the boat and had to pretend to coil ropes and all sorts of other stupid things. Eventually, the Kilchoan ferry arrived in Tobermory with six Peugeot cars onboard. At that moment, we were all frantically running down the street, having been called to the Lifeboat station, but were then side-tracked by our apparent eagerness to witness this epic arrival. It was supposed to show that even with our callout the arrival of these cars was so important. What nonsense! As the cars actually drove off, we all had to stand about looking absolutely amazed, as if we were in awe of these really rather ordinary-looking cars. I must say it was totally stupid, but other than being rather terrified I really did quite enjoy the whole episode. It is still on YouTube, but I only appear for a second or two, and you glimpse me in the chair, and then I suddenly leap out of it and run frantically down the street, wearing a tweed jacket. Basically much of the time we just sat in the minibus or ate in the big bus. Between times, all the other actors, who were professionals, just slept and did not care less, as they were well used to all the fussing about and the endless retakes. I was there for five days and on and on it went. I was initially paid about £3,000 just for being on location, but when the film finally came out I ended up with more than the farm profits for that particular year – it was in five figures! It really was quite incredible. Actually, looking back on it, it was absolutely wonderful because I could do the milking at Sgroib-ruadh and did not miss anything important at home, other than one day's silage making.'

I recently asked Jenny if she had ever thought Lawrence had any resemblance to the actor Robert Redford, a man of almost exactly the same vintage. There was a long pause and she replied, 'Good heavens, no I have never ever thought of that before you mentioned it – and we better not suggest that or he will be even more unbearable, won't he?' We both laughed and I told her that a few people had mentioned it, having seen the craggy actor in his latest film, where he appears particularly weather-beaten and rather rougher than usual, struggling with the elements while shipwrecked. But a little bird from Muck told me that Jenny has always been mad on Robert Redford and once watched all his films, but she was certainly not admitting to it. Perhaps Lawrence has missed his vocation.

Peter

'Peter MacRae lived in Pier House with his uncles and aunts – he was one of the eleven people in that wee house with just two bedrooms. We always used to joke that they had to sleep in shifts. In fact, perhaps they did, only we never really found out. His father was a wandering shepherd who struggled to keep a job. He had worked in many remote parts of the country, such as Knoydart, and Drimnin on Morvern. Eventually, Peter came here with his three sisters, Katie, Annie and Jessie, to join his uncles. He was a very good worker and he was particularly good with our work horses. He used to look after Dick, who was a nice placid beast, while Alick, who was much more fiery, looked after Dan; his temper did not help the horse much, as he too could be fiery. I used to like working with Peter because he never said much for hours on end and then suddenly he would come out with something appropriate. Unfortunately, he had a major drink problem, so things were only smooth when he was sober. Father contrived all kinds of schemes to try and keep money out of Peter's hands – he even opened a savings account so he could pay Peter's wages directly into it, in the hope that if he found it hard to withdraw it that would help the situation and there would be none to spend on booze. When Peter did get money, he went off on a blinder. He would stay away from work till one of us went to fetch him back again, and then it would all start up again. It would be fine for a while and then there would be the next episode. He was very much a single man and that probably didn't help much either. He was in many ways rather a poor soul, but I really liked him. He was also very good with tractors. Being much younger than Alick, he adapted to them very much more easily.

'In the early 1960s, Father acquired a battery-operated record player on which he used to play Jimmy Shand and Bobby Macleod records. We really wanted to learn to dance, so we had classes in the old school and then had parties. One particular night there was a dance in the school. Peter clearly wanted a bit more alcohol: sometimes, unbeknown to us, he would hide it in various places, but on this occasion he had other intentions. He crept up to Gallanach farmhouse, to where Father kept the wine under the stairs, and pinched two bottles. However, his uncle Alick, who lived at Gallanach Cottage at that time, saw him and came hotfoot to the school in search of Father and told him what had happened. Alasdair and Father then set off back to find Peter; they went on two different routes, hoping to catch him red-handed. Father went over the hill and when he was passing behind the Rock Park he heard Peter coughing. There he was, behind the wall with two bottles of stolen wine. In desperation, Father thought it might teach him a lesson if he reported him to the police. A policeman was sent out, and Peter was apprehended and eventually hauled before the beak some weeks later. He was fined £10, but the irony of all this was that when it was finally time to pay it, he came to Father to borrow the cash. This is the only crime that has ever taken place and been reported on Muck.

'In 1974, we were gathering turnips in the fields at Middle Barn with Peter. Someone had just gone off to tip a big load of them into the clamp. Peter seemed fine, but there must have been a bit of a time lapse and during that period he must have had the chance to go off and have a drink or two. He must have had a hidden stash of drink in the barn. However, none of us noticed anything different, as he was silent for most of the time anyway, and we were working flat out. At lunchtime, he had the Fordson Major tractor as usual to go down to Pier House for his lunch. This was totally normal, as often the men took their tractors home because it was quicker for them. He shot off down the road at breakneck pace and seemed to gather momentum on the way. As he went through Port, he flew past Pier House – his aunts rushed out because they heard the roar of the tractor. Forgetting to throttle back, he was still gathering speed as he passed, heading straight for the pier, where he took a sharp right-hand turn straight onto the pier and continued right over the edge onto the beach below. The tractor just went straight over on top of him and he was killed instantly in front of his horrified family. It was another appalling incident that we all found very hard to cope with.

'At an inquest later, the sheriff said it was a grey area as to whether Peter was on or off duty at the time of the accident, but basically he was found with alcohol in his system and so, as it was during the lunch break, it was deemed to be a tragic accident and we were therefore not liable. Once more the residents of Muck were left in a total state of shock. Poor Peter was only in his 40s.'

The Merino Tup

When Jenny decided that she would like to try to spin some finer wool instead of the usual island fleeces, she looked into buying a Merino tup. She and Lawrence found one of the very top Merino breeders in Scotland – a man who was so serious about the production of the world's finest wool that he sent his fleeces by air to Victoria in Australia to have them properly graded – and a tup was duly found for Muck. When it eventually arrived, it was hoped that by using him on their ewes the isle of Muck fleeces could be vastly improved and subsequently become more valuable once hand spun.

Shearing Merinos, with their mass of delicate, wrinkled skin folds and different stapled fleece, usually referred to as fibre, is no easy task. When it was time to remove the new boy's jersey, there were problems. After a great deal of trouble, the poor beast was left looking like a shag-pile rug. As well as having his beautiful fibre slightly marred, Lawrence and Jenny had also succeeded in cutting some of his skin folds, too. 'It was really awful,' says Jenny. 'We just had no idea at all and made a total mess of it.'

Though the tup quickly recovered from his accidental cuts and the indignity of having his beauty spoilt, the repercussions of their lack of experience came home to roost the following year. The new Australian lad was put to a select a few ewes at that time and appeared to be working well. When it came to lambing time, though, not a single ewe bore fruit. Lawrence and Jenny, thinking that he was surely infertile, felt that perhaps they had literally had the wool pulled over their eyes. On closer inspection, however, it was revealed that this was far from the case. Their clipping had been so bad that they had managed to leave a pad of dense matted wool right over his pizzle, with the result that the frustrated animal must have been trying his utmost to perform to no avail. It was a case of literally having the wool pulled over the penis rather than the eyes. Luckily, as they both have a superb sense of humour, they saw the funny side.

The following spring they did get some lambs from him, and they were much easier to shear because they were not pure Merinos, but it still seemed impossible to make more money from spinning the better quality wool. I suggest to Lawrence that perhaps they had missed a golden opportunity – a golden fleece, in fact . . . that they could have fleeced people by marketing Isle of Muck exclusive Merino wool condoms – he laughs loudly: 'Jenny was not really doing much spinning anyway, when we got that tup, and can you believe it, he cost £500 too, at least the equivalent of £1,000 today? Jenny is very good at spinning, but the problem is she tends to fall asleep while doing it, it's just so time-consuming, and I think the Merino wool was just so fine it was really hard. I know – it was just another of our crazy ideas.'

[105]

I still think they should have explored the possibility of fine-fibred prophylactic products, as I am sure there would have been bumper sales; visitors to Jenny's well-stocked craft shop would have been intrigued! Perfect for Christmas for the man who has everything. And a change from socks . . .

Ewen's Return and the Building of Port Mor House

'There were probably a few contributory factors in Ewen's decision to return home to Muck. He was a highly successful field geologist with Rio Tinto and had travelled all over the world from Aberdeenshire, Wales and Iran to Argentina and Patagonia, and he spoke fluent Spanish. He had also been quite ill with hepatitis, though, needed some time to recover from that. He was certainly due for promotion and he definitely did not want to end up stuck in an office, so I think there were several reasons for coming home. We were also going through a very bad patch on the island, as the old Gaelic-speaking element had almost died out. Alick MacDonald had received a legacy of £500 from my father and had decided to leave the island and move to Tobermory to work on the pier there. Archie MacKinnon senior, our excellent shepherd, had died. Sandra Mathers, Charlie's daughter, was looking at a croft in Aberdeenshire for her parents, so they too were contemplating leaving the island. We were really in a depressed state. So Ewen's return, and the arrival of Bryan and Clare Walters in 1973, greatly helped. Ewen, who is an incredibly hard grafter, began working on the farm and I was thrilled about this.

'In June of that same year, I went off to the Highland Show. I was getting a wee award from Merk, Sharp & Dohme, one of the major animal drug companies, for recognising sheep breeds. Rather amusingly, I was also to receive £100 as part of the award. It was while I was away that Ewen began one of his many epic new projects.

'At that time we didn't have a digger on the island, but we did have a McConnel back actor for the Fordson tractor, and so he began to dig the foundations for Port Mor House, the new guesthouse hotel. Ewen was also supposed to build Sandra's new house, so he started that at the same time, while working at the farm. I don't think he can have had any conception of how much work this would all prove to be. I am sure he certainly never realised it was going to take at least two years alone to lay all the blocks. Ewen is an amazing workman and a real perfectionist – remember the gargantuan effort it took a few of us to get the blocks to the island in the first place and what a saga all that proved to be.

'Well, Ewen was very lucky because, as fate would have it, just as he was embarking on this major undertaking a young Irish geology student called Colum Beagan came to survey the island for his project. I really did not take much notice of him at the time. I suppose he was just one of many such students who came to look at the island's interesting geology. One night he was camping right near the site of the proposed Port Mor House and was lying reading his book by candlelight in the tent. He must have fallen asleep and some of the tie tapes inside caught alight on the candle flame and set his pillow on fire, too. It gave him a dreadful fright. Poor Colum. At that point, Jenny had still not arrived in Muck, but Clare Walters was very kind, so he went straight to her house in the middle of the night and she gave him a bed. Anyway, before he left he offered to come back and help Ewen with the various building ventures. Colum was a very good worker too, but I don't think he appreciated what a stickler Ewen would be for a perfect job – or moreover how long it would all take. In that respect, Ewen is very unlike me. I admit I am a bit of a bodger, while he really does do things properly. So the two of them laid endless blocks. Ewen, with his spirit level, was constantly checking the vertical and horizontal. I think they must have been the most perfect blocks anywhere in the country.

'We had a builder friend who lived in the Central Belt called James Potter and he came to the island a few times. He offered to get Davy Jones, one of the stalwarts on the farm, a second-hand JCB for various projects – this was the first one that came to the island, then Ewen got one too, which was a real help. Eventually, after about two years, all the block work was complete, but what a long haul. The next saga was going to be the roof. James kindly offered to come and help put this on over Christmas and New Year, when most of his men were off. He also managed to persuade a couple of them to come and help too. James loathed the sea and, needless to say, the weather was awful. In the end, we had to go over to collect them from Fascadale in Ardnamurchan and it was a hair-raising trip. Due to the weather, the roof A-frames had to be prefabricated in the barn; it was then that things began to go badly wrong because they must have all got muddled up. They thought they were all the same size – it was a bit of a nightmare because apparently they weren't.'

Ewen later explained that they were indeed all the same size, but the pre-drilled holes varied with each frame and though the components were numbered they all got muddled up. He also re-emphasised that it was indeed New Year. Lawrence at this point starts to laugh quite loudly and I detect a little tail-pulling at his poor brother's expense. He is clearly revelling in this story.

'Well, the roof was far from level, unlike the blocks, and next thing, after the helpers left, there was a great deal of what I will call "re-assembling" to be done. They did eventually get the roof on and the sarking as well, and then the Velux windows went in. Actually, it was all no mean feat.'

Lawrence is now clearly giving a bit of ground.

'There was no expense spared; the lintels were pre-cast in concrete and were massive and very heavy indeed. Getting them into position was another taxing operation, using tractors and a lot of manpower and Heath Robinson methods; in fact, any schemes we could muster.

I tell you, those things are solid. Ewen did bring in a plasterer for some of the interior, though as well as this we collected five tons of plasterboard in *Wave*, while another 15 tons were delivered to Muck in the Arisaig landing craft, which was slowly sinking. The house exterior was all rendered, along with Sandra Mathers' new house.

'In 1980, Ewen miraculously managed to complete Port Mor House, but there were perhaps still a few things lacking. The first guests had to come and stay with Jenny because there were still no locks on the bathroom doors. When it was finally ready, they were so happy with Jenny that they did not want to move down to Port Mor House and preferred staying put.

'Then Ewen took on his first and only member of staff. He had no idea how few visitors he would get, but this lady from the south of Scotland arrived all set to help, however that didn't work out and she soon left and Ewen did everything himself – and probably far better, too. He is a fantastic self-made cook – he works amazingly fast in the kitchen, despite being amazingly slow in building mode. God help anyone who has to sort out the plumbing in that house, though.'

At this point I can detect that the two brothers, like the bulls on the island, have probably locked horns more than a few times over various projects. However, Lawrence admits that he is no use whatsoever at joinery or building projects and that it is Ewen who has all the talents in that area, as well as in the culinary department.

'When Ewen was actually working on the houses, he stayed in the farmhouse at Gallanach and he would come home from perhaps 12 hours of block laying and then conjure up a superb dinner. When he finally finished Port Mor House, Ewen gathered a considerable fan club of guests who came annually, but it was always difficult to get enough people – sometimes if it was only one couple coming to stay, they would be turned down, then as soon as that happened, sod's law others rang. It was all far from easy.'

Anyone who stayed with Ewen, and later his partner Judy Taylor, in Port Mor House in its heyday, claims it was a fabulously unforgettable experience. Indeed, many of my island-loving friends from the mainland cannot praise the atmosphere and craic of a stay with them highly enough. In her wonderfully evocative and amusing book written in 1989, *An Eye on the Hebrides* – Mairi Hedderwick writes:

> *If you have to be stormbound, where better than on Muck? Ewen MacEwen's guesthouse, furnishings, menus and hospitality are all home-made – in the most sophisticated sense of the word. A house-party atmosphere obtained: maybe encouraged by the tiny size of the island and latterly by our adventurous condition.*
>
> *Ewen bakes bread and rolls in time for breakfast. And will go out to his creels for a lobster for dinner should you wish. In between he weeds the vegetables and dusts out the bedrooms, and wonders when the storm will let the old guests leave, and have the new ones stranded at Mallaig or Arisaig given up waiting . . .?*

In his book *The Other British Isles*, Christopher Somerville was equally effusive about Ewen and Port Mor House:

> *The meal I ate there that evening with ten other guests round the big communal table would have cost a king's ransom in London – a vegetable soufflé tangy with spices, a dish of lamb covered in subtle sauce, fresh carrots, potatoes and cauliflower, a belt-loosening raspberry and strawberry pudding.*

'Eventually Ewen gave it up,' says Lawrence. 'And actually, I think he always preferred building to dealing with people.' Despite his brother's comment, it appears that Ewen to the contrary dealt with people exceedingly well.

More About Colum

Lawrence thinks for a minute about Colum Beagan and his work with his brother Ewen on Port Mor House. 'He was excellent,' he says. 'Another person who made his mark on the island. His family came from a croft in County Armagh so he was very conversant with livestock. He was one of fourteen children, and he was somewhere near the middle of the brood. I always felt that his poor mother must have been a bit like a cow, having one a year. Colum was excellent, and also had a lot of good ideas that sadly did not always quite work out. He assisted with several building projects. When he eventually finished working with Ewen, he left for a while, but he was clearly taken by Muck and in 1986 returned with his wife Bridget and their children. During his absence we had kept in touch from time to time and knew that he had been teaching at a Steiner School in Edinburgh. His aim was to return to Muck to set up an outdoor training centre for teenagers. He wanted it to be available for other schools too, sent through various councils. We gave him an area of the square where we used to have the stirks at Gallanach. He actually converted this into a house and was aiming to convert the barn into hostel accommodation. The organisation was called Muc Mahara and it was designed to teach young people about countryside skills. Soon after the Beagans returned, Barnaby Jackson, a young man who had been educated at a Steiner School and who had studied electronic engineering, came to help with the new venture. He lived with us for some time before he eventually moved into his own accommodation and he has been here ever since. He works part time with Colin on the farm; he is quietly versatile and extremely good with mechanical things, as well as electrics. It was really due to his hard work that the second of our wind-power schemes kept going for as long as it did.

[111]

'Sadly, Muc Mahara was not to be, though Muck should have been a great place for it, but I suppose the logistics of getting on and off the island, with all the erratic weather, and then the rules and regulations with local councils made it all rather impossible. In the end, Colum really lost heart. He was also working for me on the farm – and what a fantastic worker he was, too. He did get one or two school parties to come out as a template to see if it would work. Rosie Soutter came out with him to help too, and like Barnaby she has been here ever since. She recently took charge of the bunkhouse accommodation and also sometimes helps Jenny with various projects, such as the craft shop.

'One of the problems for Colum was schooling. When his children were in the school, we had Norma Lutas as the teacher, but he really did want to send his own offspring to a Steiner School. So he was never happy about it, and as they got older and had to leave the island for schooling anyway, he felt that it was time to move on. As with so many things, there was also a lack of money for Muc Mahara. Sometimes Colum was a bit difficult to get on with and he struggled with some of the other islanders. He had lots of opinions, but I admired him because he worked so hard. He was excellent at things like haymaking. I was sorry when he left.

'It really is amazing that when people depart, and we are really worried about how we will cope without them, as if by magic someone always seems to arrive just in the nick of time to save us. When Colum left, Theo and Cathy Nells from South Africa appeared. Cathy was unsuited to Hebridean life – she was rather too glamorous. She was the one who regaled our daughter Mary with the facts of life!' Lawrence laughs very loudly in a rather prudish fashion. I am quite sure that, living on Muck, even from an early age, the MacEwen children must have been fairly au fait with this, given the amount of regular ovine and bovine births they witnessed. However, it seems learning them from Mrs Nells was not something Lawrence was too pleased about, especially as it appears that she gave Mary a little too many of the finer details.

'Eventually, Mrs Nells ran off with another man who lived in the Cayman Islands – that must have been a change from Muck. Poor Theo was left on the island and I gave him enough work to earn himself a ticket back to South Africa. He did a great deal, including making septic tanks and a porch for the farmhouse, and laying concrete paths, as well as building chimneys for the bothy bunkhouse, though his cement mixing wasn't too hot. He seemed very sad and I used to find him wandering about in misery first thing in the mornings till eventually he too left.'

Electrifying Experiences

It never ceases to amaze me how quickly we have lost touch with reality. When there are power cuts on the mainland, the majority of people tend to go into a total meltdown; they appear to have forgotten how to be resourceful. When I was growing up in Ardnamurchan at the end of the 1960s, we still relied totally on generators for power. My parents, who owned the Kilchoan Hotel, had to adapt frequently when the whole place was plunged into darkness due to inevitable breakdowns. The kitchen was largely run by gas, and there were gas lamps in the main rooms, and torches or candles in every bedroom. Most southern visitors, who'd first had to dice with the 50-odd miles of single-track road from Corran Ferry down the peninsula, usually understood they were entering the dark ages and there were few complaints. Sometimes the breakdowns might last days, or even weeks, especially if parts were scarce to come by. There was also the issue of weather, when boats perhaps did not appear with supplies; the post, too, was far from reliable. Many of the crofters and locals did not have generators, so their houses were lit entirely by gas and that too often ran out. I do not think I over-romanticise this issue, but amongst my fondest childhood memories are those of long evenings with local families and friends spent around a peat fire, chatting and listening to a wealth of tales. Sadly, our illuminated lifestyle these days, and the constant prattle of the television and computer, all too often puts paid to that. Losing the oral tradition has not been a progressive step.

In 1969, Muck, like Ardnamurchan, also relied on generators for electricity; Lawrence was at this stage wiring up the byre at the farm, the island on the verge of entering its first era of electricity. By 1970, a generator shed was being built at Port and he was fitting out the farmhouse, too. Though he did much of the work, Fitzsimmons, the electrical contractors from Fort William, came to the island to fit the rest of the houses in Port.

'When it was all finally done, I thought it would be a nice gesture to invite Robert Grieve, the first chairman of the Highlands and Islands Development Board, to come and open our new power scheme. The event was to take place in Charlie and Katie MacDonald's house, but as usual for Muck there was a problem and we weren't actually really ready for his arrival. Though their house was all wired up, there was still an issue, as the generator was not working on Start-O-Matic. Robert Grieve made a good speech about how important the periphery is, as well as the centre – the usual sort of thing, saying that basically the islands are just as important as the mainland, though that of course does not always hold sway. Due to things not being quite ready for the off, I had arranged that someone would stand above the generator shed where the electrician was waiting inside. I also arranged for someone to put a hand out of the house window to give the person above the generator shed a quick wave, and then the electrician inside could get the starter handle on the generator going. It worked, but there was rather a long pause before finally the electricity came on. Then everyone clapped and cheered. It was all most amusing.'

POLLY PULLAR

Several generators ticked away for years, breaking down, as they do, and the island power was intermittent, sometimes off altogether and never on for more than part of each day, but no one complained. Moving further into totally electrifying times was to prove a long and laborious saga that went on for years and years.

On my first visit to Muck, there was much evidence of two failed wind-power schemes, with the associated clobber and detritus left *in situ* on Carn Dearg hill. However, the island had had seven years of intermittent 24-hour electricity provided by a Scottish Power scheme, though this had been erratic and only worked when it was windy. Now work was well underway to install a third. The islanders still relied on a generator that ran from 8 a.m. to 11 a.m., and then from 5 p.m. until midnight. Nobody I spoke to had a single complaint about this and said that days were planned around the electricity schedule: washing and cooking could only be done when it was on, unless they had gas cookers for the latter, which most did. Though they were all looking forward to the prospect of 24-hour power, the interesting part was that they were in fact managing fine with a limited supply. I suppose I did wonder how the final electrification of Muck would alter the whole ethos of the place.

'In 1991, Ewen took up the electric scheme wholeheartedly; Murray Somerville of Wind Harvester gave us a presentation for a single 100-kilowatt generator on top of Carn Dearg and there were no batteries involved for that one. They had already successfully installed similar systems on Foula and Fair Isle. Next, Wind Harvester set about securing funding from Brussels; this was a long and complex process that took six months. Finally, on 24 April 1992, we heard back that we had been successful. The funding package included a substantial community contribution in labour. Ewen then got everyone together and basically told us that we just had to start digging. The first thing was to lay the cable to the houses, and for two solid years we did just that. Though Ewen dug most of the trench with the JCB, there were many places he couldn't and had to dig by hand, and then he insisted it was all filled in by hand too. I remember using a pick to dig about 50 yards of trench into solid rock in the middle of the island, with the help of a lad called Lucas Chapman. It was supposed to be two foot six inches deep, but in areas of solid rock it probably ended up being a foot shallower than that, and then there was all the backbreaking work of backfilling it by hand. We laid about four miles in total. At the start of all this, we had quite a lot of snow and it filled in all the trenches. I really cannot take too much credit for digging in the cable because I was usually pretty tied up with the farm, but other islanders did a massive amount of work on it to help Ewen. The worst bits to fill in were where Ewen had got far ahead with the JCB and the earth had been lying for up to a year and was compacted with grass and weeds. I really couldn't believe that Ewen was insistent on the filling all being done manually. I had even bought a back-actor to fit on the tractor for this purpose. I thought this would be the ideal way to deal with it, but he wouldn't allow it because he was worried that the machine might heave big stones down onto the cable. In some places he even fetched sand from the beach and laid this on top first to protect it in the roughest areas. A foot above the cable we put in the BT telephone line, and then a foot above that we had the yellow plastic strip to warn future diggers what was there. By doing it all by hand, Ewen ensured it was all in the right position, so he was dead right, though I most certainly did not think so at the time.

'As Ewen had recently finished Port Mor House, he was really keen on putting all his endeavours into the new wind-power scheme. He had spent part of the year building a road, from the low pier down to the site of the new pier, and mostly just using a pick and shovel. He is far tougher even than me and also laboured away with a crowbar, levering out huge rocks. What he has achieved is really quite astonishing; he did it so well, too.

'As the main run across the island was 3,000 volts, that meant we needed a cable of a much lower cross-section because the higher the voltage the less copper you need to carry it, making it relatively cheaper. We eventually reached Gallanach, and had transformers there and at Port, and at the branch going to Scilachan, Dun Ban and Godag. We finally connected up all the houses, and then later the big stuff appeared, including the main nacelle and the tower. The next marathon began in June 1993, as we constructed the block to hold the tower. Ewen had worked away on the top of the hill, excavating into solid basalt with mechanical picks and shovels to enlarge a huge hole blasted out with explosives. It had to be at least five feet deep for the concrete block to hold the tower. So Wind Harvester got a second-hand batch mixer, and quantities of cement in bags, plus sand and gravel. It was supposed to be cast in one piece, but that proved impossible because the batch mixer had been knackered by one of the men who had come to the island to help. The gears had gone haywire and it broke down. They had hired in a vibrator, too, and we had a special cage to reinforce the concrete. After a few setbacks, we started at 3 p.m. one afternoon and had to work in shifts of four hours right through until 9 a.m. next morning, when we were revitalised with some beer. We had to scratch some of the block with a pick to put a rough surface on it before we could add more cement after a few days' stoppage due to breakdowns. And then after all that, within a fortnight of finishing the work, we heard that Wind Harvester had gone bust. So the block was never used and is still sitting there, with all its bolts intact on top of the hill, and that I am afraid was the end of that.

'We had an eight-year wait for the next go at it. Poor Ewen took the brunt and tried again for further funding from Brussels, but he was immediately turned down.'

It wasn't until 1999 that the newly formed Isle of Muck Community Enterprise (IMCE) Ltd applied to the National Lottery for funding for another wind-power scheme, with the backing of local enterprise company Lochaber Ltd. IMCE Ltd had been set up in 1992 to own and run the first electricity scheme, with Ewen as one of three directors. 'It was all really hard, dedicated graft, but Ewen was tenacious and kept pushing. Again, it took ages before we heard anything. Eventually, we got the good news that it was all go again, as the Lottery had agreed to give us funding. This time Scottish Power Technology was in charge. There were to be two 25-kilowatt turbines and a French make, Vergnet, was chosen as being most suitable. Then there were five blocks to be cast for each of the five turbines and their stays – needless to say, the old block was no use, as it had the wrong fixings. We then had to start all over again to make reinforced blocks, as well as building a house on the hilltop for the batteries. When all the work was finished, the scheme was riddled with faults. There were issues with the inverters that deal with AC/DC, and also the "dump load", the expression used for the surplus power, caused problems; the whole thing kept breaking down, with the constant fluctuations in wind. It worked fairly well for about seven years, but the batteries boiled and lost water too, and in the end the language barrier with one French manufacturer added to endless problems. Finally, when they stopped production of the turbines, we had to give up on that, too.

'So it was back to the National Lottery again, with the invaluable help of Ian Leaver from Eigg, our project officer, to see if we could get more finance. Eventually, a new scheme was awarded, £980,000. We now have 30 x 500-w photovoltaic cells, and six Evance generators without gearboxes. The photovoltaics are none too bonnie, but we are going to plant some bushes and trees around them, though they do have to be in an open position to catch the sun. The work began in July 2012 and was finally opened and ready in March 2013, and so far it appears to be really reliable.'

Certainly, by the time it was complete Muck was one of the last places in the UK to finally have 24-hour electricity. It had taken a staggering 43 years from start to finish, with endless trials and eternal hard graft, much of it on the part of – and thanks to – Ewen. It has indeed changed things on the island, and largely for the better.

People on the mainland become unreasonably irate when power is off for mere hours during extremes of weather. Not so the islanders of Muck. No one could have been more patient, long-suffering and persistent.

Though Lawrence appears to have tried hard to move with the times on most issues, I know that he too had qualms about what would happen when electricity became a permanent fixture and worried that it might change Muck for the worse. Jenny can now bake her bread and cakes at any time of the day or night, and though she does not have to she still rises with the lark, when she gets the ultimate peace to cook. And it is now possible to watch the end of a late-night film, instead of it being cut off in its prime, which was, I gather, a constant irritation. And as Ruth told me, there are no longer the same problems of rising in the middle of the night to deal with an ailing child. Muck has finally left its Dark Age, but let us not forget electricity bills.

A New School

'The island's very first school was in a room on the upper floor of Pier House and the first teacher was Colin Campbell. After the Education Act of the late 1800s, the children were taught in the living room there before the school was moved to the tin shed by the road, which eventually became our first bunkhouse. In 1927, the education authority was persuaded to erect a purpose-built school on the hill above and that corrugated-iron building is still there, though it is now falling to bits and will probably go soon. Another new school was badly needed, but it was quite controversial, as we only had one pupil, and that was Mary. At first the council suggested that we just use a Portakabin because the roll was so low. There were lots of newspaper articles about the situation, with photographs of Mary, who was 11 at the time. The headlines read: "A Class of her Own" and other similar things. Understandably, we were not at all happy about the Portakabin idea. I presume they wanted to board the teacher out, so it would not have been feasible to get a married teacher, if one applied for the job. Councillor Michael Foxley was a great help and pressed Highland Council hard to build us a proper new school. Finally, the council bought a site from us for which they paid way below the odds. It was clearly valued as agricultural land rather than for development, and we only got £3,000. As usual, we lost out heavily. However, we all felt that the school was very important, more important than arguing over the price of the land, and therefore we did not feel it appropriate to charge a proper rate in case the council decided against it.

'The architect for the project was John Pottie, who was actually at school with me at Altyre House, so I knew him reasonably well. The building contractor employed by the council was Neil MacDonald from Portree. Interestingly, building materials were much cheaper in Northern Ireland than they were in Scotland, and MacDonald got a boat called the *Houndbank* to bring in almost all the materials from there. As usual there was a glitch. They were using a Hiab crane to lift them out of the hold when the hydraulic pipe broke. It was going to take at least two days to get a new one, so there was nothing else to be done except to knuckle down and lift the blocks out manually. We all just grit our teeth and set to. We had to stand on blocks in the hold and then passed them hand-to-hand to one another; it was impossible to extricate the last ones, so they went back in the boat. It was another exhausting job, though not in the same league as the block episode for Port Mor House. When all is said and done, Neil MacDonald got a very good deal out of us and gave us very little thanks for our efforts. We were not very pleased at all but decided to lie low over it because at least the island had got its school.

'The new school was a vast improvement on anything we had had before. On the top floor there is a palatial flat for the teacher and his or her family, if necessary, and there is masses of storage space for all the junk that teachers seem to need nowadays, and an office, and ladies and gentlemen's toilets. We were also allowed to have community events there until the hall was built. Previously, we held most events in Port Mor House, which has a better floor for dancing and there was a bit more space, as Ewen had made super big double doors between the sitting area and dining area, so it was very nice indeed. Both Ewen and I enjoy dancing, but now we have bad knees so are not so keen. Actually, to be fair, building the school compared with just about everything else on the island, apart from the block episode, had very few glitches.'

Neighbourly Relations

Eigg like Rum plays a dominant role in the visual appeal of Muck, as its dramatic sgùrr is seen from most of the island. Many of its occupants have also become an integral part of Muck life, sailing across stormy seas for parties, weddings, funerals and ceilidhs, and joining in with livestock movements and providing general neighbourly support. Over Lawrence's lifetime, relations between the islands have on occasions proved tense, although there has never been a time when the two were not closely connected.

During his father's day and beyond, Eigg provided the lifeline to the mainland and various Muck boatmen collected the post from there on a regular basis. Commander MacEwen was never particularly friendly with the other owners of the Small Isles because they only tended to visit their islands during the summer. Sir Walter Runciman owned Eigg from 1925 to 1966. Though he was not present for much of the time, he was viewed as a good landlord. For a time, from 1966 to 1971, Eigg was owned by Captain Robert Evans from Shropshire. There were then excellent relations between the two islands due to the MacEwens' friendship with Graham Murray, Evans' manager, whom Lawrence describes as a 'super fellow'.

'Alasdair and I first met Graham Murray when we went over to Eigg to collect a coffin for Father. Poor man must have found it hard to deal with us, as we were both distraught, and I will always remember how kind he was. We got on really well on the livestock side, as he was very good at his job and they had excellent stock. There was a period when we went over to Eigg a lot more for things such as Burns suppers, ceilidhs and badminton sessions. I was once invited over there to shoot – that could have been highly embarrassing, but we had a blank day . . . the only bird was a jack snipe right at the end! I missed, but I was not keen to shoot it anyway. Over the years I have only ever shot a few birds, and they were probably all sitting. I prefer to see them alive.

'When Major Evans, who was quite elderly, put Muck on the market again, it was bought by the Anglyn Trust, who wanted to open it as a trainee centre for disabled adults, and for a while it was run by its owner, Bernard Farnhum-Smith, who called himself "Commander". It was later revealed that he was a commander in the fire service, but I never knew they had such a thing. Unfortunately, the local authorities did not send them any people. Local Councillor Fergus Gowans had been part of the consortium trying to buy Eigg and had tried to acquire it on several occasions, and he was not too enthusiastic about the new owner. They once had a dispute on the jetty on Eigg. Incidentally, Farnhum-Smith was a small man, but Gowans was even smaller! During Farnhum-Smith's ownership, the farm all got rather run-down too. Farnhum-Smith's relations with the islanders, and in particular the outspoken Dr MacLean, deteriorated badly and in the end it was sold again. When he finally left in 1975, Dr MacLean waved a claymore in defiance, he was so pleased that the Trust had gone, so they were clearly not very good landlords.'

On April Fool's Day of the same year, a date that in retrospect proved auspicious, a new flamboyant laird took over Eigg. Keith Schellenberg was already making the Eigg residents a whole list of promises, including setting up an island air service and the building of a distillery. This latter was a hugely popular idea, for obvious reasons. Ironically, he himself did not drink. He did not like field sports either, and spoke much of conservation and wildlife matters, and said he would be bringing in new islanders – though he would not be considering so-called dropouts from the south – and that he would make sure the island now blossomed, with plenty of opportunities for green tourism, self-sufficiency and employment.

Soon after his arrival, Mr Schellenberg, accompanied by eight children, took a boat trip to Muck, keen to meet the neighbours

'He was a dynamic personality and had great enthusiasm and was very keen on starting up a whole range of business ventures, and he wanted to arrange regular sporting events between the two islands. I learnt very early on how extremely competitive he was. He invited us over to play hockey, and it was amazing that we actually went. It turned into a mixture of hockey and soccer all at once; he was just totally mad. Now we have a hockey match on the beach at Gallanach every New Year's Day. It has become the ultimate masochistic hangover cure, as well as a way for all the extra people who are here during that period to show off their prowess. That, too, is utterly mad.

'Thank heavens we avoided a rugby match on Eigg one November with some of the army members from Benbecula. Schellenberg had brought in some of the rugby team from his previous home village of Udny to play for us, but even so, against the army I doubt we would have had much hope. Though I have always been very fit, I was certainly not a rugby player and had not played since schooldays. Luckily, the weather intervened and the army had to cancel. Mr Schellenberg got very angry when we cancelled too, and I learnt that he was a man who always liked his own way. It was not long after this that I crossed swords with him for the first time. I used to write a small guide booklet for sale for tourists, *A Guide to Eigg & Muck*, and, having had an expedition to take ewes over to Arisaig in Mr Schellenberg's rotork sea truck boat and nearly having to ditch them over the side due to it filling up with water, I commented in my piece "the Eigg boat is less than totally successful", that was all. He went mad and became furious with me. Looking back on it, it was well worth a bit of entertainment.

'Soon after this incident he invited us to go over to the island one Sunday afternoon. Colum Beagan and a few others accompanied me. When we arrived there, we walked up to the lodge, but outside was a big party of islanders, seemingly all fired up by Mr Schellenberg, who appeared to still feel rather put out about my comments in the guide. Well, I turned around without saying a word and we all trooped out back down the drive purposefully. However, instead of turning the way they expected us to, back to the pier, I led them on another more roundabout route. Some emissaries were sent after us, but they went the other way and before they got to us we had already got in *Wave* and were sailing home.

'On another occasion, there was a ceilidh in the hall on Eigg. By now Schellenberg and I were tolerating one another, just. He challenged me to sing, and frankly I am not much of a singer, so luckily Colum Beagan, loyal to the last breath, intervened and saved the day, as he could see I was going to fluff it. He piped up and said we would do a duet, and then everyone joined in with "The Road and the Miles to Dundee", so I got away with that one.

'We played numerous hockey matches with Eigg, but there was always foul play. Despite this, we once beat them 10–3. Schellenberg loved the Island Sports Days. He liked to referee all the field events; in fact, he often liked to be in charge of the whole show. Though I do recall him leaving the heavy ones, like caber tossing, to someone else.

He had a smart Spey-class yacht called *Sunart*, but she was soon ruined, as he filled her with basic slag or something similar, and he also had another boat called *Eilean ban Mora* – the Gaelic translation is the 'island of big women', the name for Eigg – and ran a daily service in competition with *Sheerwater*. This was mildly successful, but everyone was very relieved that he never took over the MacBrayne's runs. That was another of his mad ideas, and that would have been a disaster!'

Keith Schellenberg's entire stay on Eigg proved worse than disappointing. It was colourful and fraught with incidents, court cases and rebellions by the islanders. Someone burnt his Rolls-Royce Phantom and tensions mounted. The island fell into total disrepair. He and his misdoings were never out of the papers, and it was a tragic era for the beautiful Isle of Eigg and its people.

Another short-term landlord followed on, with hollow promises, and after a lengthy battle for funding, the islanders finally decided to go it alone and there was a community buyout in 1997. It was also a headline-hitting venture and has proved highly successful. Eigg is currently thriving and relations between the two islands are once again in fine fettle.

David Jones

It takes a very particular person to survive life on Muck and during Lawrence and Jenny's time at the helm they have seen a great many come, and even more go. Some have stayed and made their mark, becoming very much an integral part of everything whilst relishing the tiny community and its many challenges. Some have come expecting paradise and have found, particularly during the long, rain- and gale-battered winters, that if you are not fairly resilient it is something more akin to hell. As one islander commented, 'Living here has its bonuses, but I can assure you that everyone knows what you have done before you have even decided to do it and that can be very stressful. If you fall out with someone too, which invariably happens with such a melting pot of different characters, then it can be well-nigh impossible to avoid bumping into them.'

Jenny is the sort of mother and grandmother everyone dreams of. Caring, compassionate and with a brilliant sense of humour, to an outsider she can seem hopelessly overworked and in need of a good rest, but as I am beginning to realise she thrives on the need to be needed. This is a woman who can muster a miracle banquet out of almost nothing and is totally unfazed when yet another boat fails to run and visitors are stranded without supplies; and she is equally adept at sorting out animal problems as the eternal human ones. Muck, however, is no place for the faint-hearted. It is certainly not the place to come to run away from a sea of emotional problems.

Jenny is philosophical about many of the people who have come to the island. She has without doubt had much to endure, housing endless agricultural students over the years, all of whom she took under her wing and nurtured. Some had little or no idea whatsoever and, though she and Lawrence are careful not to say so, probably added to the workload rather than easing it. But there are many others who proved invaluable and became lifelong friends and still return to Muck on a regular basis.

David Jones was one such soul. He had come from Glasgow to Muck in 1974 just two days after the birth of his second daughter, Sharon, for a fortnight's trial period as a trainee shepherd. Lawrence took to him at once, though he did not show a particular interest in sheep; however, he realised his potential as a very skilled joiner adept at turning his hand to almost anything and found that he was also excellent with boats. Lawrence recommended to David that as he was so keen on farming he should go to agricultural college and he duly did this for three years. It was then that Lawrence offered him a six-month placement on Muck as part of his course.

To begin with, the Jones family lived in Boatman's Cottage near the pier in Port, and David added an extension onto it. Eventually, because he was so hard-working and really seemed to want to make a go of life on Muck, Lawrence, eager to give him an incentive for staying, offered to make a smallholding for them on 80 acres at Godag overlooking Rum and Eigg. He also got plans drawn up and David built his family a house there, too. It seemed that as well as helping in many ways on the farm, and doing some fishing and general maintenance, life was going to work out well for the Jones family. Today an impressive array of immaculately made field drains in the bog at Godag are a lasting legacy of David's hard hand digging. Their daughters helped to keep the tiny Muck school going.

David, more usually called Davy by the islanders, made good friends on Muck and in particular spent much time working with Bryan Walters. Bryan's widow Clare remembers how devoted her husband was to him and how much the pair enjoyed working together. Lawrence views him as someone who really was an ideal person for the island.

In September 1987, Lawrence lost one of his favourite collies, Shona, when she jumped overboard from *Wave* as they left Arisaig. Though they searched extensively, she was never found and it was clearly a devastating incident that upset Lawrence very much. However, far, far worse was to come. Looking back on it, it was almost as if this paved the way for probably the worst year of his life.

By the end of that year, there was a looming crisis on the farm. It was still incredibly high-maintenance at that time, so when Davy resigned from farm work and told Lawrence that he wanted to pursue a career crab fishing in partnership with his friend Bruce Mathers, he was most upset. He was losing a really good man, and now they would be severely shorthanded on the farm. As we talk, an air of abject misery and a profound depth of sadness permeate the room, as the story of the ensuing tragedies begins to unfold. There is an odd stillness followed by a rattling as the wind sweeps in off the sea and teases the slates on the roof. Lawrence looks down.

On 16 January 1988, Davy and Bryan went to Arisaig on *Wave* to collect fencing materials. The weather was fair and there was nothing to fear from that at least. In fact, Davy was casually reading his book behind the engine screen, and they were apparently just gently cruising home. Suddenly, the book slipped and fell down a gap by the engine. Instinctively, Davy put his arm down to retrieve it but his sleeve caught in a stud, which instantly pulled him right into the propeller shaft and the engine. He was knocked out and killed immediately, right in front of his friend, Bryan. It was a most horrific, terrifying life-changing ordeal for Bryan. His wife Clare says he never, ever got over it; he would not even talk about it, always changing the subject when Davy was mentioned.

Bryan immediately called the police, who rushed out on the lifeboat. Meanwhile he had put *Wave* into Eigg. Bruce Mathers took Lawrence over to Eigg on his own boat, *Alert*. Nothing could be done except to try and absorb the shattering truth. Later Lawrence and Bruce returned to Muck in total darkness and drizzle weighed down with ultimate misery. Davy was only 39. Lawrence sadly describes him as a man at the top of his game, a towering force on the island, and above all someone he really liked and admired. His gravestone in the tiny hillside graveyard in Port reads, *Hope Was Never Higher*. This was a man with his life in front of him; the black cloud over the island was bigger than ever. But before there had even been a Fatal Accident Enquiry, disaster struck again.

Bruce Mathers

'Sandra Mathers and her son, Sandy, are a few of the only people left on the island that were born on Muck. Sandra's great, great-grandfather originally came here from Rum in 1876 as a shepherd. Charlie MacDonald was Sandra Mathers' father and he used to go over to Eigg for the mail, and it was there that he met Katie, who became his wife. As I have told you before, she was without doubt one of the finest people I ever met. They were all native Gaelic speakers – sadly, now Sandra is the island's last remaining native Gaelic element. Charlie's uncle ran the farm for my father, so you will understand that they have always been a most important part of Muck. When Father died, as he did with Alick, he left Charlie a legacy because he held him in such high esteem.

'Sandra and her sister Ellen were both brought up here but had to go away to senior school in Portree in Skye. Once Sandra left high school, she went to Domestic Science College in Aberdeen and it was there that she met her future husband, Bruce Mathers, a tax inspector with the Inland Revenue. After they were married, they eventually returned to Muck and had their family, a son Sandy, who now fishes around the island, and a daughter Sheena, who trains racehorses and lives in Northumberland. I made another smallholding of 30 acres on the island so that Sandra and Bruce could croft, and Sandra still retains this with Sandy. She is a very good stockwoman.

'Bruce sometimes helped out on the farm, as well as working as a woodturner and also fishing. At one point, he got a contract to make 3,000 wooden light pulls for bathrooms – I think this probably finished him off and he decided to become a full-time fisherman after that. He bought a boat, *Alert*, from my brother Ewen and altered it by fitting a higher deck so it was suitable for creels. Having suffered the loss of his future business partner, Davy Jones, Bruce advertised for another man to fish with him. Roddie Murray from the Isle of Mull came to stay on the island and work with him, along with his wife Catriona.

'On their very first trip out together on 3 May 1988, just a few months after the death of Davy Jones, they were travelling towards Ardnamurchan in a strong north-easterly wind. The boat was laden with creels and the pair must have been filled with enthusiasm for their new venture, though this was surely marred with sadness for Bruce by the loss of Davy. We think it must have been the spray coming on board that filled the boat, though it is all just speculation and we will never, ever know what really happened. But she must have quickly sunk. The alarm was not raised until the evening. Roddie's body was eventually found weeks later in Uist, but Bruce was never recovered. Sandy and Sheena were still at school at the time. Sandra had also lost her father, Charlie, in February of the same year. The island was totally shattered.'

Sandra told me that the worst day she can remember was when she had to go to the Fatal Accident Enquiry, as no one knew what had happened. Once more the sea's treacherous nature had been revealed.

Dougie the Dyker

A casual day visitor arriving on *Sheerwater* for their fleeting summer sojourn cannot fail to notice the island's impressive dry-stone dykes. Dougie Irving, a dyker from Bridge of Weir, has recently repaired some of these. He turned up totally out of the blue on one of the saddest days the island has ever known, during the funeral of Izzy Fichtner-Irvine, Lawrence and Jenny's beloved five-year-old grand-daughter. Dougie, who Lawrence says was a total godsend, ended up staying for three months. The MacEwens had never previously met him, but he made a big impression on them all. His work leaves a lasting legacy, providing not only an impressive visual addition to the stunning land and seascape but also valuable shelter for stock and wildlife.

While he was working on the island, Dougie stayed at Sellachan Cottage and completed a large section of dyke near the farm at Gallanach. He was to be seen working in all weathers.

'He is only very lightly built, and I was hugely impressed with his work ethic, as even the worst days never seemed to put him off. In one place where he was building in particularly savage weather, he could have kept the dyke much lower but he still built it up to six feet and did a beautiful job, even though there was no shelter for him whatsoever. In fact, he went straight into the "Muck Heroes" category, along with Ewen, who has had this accolade twice – once for filling in the trench for the electric cable by hand, and the second time for building the road to the new pier site.

'Basalt is not good for dyke building, as it tends to fracture in hexagonal blocks, as seen on Staffa with Fingal's Cave. It's not like building on sedimentary rock, where all the stones tend to be flatter, and it's important to have big stones to help stabilise the wall. He used a plank to slide the bigger ones up into position. He also worked on Canna and Pabbay, and seemed to really like building walls alone in remote places. He is a most interesting multi-faceted person. He sometimes used to do a bunk, and go off and camp up the glen alone; I think he loved the peace. He amuses me with his mix of characters: shy one minute, then he would totally surprise you by doing amazing sessions at ceilidhs, especially if he'd had a few drinks. At one party he did a wonderful song he had composed about Colin's dog, Shona. It was in the form of a rap and amused everyone greatly. He is very musical and is a great fan of the Proclaimers. He was doing a librarian course at Aberdeen University, but then quickly tired of that. I think he really needs to be outdoors. He speaks several languages, including Spanish and German. Like his mother, who is a fantastic knitter, he also knits very fine socks, something that always seems rather surprising, but he and Jenny had lots to talk about because she knits wonderful socks, too. Dougie's mother is a real character; she came here to do some of Jenny's basketmaking courses and we all really liked her. He certainly made his mark here on the island, and I always looked forward to his visits. I suggested he went to my friends, the Reades on Mull at Sgroib-ruadh, but that did not work out, as they asked him to do a wall right by the roadside and I think passers-by stopped to chat to him and he could not stand it. I think he did the work very fast and then did not want to do any more because there were too many people around.'

Dougie's take on Lawrence and the island is equally glowing: 'Lawrence told me that in his lifetime he never thought he would see the dykes repaired. Maybe he just said it to get the work done, but actually I don't think so. He was genuinely so pleased. You know he used to come up to see me working and would always bring me stones in the back of his transport box on the wee red Fergie. They are a ridiculously generous family; Jenny is just so generous, and I can now see that rubbing off on her daughter-in-law Ruth. While I was working on one particular part, we needed a big flat through stone and eventually found one. I was also making steps in the dyke, so Toby, Mary's husband, could go back and forth to feed pheasants. Lawrence came up and saw the stone and asked me, "Is that your gravestone?" Toby is a big bear of a man and I must admit I did feel it had to be a big one to take his weight. It always used to amuse me that Lawrence would travel around the island on his bike and just leave it anywhere. I was so impressed to see him up ladders on the roofs putting slates back on, and always doing all manner of mundane jobs. He has a child-like adoration of Muck, and the farm is his life. I once knitted a pair of socks for him, but of course he never wears them.

'I am a big fan of Colin and Ruth. He is a real gentle giant; a soft-hearted guy who has a very different role to play than his father.

Lawrence has always loved publicity, but Colin is totally different. The MacEwens are always so welcoming and kind to me on Muck, and I love being there. It is entirely due to them that it is thus.'

Duchess

The story of the acquisition of Duchess appears to vary somewhat depending on whether it is Lawrence or Jenny who relates it. I first heard it from Lawrence and found the whole episode hilarious. However, I was sitting having lunch with them both one day at Gallanach and felt that Jenny's version of events was somewhat different and perhaps even funnier, as was the considerable amount of stick that Lawrence had to take for moderating it. I suspect, too, that Jenny's will be the more accurate, for I have already learnt that Lawrence tends to underplay some of their more hair-raising exploits, in particular, those relating to weather and livestock.

Lawrence, however, begins. 'I will tell you about my wonderful 45th birthday trip to Mull to buy a cow. As you know, I just love dairy cows, and I also love boat trips, and I just happened to notice that there was a dispersal sale of dairy cows on a farm near Craignure. The woman who owned it had all the best intentions but probably had not realised just how difficult it is to get milk distributed all around Mull.

'Anyway, though she wanted to be a dairy farmer, she sadly had not done her homework and it had not worked out. When I read that she was selling up, I thought to myself what a great day out it would be for my birthday. Jenny was agreeable, though if she thought it was just another of my hair-brained schemes she was not saying so. We made plans to go across to Mull and she made her usual big picnic to take with us. We had to leave Muck about 6 a.m. in order to get to the sale in good time; it takes two hours and twenty minutes to reach

Tobermory, and then we had to travel down the Sound of Mull on to Craignure, which takes about another hour. We had not only Colin and Mary with us but also Bryan and Clare Walters' girls, Emma and Ishy. The morning was fine and we set forth in good heart. When we finally reached Craignure, we moored *Wave* and then had a considerable walk before we got a lift to the farm for the sale.

'There, in amongst the cows, I spied this unusual, chocolate-coloured Jersey cow and I bid for her and got her. She was very different to the normal Jerseys I had seen, and I thought she was lovely. Just a young cow, I was thrilled with my purchase, as buying livestock is another of my passions. My sister had always milked cows and had Jerseys on her farm on Lismore; she had given me a Jersey cow called Arran, who was more of the conventional light-coloured type. Luckily, the Shaw-Stewart's obliging farm manager, Bill Henderson from Traigh Farm, Arisaig, was there with a trailer. He has frequently helped people in the islands over the years and has kept tups for us when we were unable to fetch them in bad weather. In the end, he did not buy anything, so his trailer was empty and he immediately offered to transport Duchess to Craignure for us, then to help us load her onto *Wave*. The day was still young, so we agreed a time to meet him back at the pier.'

It is at the next phase of the tale that Lawrence's and Jenny's versions differ, but for now Lawrence continues. 'We walked back from the sale through the beautiful Japanese gardens at Torosay Castle, as I really wanted to make it a nice day out and see lots of things too. We then had a quick look around the inside of the castle. By now, it was raining quite heavily. I am also a passionate railway enthusiast, so we had made plans to go on the little narrow-gauge railway that then ran from Torosay Castle to Craignure. We must have also had our picnic in some sheltered spot, as it was by now a bit damp. When we finally got back to Craignure, we were quite wet. We went out to *Wave* and brought her alongside the linkspan, where they load the car ferries.

I got the chap who works the lift to suit the level of the tide and he raised it for us so that it was exactly at the right level, with the gunnel of the boat against the pier. Then Bill arrived, together with a few other people from Arisaig who clearly thought that putting a Jersey cow on a boat might be quite amusing and worthy of a closer look.

'We got Duchess out without any problem and found that she was a very nice, quiet cow, but unfortunately the last six feet of the roadway were not tarred, they were made of steel. She took one look at this and then refused point-blank to budge; she would not walk one step further onto the different surface. Then she resolutely lay down. Well, we pushed and we shoved and we did all in our power to get her back up, but she refused. So in the end a lot of us had to literally manually roll her onboard *Wave* without further ado. This, I might add, had lured an even bigger audience, and I think there was a cheer when she landed on the deck of the boat. It must have been a really funny sight, and all in the rain too. By now the weather was not too good; in fact, it was turning very wet indeed and, as we started to round Ardnamurchan Point, it got worse still. Jenny had to take the helm and steer, throttling back each time a big wave came over us, while I stayed with Duchess, as I was frightened she might lose her footing and hang herself by the rope we had tied her up with. It was all a bit tricky, but not that bad really. Jenny was always very good in boats. She is a far better sailor than me and has never ever been seasick. I think she had plenty of practice in rough water boating with Tex Geddes on Soay. As ever, she helped enormously; as well as taking the tiller from time to time, she had to cope with the children, several of whom were being a bit sick, even though it was not that rough. Eventually, after passing Ardnamurchan Point, we altered our course and this made it far easier. We got back home to Muck safely with our purchase. Thankfully getting Duchess off was a whole lot easier.'

As we sit eating our soup a few days after I hear this tale, I raise it with Jenny and mention that it sounded a great trip. She asks me what Lawrence told me. Then, giving him a very stern look, she says, 'Lawrence you have not told her the truth. It was a horrendous trip! A bit damp? It was absolutely torrential rain and we were all totally soaked right to the skin. In fact, I was mortified when you were insistent that we all trooped into Torosay Castle in our bedraggled state. We each left deep pools of water and mud from all the bogs we'd had to walk through all over their highly polished floor. And you did not even seem to notice. And as for the journey home, it was a dreadful day by then, and the waves coming over the boat were immense, and *all* the children were dreadfully sick and drenched and thoroughly miserable. *And* Duchess was as stubborn as a mule, and it took ages messing about getting her onboard in the first place. You never really much liked Jersey milk and cream anyway, and always said you preferred Ayrshire milk! Oh, he will insist on us taking to the sea in some dreadful weather and we have had numerous miserable boat journeys for livestock, but somehow he does not seem to notice.'

There is a giggle from Lawrence as he pours himself another cup of tea and sups it loudly to cover up his embarrassment, then Jenny winks in my direction.

'I do much prefer Ayrshire milk, as Jersey milk seems to have a bluish tinge. And it's so thick with yellow cream on the top. But Duchess was a lovely cow, with a nice temperament. I suppose I never took to Jerseys as I did to Ayrshires. We were supplying the whole island with milk at that point. It was amazing in the end because we put both Jersey cows in calf to a Simmental bull and it was incredible that the calves made £550 each in Oban, a very good price at that time. That really was a huge surprise. I think the buyer thought they were Limousin crosses, as obviously Jerseys are at the bottom of the heap when it comes to beef cattle production, but we were not going to explain that. I admit we beat a hasty retreat!'

Though Lawrence has a fantastic memory, it seems clear that he is never one for remembering the worst abuse the west coast climate has hurled at them during their many excursions. 'I suppose,' he adds rather wistfully, 'it was not the most exciting trip for Jenny, but I thoroughly enjoyed it. And ten days after we got Duchess, she produced a fine heifer calf.'

The Noble Sensation

Keeping enough children in the school has long been a problem for Muck. Families come and go. Often once their children have to go to the mainland for secondary education, it is a real wrench for them and the families move on, particularly given the fact that even getting them home for weekends with erratic weather and lack of boats is never guaranteed.

Trying to find suitable new residents is a hard task. Many people love the idea of island living but have no conception of the challenges it presents: they don't fully appreciate how hard it can be to get on with only a very small number of other people. Some of these families are of particular note. In 2001, in a bid to find suitable islanders, Lawrence put an advert in the papers.

'Carn Dearg was empty again and so I thought this would be a good idea. Bryan Walters knew Lamont Howie, who works for Radio Scotland, and contacted him to see whether he would give the island a little publicity. Before we knew it, Howie, who is a wonderful chap, came out with a *Sunday Post* photographer who had me parading up and down the beach endlessly with my dog. The sand was wet and there were very beautiful reflections, and the subsequent picture appeared splashed all over the national press with the story that we were looking for a new family. Needless to say, because the image showed Muck in a good light, soon after we were inundated with about 100 applications and we had to go through each one, endeavouring to gauge its suitability. Some of them were hopeless, we could tell that just from their CVs and the way they wrote about what they wanted. The Hebridean Press Agency, which operates out of Stornoway, then got in touch with me to find out more about our aims. I told them that in these days of democracy I thought it appropriate to have an island vote, so that everyone had a chance to choose the best-suited family for Muck. At about the same time the BBC were running a very popular programme called *Two Thousand Acres of Sky*, about a fictitious island idyll, and that must have also brought the dream of escape to an island to the fore. Unless you are media savvy, you just never know the moment something is going to cause a sensation, and this did just that.

'After much work we had whittled the applicants down to six families. Ideally, we wanted people who had a country background, as well as primary school-age children, the younger the better to keep the school going for longer. The Nobles were amongst those that came to have a look and, with two wee girls only just primary school age, they seemed ideal. Some of the others did not like the look of the island and did not turn up. When it came to the vote, despite the fact that they did not know the west coast at all, the Nobles won. The husband was into computers in a big way and we thought they would be able to support themselves because he could do his work remotely. Frankly, I always thought, as with so many of the new families that come here, they were a long shot. They were from Leeds, and I always worry about how people will keep body and soul together. One thing was sure, they loved all the media attention: they kept appearing on the television and in newspaper articles; it was all about them leaving an area where there were drugs and joyriders and other perils, and swapping it for heaven on earth in a place where no one locks doors or carries any money and there are less than a handful of cars.

'We took all their furniture over in *Wave*, but they themselves arrived on *Sheerwater* in a blaze of glory, with an entourage of press.

The idea was that they would step ashore on their new island home and the press would record every second of this epic event. I stood back somewhat and took it all in. In the evening, we had a welcome party in the craft shop.

'To begin with, they actually wrote a few articles for English women's magazines about their new ideal lifestyle. Sadly, he got very little work and was not so able to help around the place as others do. They were here for about three years and then they left. They left of their own accord, though the media tried to say otherwise and there was more coverage. It was not a big deal, as far as I was concerned, though obviously I was sorry it had not worked out.

'Mrs Noble was scared stiff of cows and, as you know, there are cows all over the place at various times, and she always had to escort her children to school on great detours to avoid them. Just that alone was enough to show that this was not really the place for them.'

And as such, another family bit the dust and left.

John Morris and the Postal Bride

The Nobles were not the first family to be enticed to Muck as a result of Lawrence's ingenuity. There had been an earlier attempt to increase the population on the island and likewise the story had attracted the attention of the national press. As Lawrence puts it, 'Obviously, when there is a slow news day, the press go mad for small things like this and Muck gets masses of publicity. The island's name also has a great deal to do with it, as there are all the usual puns and plays on words.

'The Morris family came from Wilmslow in Cheshire. Husband John was very mechanical and that attracted me, as I am ever on the look for people who can help out here. He had been in the British Army in tank maintenance, and he had also worked for Foden's in a diesel assembly line in Cheshire. He had a young wife and four children, and all seemed rosy. Within six months, his wife and family had upped sticks and left him. At that point, he understandably seemed very dejected and sad, and Rosie Soutter, who has a very kind heart, took him under her wing. I was a little concerned that he was perhaps rather too keen on the bottle, as you know that is somewhat of a peril in the Hebrides.

'Then one day Bryan Walters, who was postie at that time, received a letter. It was simply addressed: *The Postman, Isle of Muck*. When he opened it, he found it was from a single woman in Guernsey who said she was looking for a man! She had clearly seen something in the press about the island and thought it would be fun to just send a letter to see what happened. So Bryan thought this was highly amusing and said to John, "Here, you are single, you better have it." The whole thing was quite extraordinary. The lonely John started corresponding with her and the next thing she came out to Muck. She seemed really nice. Before long it had progressed much further and he announced that they were getting married. I was never sure if he was still married or not – either way his wife and children were never seen here again and he did not even appear to communicate with them.

'Excitement mounted on the island. It was a beautiful day when they were married by the charming minister, Alan Lamb, in a field of thistles near the graveyard at Port. I made a speech at the event. It was a super day; actually, it was the day after the Nobles arrived, but we did not tell the press or they would have been around too. Afterwards we had a nice party in the craft shop. The Postal Bride stayed about four years and certainly did not make too many waves, but John never seemed very enthusiastic about her, while she to the contrary was mad about him! This seemed rather sad to me. Actually, I was always surprised that he did not even bother to scythe all those thistles!'

Lunchtime Drinks at Inverockle

Lawrence's boating forays are legendary. There are those who refuse point-blank to venture to sea with him, while others claim that taking to the ocean wave with him often turns into an epic adventure. Personally, I was hugely disappointed when on numerous occasions plans to sail to Mull in the winter to fetch calves had to be postponed due to the abuse the weather hurled in Muck's direction.

Jenny regales me with another good tale about one of Lawrence's boat trips. 'Over the years I have never doubted Lawrence's capabilities in a boat, but perhaps I should have because we have certainly had plenty of hair-raising experiences. During the summer, we quite often used to go off on Sundays somewhere in *Wave* and usually had a few extra children with us. We once had a great trip to Coll and cycled around the island, and we frequently went to Rum, and sometimes back to Soay, too. On one particularly notable occasion, Lawrence had the idea that he would like to pop across to Ardnamurchan to take some gravel off the shore at Inverockle. Off we set with Colin, Mary, Sarah and a French student called Gilles, whose parents owned the House of Hermès in Paris. This is a very upmarket Parisian fashion house. We also had Haig Douglas's grandchildren and a couple of other students as well. Lawrence's idea was to collect gravel for the yard. Once we got across to Inverockle, we anchored in the bay and then rowed ashore, and soon began filling about 50 bags with shovel-loads of gravel. Then the mist came right down. Inverockle is a lovely little cove and there is a beautiful turf-roofed house on the other side of the burn there. We were a bit concerned about the mist, then suddenly it began to clear a little and we noticed this group of people by the house all waving at us. I was so embarrassed because we all looked like raggle-taggle gypsies, we really did. They had been having a lunch party and had just finished, and were rather jolly and on to more drinks and tea.'

This turf-roofed house was the part-time home of Arthur Kellas, who was a soldier and distinguished diplomat. He had seen serious warfare with the Parachute Regiment and the SOE, and was ambassador to Nepal and Yemen, as well as the High Commissioner in Tanzania. He and his equally charming wife Bridget spent much time in Ardnamurchan at Inverockle and visits into their amazing house were always at a premium as I myself experienced over the years.

'He really was a most charming man and he insisted that we came straight across for tea and drinks and what have you with them. Lawrence had taken a South African chap as crew with us as well, so we really were quite a big party. I was mortified when Lawrence in typical fashion agreed to go in because we must have looked like real down-and-outs. So, over the burn we traipsed. Once inside we found that the house was full of wonderful antiques and artefacts, and it was all so immaculate and artistic. Mr Kellas poured some huge gin and tonics, but I had a cup of tea, as I was worried about what the children might get up to in that gorgeous house and I certainly did not want to be fuddled. Mary and Colin were very small and both they and the other children were awful, as they just would not stop fiddling with everything. I was scared stiff that something would get broken. Meanwhile Gilles and Mr Kellas were deep in conversation in French. Poor Gilles had found English very hard and was clearly so happy to be speaking his own language once more. He was on the gin, too, and was becoming quite tiddly. Well, Mr Kellas's French was probably better than Gilles's.

'Meanwhile the children were wandering about causing mayhem and, though the Kellas's and their party were all so charming about it, I just wanted the ground to swallow me and for us to get out quick. I was also cringing about us pinching all that gravel. Eventually, the mist cleared and I just grabbed everyone and bundled them all out of the door again, as fast as I could, and home we sailed. What an experience!'

The Catering and Craft Department

I am sitting in the dentist's chair with mouth agape, nodding as Morag Anderson probes my teeth while cheerily chatting. On my arrival, before I was able only to mumble a response, we had been briefly talking about summer boat trips. She then said, 'We went over to Muck recently and the tearoom there has got to be the best in Scotland. It is absolutely fantastic.' Until that moment the subject of the Isle of Muck had not been mentioned. It is a much-deserved accolade, as the well-trodden path from the pier to the island's craft shop-cum-tearoom bears testimony. With fresh shellfish caught by Sandy Mathers and a quite surprisingly diverse menu of mouth-watering goodies, it offers some of the Hebrides' finest fare. Jenny rises at dawn every day to bake, and almost all of the food is home produced. Squat lobster sandwiches on thick, freshly baked brown bread, with salad grown in the island's poly-tunnels, and unusual soups often with a hint of spices and herbs are just a few of the gems on offer. And then there are Jenny's cakes; the selection is astonishing and it means that day-trippers tend to be a good deal heavier on their return crossing. The craft shop is full of fascinating stock. An eclectic mix of reading matter, as well as fine hand-knitted garments, cards and treasures make this an emporium not to be missed. Jenny's opening hours coincide with the year's first visitors, who arrive on the *Loch Nevis* on Tuesdays, when they have a couple of hours ashore before being whisked back to the mainland. When Ronnie Dyer returns with *Sheerwater* loaded with visitors, the tearoom never seems big enough, and on fine days outdoor tables are at a premium. Once it closes again at the end of the season the craft shop becomes the venue for shooting lunches, where a delicious four-course meal is served and sportsmen dry off in front of the wood-burning stove. Their healthy glow is down to not only the elements but also probably to the lavish amounts of liquid refreshment served by Toby Fichtner-Irvine, Lawrence and Jenny's generous son-in-law. Despite the building of the new hall, the craft shop still remains the hub of the island and has become an institution.

The building was formerly Kiel House, and when it was taken on as the site for the craft shop it was just a typical croft cottage in a poor state of repair, without a roof. When Ewen returned home he found time to roof it with felt despite the fact he was already working on two other houses. Lawrence's mother had already started a small craft enterprise in an outside bedroom beside the farmhouse where visitors could buy a few items made on Muck. Jenny, who is an exceedingly fine cook, is also intensely creative and had always had a vision for a craft venture.

'Initially, I just had a few old tables and chairs in it. It was all very simple and I only really made people a cup of tea and they had a piece of cake, and I sold one or two crafts but not much more. At that stage, whatever money I made I ploughed straight back into the business. Various people have had an input in making the craft shop the attractive place it has since become. One student was given the task of pointing up the wall inside. John Low, who built his house, Dun Ban, had some leftover slates, so Davy Jones slated the roof and lined the interior with pitch pine, adding to its cosiness and charm. He also put the porch on. Lawrence had already built a stone chimneystack by then, so that we could have a fire in there.

'We soon found that there was not nearly enough space. Architect Mandy Ketchen, who lived here with her husband Ian, designed the extension – that's why it blends in so well with the rest of the building. She persuaded Pod Carmichael, a very busy local builder, to come and complete the work and together they made a really good job. Lawrence had to find precisely the right five-inch stones to face it all off so that the new bit was in keeping with the rest, but I think he liked doing it. He certainly mentions it quite a bit. We had an open-ing ceilidh and I remember dancing on the newly concreted floor. We have had many events in there over the years: Mary's christening, church services, John Morris's wedding reception, and various other things.

'During their time on Muck, both Mandy and her husband made their mark. She was the founder of CAMUS, our community arts organisation. Lawrence and I were very sad when they departed due to Ian's poor health. Originally, Ian had been a stonemason in Edinburgh; he made Northumbrian pipes and played them, as well as selling them sometimes to America.'

Jenny has seen many come and go and seems genuinely sad to have lost people she considers to have been close friends.

Having the craft shop fully operational by the time of Muck's first Open Day nearly 30 years ago was a real bonus. This successful event has continued annually and is usually held on the first Sunday in June. It is something that Lawrence in particular relishes.

'I had this idea that it would be good to meet other farmers, as I really miss having the chance to swap ideas and chat, and other than in the market Muck provides little opportunity for that. I put an advert into the *Scottish Farmer* and got lots of interest, and the first Open Day was great fun. We sometimes get farmers from quite a long way away, too.'

'In the beginning, there was no steamer pier, so that meant if the tide was unsuitable we had to ferry everyone ashore in as many din-ghies as we could muster. Ronnie Dyer, who frankly has done more for this island than anyone, brings the groups over in *Sheerwater* and waits to take them back again. Sometimes Catriona brings groups over from Lismore. We may have a fund-raising stall and everyone bakes and makes various things to sell. We take people around on tours in two tractors and trailers, with straw bales for them to sit on. Someone else drives while I do the talking and tell them about the island and the stock. I bring cows down for them to see and put some attractive Jacob-cross Cheviot ewes with their lambs in a pen too. The only problem is that I tend to talk far too much, as you know, and then on some occasions they don't have enough time to buy produce, as we are so late back. We also have a little Berber tent for the day, and do sandwiches and draught beer operated with a foot pump, initially provided for us by Murdo Grant of Arisaig Hotel. If it's a bad day and not many people come, then we are left with an awful lot of drinking and eating to do, and usually have a good party afterwards. It is a huge amount of work for Jenny and she does such a good job. I would quite like to do more with the Open Day to provide further entertainment. Colin hates it though, so the whole thing will probably die with me, but I admit I really enjoy it.'

Muck's ambassador understandably loves to show off the island he lives and breathes.

As if Jenny had not got enough to do, she was an active member of the Lochaber Craft and Food Producers Association and became involved in discussions to develop an outlet in Fort William. When the idea was first put forward, others seemed to be lukewarm about it. It was organised by Kate Campbell of Strontian and though the thought seemed good it came as rather a surprise when Jenny suddenly found that she had inadvertently agreed to run the new venture, based in a small retail outlet at the station called the Siding. Luckily, Mary was at home at the time and during her mother's absence running the Siding enterprise took over the reins in the tearoom. Jenny quickly realised that the only way the new Siding cafe could make money was if she ran it herself. A flat in Fort William was bought and she stayed there.

'It was all a bit of a nightmare and proved to be three years of exceedingly hard graft for nothing at the end of the day; in fact, I think we really lost money. As well as providing sandwiches for people on the overnight sleepers, I made copious amounts of food for other outlets too, including the Fired Arts Centre at the end of town and the restaurant car at Glenfinnan Station.

'Lawrence was in Fort William quite a bit too at that time because after years of campaigning and fund raising, auctioneer's wife Isabel Campbell had succeeded in realising the dream for a state-of-the-art auction mart, built just outside the town. Lawrence agreed to take on the role as one of its new directors but, given the logistics of getting on and off Muck for meetings, eventually felt he was unable to make a worthwhile contribution and therefore gave it up. He had also been running a stall at Farmers' Market there, selling apples, and I provided loaves, which were very popular.' Jenny laughs, 'Really, though, the Siding enterprise was a farce because there was more than enough to do at home!'

While the Siding was perhaps a white elephant, Jenny has certainly made a real success of expanding the island's craft shop.

'I had the idea that I would like to produce a yarn on the island and as we had some beautiful soft Jacob fleeces with lovely markings I felt I should learn to spin. It was then that I met Marci King, who came from Norwich to teach me. She went on to become one of my greatest friends. I also learnt how to felt wool. Then I saw a very good article in a magazine on basketmaking and followed this up. Sheila Wynter, a professional basketmaker from the south, came to run an initial course and I became totally hooked. We have been running basketmaking courses ever since. I am happy to show absolute beginners how to make a basket, but various people come to teach a more advanced level and we usually have plenty of takers. I wanted to grow our own willow and started to plant some at Dun Ban in the wood there, however it did not last long, as along came Toby with his pheasants and you know what they are like.'

Jenny smiles wryly, as no one is keener that her family have the opportunities to run their own successful businesses here. Pheasants, however, can be destructive, with their pecking and scratching and, like the expanding population of geese in the Hebrides, often come into conflict with agriculture and horticulture, though few on Muck complain.

'There always seems to be so much else to do that I don't get enough time to put into the crafts. I have a few other knitters who provide garments for me. There is a lady in Arisaig, and Dougie the dyker's mother is a great knitter. I spend a lot of time knitting shooting stockings. When the shooting parties arrive, I often get commissions for made-to-measure ones as well. I once made a pair in a fortnight, but that was because I had to. Normally, it takes longer than that. It is marvellous that we have 24-hour power now and I don't have to struggle to knit by candlelight at the crack of dawn when I can knit in peace. '

Jenny also keeps bees. She has a laissez-faire approach to their husbandry, doing it all herself with little fuss. One lot swarmed down the chimney, but Lawrence, dressed in Jenny's bee suit, managed to extricate them; she claims she is not much use on a ladder. Muck's abundant wild flowers make the resulting honey exceedingly fine.

'Clare Walters and I kept a few goats and their milk was great for pet lambs and calves. I really loved them; they are very human-orientated animals. I used to drink their milk, but, though Lawrence is so passionate about his own cows' milk, he never liked it.'

Her house reminds me of a motorway service station, with a constant throughput of people. It bulges at the seams with children and their toys, and Jenny's ginger dog Mattie wrinkles her sweet face in a canine smile as more pile in amid the heaps of cast-off steaming wet clothes, filthy muddy boots and boiler suits, with buckets of hen and pig food awaiting collection at the doorway. The kettle is glued to the Raeburn, there is always some fabulous cake to tempt the unwary, and she seems ever smiling despite the constant intrusion – and eternal washing-up. And then it is lunch or dinnertime yet again; and rare for it to be just the two of them. She has had endless students living as family with them and appears to be an agony aunt to everyone with problems, both real and imagined. Most days, she has some of the grandchildren at some point, something that makes her happiest of all. And somewhere in amongst all this she manages to run her highly successful business – the best tearoom in Scotland.

Snow Business

'Snow is a very rare occurrence here and seldom lasts any length of time. Due to the sea being warmer than the land in winter, and Muck's small size, it seems to melt fast. I can only remember one major fall. In 1995, snow lasted for a week. Each morning I can look across to Rum and see how low the snow level is on the hills over there. Compared to us, they have a great deal and it lasts due to the height of the hills. The same year there was quite a lot of snow all over the west coast. Lewis had an unusually big fall, too. It fell on Christmas Eve and totally transformed everything. Every year we sing carols by candlelight in the byre with the livestock, but this particular year Mandy and Ian Ketchen had offered to host it in the sheep pens near their house. It was so cold that they lit braziers and there was a near gale blowing. Holding the candles was very hard and everyone had cold hands. The previous year it had been so calm and frosty that we had moved outside into the silver light of a full moon. Our candles had hardly flickered.

'The year of the snow we rose on Christmas morning to about five inches and it was really lovely. On Christmas Day, I conduct a carol service somewhere and various people do readings. It really helps when we have good singers on the island – frankly, I have never been a singer, but Judy, Ewen's partner, is very good and sometimes organises this side of things.

'Afterwards we all got going with sledges and used home-made ones constructed of wood and plygene, a strong plastic that we used for the runners. Bryan Walters had a quad bike then, so he towed the sledges through the snow and we had great fun on the slopes behind the farm; some of us also snowboarded on the hillocks. In Port, they used a rubber dinghy as a sledge and it flew swiftly down the hill and was most successful. By our standards, the frost was quite hard, so that helped with the sledging, but even then it only fell as low as minus five or six at night. I have never known it lower than that. During the snow, I went up Beinn Airein because it was so clear and I could see right up to the hills of North Uist peeping out behind Tarbet on Canna. This is quite unusual; it was stunning. Sadly, by New Year the temperature had risen and the snow had disappeared.'

Pier Pressure

'The original pier was probably made in the 1850s. At that time, some of the islanders had left to go to Tobermory to fish, as Muck had become very run-down. However, when Captain Swinburne bought it in 1854, he also bought two fishing smacks and some islanders came back because he intended to build up a fishery. Soon they were fishing as far out as the Rockall banks, west of St Kilda. The only way to preserve fish then was by salting it, so Pier House was built as a salt store. My grand-uncle put the parapet around the old pier; it was dry stone with no cement surface and tended to wash away during any storms, so one of the things I did very early on was to put concrete on top of it with a wooden edge and that has been very successful. It's not very clear, but there was another pier about 100 yards down the shore. The big pier was covered at really high tides, but the next one was built of large boulders and you could get *Wave* alongside a bit earlier with a rising tide, maybe about an hour sooner. However, we still did not use it much because the road down was far too rough even for tractors.

'In the 1990s, I thought we should rectify this and make it easier for visitors coming ashore, particularly off Shoormowuu. It was a typically long, protracted "Muck" task, involving copious amounts of concrete, hard graft, blood, sweat and turmoil. The sea and a large swell smashed the first endeavours overnight and all the work had to begin again from scratch. I bought Greenheart, a tropical timber from Guyana often used for making piers, and personally shovelled some 13,000 shovels of gravel for the concrete.' I have no reason to question him as he is a man who appears undaunted, even relishes, life's greatest challenges.

'Though the advantages of using that pier were perhaps marginal, it did mean that when we got home from Arisaig we could get to it an hour before we could get to the higher one and unload whatever we had. So it really has been a big help.

'We also built a little extension with steps so that visitors in dinghies could get alongside because when the tide was really low there was nowhere for them to come ashore without getting their feet wet – they always had to wade. Of course, when we were young, Alasdair, Ewen and I were often down at Port to meet the boats coming in and if the passengers were pretty girls we'd heroically carry them ashore and wade through the water barefoot. They thought this was wonderful, and so did we. However, I have to admit, I have also carried quite a lot of men.

'In the 1980s, there was pressure and a great deal of talk about building a proper new pier. Up until then, we used *Wave* as a flit boat for everything. It was not only laborious but also considered dangerous. However, no one ever went into the sea when they were being transferred, although one woman did end up on her back on *Wave* – and this was nothing to do with drink! Our boatman Bryan Walters was particularly good at operating the flit boat and he would insist that the big CalMac boat was in just the right sheltered place to make it safest. There was one relief boat, *Pioneer*, that was particularly dangerous and difficult to come alongside, and often it was risky. We had a pile of pallets stacked in the hold to use to help us reach the steps protruding from the *Pioneer*. We also used another set of steps to get the passengers off the pallets. To offload parcels, we had some heavy plastic sheeting that the crew of *Pioneer* attached over their steps to serve as a chute and we caught the parcels as they tumbled onto the pallets below. If the health and safety officer had seen the Heath Robinson set-up, he would have had a fit. Things really have changed.

'One summer in August the weather was so bad that we had to take *Wave* around to Gallanach and keep her there for a fortnight. Visitors, luggage and provisions all had to be rowed ashore from there. On another occasion, Colin had 26 friends coming over for New Year and we had to meet the *Loch Nevis* round at Gallanach too, because of the squalls and the swell. Everyone got really soaked and all the cardboard boxes of provisions and booze literally turned to pulp.'

After endless discussion and procrastination, Construction Centre Group (CCG) started building Muck's new pier in the spring of 1999. CalMac had advised that the best place for this would be on the Gallanach side; there was also an island vote about it, and the only one pro this idea was Ewen. Lawrence and the rest of the island felt that having a pier in such a beautiful spot would totally ruin one of the best views on earth. So the pier work began at Port, despite the fact that they had been advised that if they put it there, then there would probably be many days when it was far too difficult and risky for the CalMac boat to get into the harbour due to the exposure and the narrow channel. Lawrence felt that most of the infrastructure was already in place at Port and obstinately stuck his heels in, no matter the advice to the contrary.

To begin with, it appeared that CCG had far too much money; they were very lavish until it began to run out. One day after the work began Lawrence had pedalled down to Port to see how it was all going and commented in his diary that there was more shipping in the harbour than they had on the Clyde. Work had truly begun. There was much dredging, and the new base for the slipway began to take shape as the enormous blocks that had been cast in Mallaig and brought over by barge were put in place. Over the winter work had to stop due to the weather. By the second season, CCG had realised that they were spending far too much and most of the shipping vanished. Ewen and Lawrence fell out over taking stone for the pier from the small quarry on Muck. Lawrence did not see why not; Ewen, understandably, was adamant that it should not be removed. Tension mounted. Pier pressure was beginning to get to them: it was turning into yet another typically protracted and difficult Isle of Muck job.

By the third season, much time was being spent trying to extricate more money from Highland Council; this drew a blank. Meanwhile CCG frustratingly only maintained a token presence on the island and work ground to a halt. They were also making a pier on Rum at the same time.

Then, at the end of the third year, CCG's marine division went into liquidation and Briggs Marine, a large firm from Burntisland, was brought in. The Rum and Muck piers ended up costing in the region of £9 million, to say nothing of the cost to the nerves. Eventually, at the end of it all, Muck got its proper pier. Now there was no need for linkspans, used to allow for tidal changes, because the new CalMac, *Loch Nevis*, was constructed with an extra long ramp that could be lowered onto the slipway. And, of course, flit boats were no longer needed either.

Though only islanders are allowed to bring cars onto Muck, it means that all goods, passengers and livestock can finally be transported back and forth with a great deal more ease. On 5 March 2004, the *Loch Nevis* came to use it for the first time, and in August MSP Nicol Stephen officially opened it. It was the end of another long saga.

Once again it is the weather that dominates its existence, however, and determines how much it can be used. As I was to witness on numerous visits in severe weather, frequently the CalMac boat just cannot come into Muck's harbour – to see the boat coming near but yet so far, and it having to turn back, is very frustrating for all concerned.

Lawrence grudgingly accepts that his brother Ewen was right, but despite the fact that the *Loch Nevis* misses up to 50 calls per winter, if the slipway had been to the west side of Gallanach not only would one of the best views on the island have been ruined but it would have been of no value to any other boat operator except CalMac. *Sheerwater* has no problem entering Port. 'CalMac should charter *Sheerwater* as an island service for us in winter,' says Lawrence. He frequently grumbles about this issue in his regular column in the community new magazine *West Word*. He is adamant about it and remains immovable on the importance of safeguarding the view. There are times when you have to take the rough with the smooth.

Amy

New island visitors coming to Muck on the *Loch Nevis* can find themselves being scrutinised by a small crossbred terrier with a very comfortable little figure. She may go up the ramp and sniff them out to see if any are worthy of her companionship during their sojourns. This is Amy, who has accrued the size of fan club that would put many arrogant celebrities to shame. Her presence dominates the holiday house visitor's books and no one has a bad word to say about her.

Sandy Thomson, who worked for CCG on Muck during the time

of the pier construction, bred Amy. He had a black Patterdale cross Border terrier bitch and she produced a litter of wonderful puppies. He had them in a large box adjacent to where he was working and there was a certain inevitability that Jenny, who adores animals, would fall under their spell and agree to keep one. Sandy had decided that he would like to leave a puppy on each of the islands where he had been working. At first he gave Jenny a dog, but as only bitches are allowed on Muck she had to ask him for a swap, and Amy was the result. Much loved by all who meet her, she uses Jenny as her main base when nothing better is happening, but for the rest of her time – and in particular during the summer, when the holiday cottages are occupied – she prefers to make the acquaintance of temporary residents, who end up falling in love and feeding her a most varied diet. She now tends to spend much of her time with Gareth and Zoe Moffat and their three children, and the adoration is mutual. When they go south for holidays, Amy returns to Jenny, who is always pleased to see her, despite her lack of loyalty.

Amy has always moved around the island from house to house and likes to find keen walkers. Then she acts as an expert guide, steering them away from the worst bogs and other hazards and generally ensuring they don't stray in the wrong direction. When the *Hebridean Princess* came to Muck, Amy saw the chance for a little hob-nobbing with the more upmarket type of tourist, accompanying one extremely fit gentleman right to the top of Beinn Airein, much to his absolute delight.

There was one dog that managed to sneak onto the island, and Amy, with her wanderlust, saw fit to pay him a visit, too. The resulting liaison was Mattie, a delightful ginger girl, who is the complete opposite of her mother, being so faithful that she seldom leaves Jenny's side. Jenny finds it hard to leave the island now, as Mattie cannot bear her to be away; she has never yet been in a boat or worn a collar and lead.

It would appear that Mattie is becoming just as popular with visitors. An entry in the Seilachan Cottage visitor's book by Ruby Baird Allan – aged 8 – reads as follows:

I have super duper loved Muck. It was a shame I didn't see Mattie this time but my friend saw her and said that she was getting a little chubby. I played on the beach and met new friends. For marks out of ten, I give Muck . . . 100,000.

Blackie

'Blackie and her companion were two Luing-cross Holstein cows that came from Mull in 1992. I was particularly attached to Blackie, as she was so good to hand-milk, and was also so good with calves when we twinned on others after she had given birth to her own. This is something that many farmers do. As most cross dairy cows are well able to rear two calves, a new one is given to them soon after they have given birth to their own, in a satisfactory system called "multiple suckling". Some cows, unlike sheep, are very happy to accept another calf and Blackie was one of those. One summer, when the two were still heifers, they were out in Glen Martin with the rest of the Luing hill cows. On a particular June day, they must have taken a wrong turning and went on a path across the cliff on the other side of Spichean, the rock pinnacle that is so distinctive on Muck's south-west side. The ewes use it the whole time, but for cattle it is impossible because a rock juts out and means they cannot turn around to come back. When they reached this part, these two cows must have fallen about 30 feet onto a very steep grassy slope and then they must have literally rolled right down. It was an awful place for a cow, and very hard to find them too. They could have been there for a long time had it not been for James Alexander, a minister who comes every year on retreat. When he told me, I rushed over to have a look at them. I found them both very bruised and scraped but miraculously seemingly uninjured. Getting them out was another matter altogether: while humans can scramble out at the top with difficulty, not so cattle. For these two, the only hope – apart from swimming – was to wait for a low spring tide and then they would have to cross a boulder beach covered in slippery seaweed. Blackie, having been reared in the byre as a calf, was very quiet and I fitted her with a head collar and led her slowly down to the rocky shore. Others helped me by pushing from behind and Blackie's companion duly followed on. Eventually, after a very hazardous passage, we reached Camus Mor and safety.

'The fall did not seem to affect either cow in the long term and for the next four years or so they went on to have their calves without problem. However, one particular year a long while after Blackie had calved, when all had been going well, I went in to find she could not get up. This often happens with newly calved cows: known as "downer" cows, it happens when a nerve is trapped in their pelvis area following a bad calving. But this was several years after her fall, and indeed months after she had calved again without problems. We tried everything, but something was clearly wrong. In the end, we transferred her to a rubber mat and dragged her on that out to the field with the tractor, as it would be so much easier for her to get up on soft ground. However, try as we might, it was all to no avail. She never managed to get up again. I was very upset about it, as I was so fond of her and she was such a good cow. In the end I waited until it was so dark that I could only see the outline of her head and I shot her.'

An Unusual Migrant Bird

It was 1 May 2002 and a beautiful spell of weather had put the MacEwens in fine fettle, as the lambing was going well. Spring migrants were arriving steadily in Muck: snipe were drumming over the bogs and the cuckoo was calling, as skylarks rose higher into a sky of eternal blue. Wildflowers were dotting the landscape with a profusion of colour, and Lawrence was bouncing down the road early to check his ewes and lambs. He suddenly spied a couple walking up the road from Port towards him. It seemed too early in the season for casual tourists. Work was ongoing with the new pier, and Lawrence somehow thought they looked rather familiar.

'I had my dog with me and, as they approached, I said to them, "Are you from the pier construction company?" Even before I said it I knew exactly who they were, but I thought I might as well say it anyway! They grinned very broadly and said no, that they had come in on a yacht. It was Princess Anne and her husband, Tim Laurence. Soon we got onto the subject of farming, and she asked how the lambing was going and also about a Highland mare on the hill who was shortly to foal, then she told me that they had White Park cattle, so we chatted a bit about that too. I just carried on conversing casually, as I usually do, and then they went off for a walk to Camus Mor. When they came back down off the hill, they called at Port Mor House to ask if it would be possible to have a shower. However, Judy and Ewen, who were running it at the time, had not got the hot water turned on, so had to tell them and it was apparently a little embarrassing. Anyway, instead they had a cup of coffee and some cakes with Jenny in the tearoom. Princess Anne also bought a pair of hand-knitted socks. We were absolutely delighted about this, as we could then send a note to the lovely old lady at Glenuig who knitted various garments for us and tell her that Princess Anne had bought her socks. Of course, she was thrilled to bits. Feeling rather inspired after this impromptu visit, I did endeavour to get the Queen to come to Muck.

'I had read that the Queen was chartering the *Hebridean Princess* instead of using the decommissioned *Britannia* to tour the Hebrides, and while I was at a cattle sale I bumped into freelance journalist

Clare Powell and we got chatting and I mentioned the Queen having the *Hebridean Princess* and sailing around the Western Isles. I said rather blithely, "It's a pity the Queen won't come and see us, as we have just had Princess Anne." Anyway Clare wrote to the Queen for me and sometime later we got a very nice letter from a lady-in-waiting thanking us for our kind invitation but telling us that the Queen wanted to revisit all the places she had been in *Britannia*. All is not lost, however – we have had the late Ben Coutts!'

Lawrence and I laugh uproariously about this, as Captain J. Burnaby Coutts – Ben, to his friends – was not only a huge farming character and a good friend of us both, but also a great fan of both the Queen and Princess Anne. In his capacity as a knowledgeable Aberdeen Angus cattleman, he was frequently to be heard talking about his meetings with members of the royal family.

'Yes, indeed. He arrived here off the *Hebridean Princess* and I gave him a little tour of the farm, just as I would have done for the Queen.'

There are times when you have to take what you can get, and I am still giggling to myself about Lawrence asking Princess Anne and her husband if they were from the pier construction company. He has a very devilish side.

John Low

During an autumnal stay on Muck in 2013, I went with Lawrence, his daughter-in-law Ruth and her two children, plus a pack of dogs, including mine, to pick brambles and apples in an astonishing area of mixed woodland behind Seilachan. Despite the salted winds blowing straight in from the shore, the trees have grown dense and strong, dominated by hazel, rowan, sycamore, pine and spruce. In amongst them is a large orchard latticed with a thick cover of brambles. The apple trees were laden and there were fat succulent brambles everywhere. It was a happy family party; Tara strapped to Ruth's back, her cheeks red and her smile summing up the expedition. We left the dogs sitting by Dun Ban cottage, with one collie surveying the scene from a fish box on Ruth's quad in a bid to leave Toby's pheasants in peace. Wee Hugh's lips were stained purple from bramble juice and Lawrence was busy loading large baskets with apples, whilst chatting to us all. This surprising wood was the work of one John Low, who came to the island for some years and left a particular sylvan legacy behind.

'I have always been very interested in forestry, as you know, and was much inspired by Haig Douglas, who used to plant trees on his farm on any available uncultivated land. I have kept planting schemes going on the island, following in the footsteps of my father. There were really no trees on Muck before he came to the island, except for a few aspens.

'John Low came here on holiday during the 1970s. He was visiting some of the Western Isles with a view to finding a suitable place to build himself a house for retirement. After a few visits, it was clear that he liked Muck and he had softened me up enough for me to agree to him building a house here. Not only did I agree to that, but I also agreed that he could have about nine and a half acres adjacent to the plot on which to plant trees.

'Once he got the go-ahead for the house, he spent hours demolishing an old paper mill in Penicuik and salvaging slates and timbers for his own use. The timbers were full of nails, making planing and sanding far more difficult. Overloaded lorries kept arriving at Arisaig with all this stuff, all to be shipped to the island. Needless to say, we obliged with *Wave* and brought most of it back for him. He wanted to build in stone, but the cost was prohibitive, so in the end he had to change his plans to use Fyfestone instead. He built outhouses as well, and one of them was eventually converted to become Seilachan, one of our holiday cottages.

'He was absolutely passionate about everything related to forestry, and as well as planting around his house at Dun Ban he offered to plant trees for me too. He managed to grow trees in all sorts of places where normally it would have been impossible. Much of this was due to his knowledge, but it was also due to the fact that he got trees of many different provenances that were acclimatised to the severity of the weather here. Many of them had Alaskan origins. He had a tree nursery on the island and worked very hard – it was probably largely due to his determination and stubbornness that he was so successful. The small woods have certainly made it far more possible for Toby and Mary to succeed with their shoot. I later received a Small Woods Award for my work. Dr John Morton Boyd, the zoologist, writer and conservationist, was an assessor and was most supportive about what we were doing on Muck.

'Once John had finally completed the building of his house, his wife suddenly decided that Muck was not for her and left. He then met a nurse in Fort William, but she did not want to live in Muck either, so it was all a bit of a disaster for him. At first he wanted to put the house on the open market, but this was the last thing we wanted. Rather than come to some gentleman's agreement over a dram, we each put in a widely differing valuation and ended up going to a hearing in the Land Court in Morar. Lord Elliot did not appear to have much idea about the value either and we ended up splitting the cost in the middle. By the time we had both paid all our lawyer's fees, I am sure it cost us far more at the end of the day. It was exasperating. But though it made me mad at the time, and I always felt he did not have a sense of humour, he certainly left us a wonderful array of woods.'

Ronnie Dyer .

'As I have said several times, Ronnie Dyer, the skipper of *Sheerwater*, really has done more for this island than any other outsider. Arisaig Marine, a small family-run business started by Murdo Grant, has been organising superb boat trips and wildlife cruises to the Small Isles for over 35 years. Ronnie is the best man for the job and is their lynchpin. Murdo is an entrepreneur and is highly professional: he owned the Arisaig Hotel, where he was an excellent host, and then he began the boat side of the business. He really appreciated the need for a good pier in Arisaig and first tried to achieve this in 1964, but he hit all sorts of problems over landownership and feu laws and it was not until 1998 that the pier and breakwater was finally completed, due entirely to his tenacity. It has since transformed travel for thousands of tourists coming out to the islands every summer. Previously, there had just been a small pier at Rhu Arisaig, so they'd had to go out over rocks and slippery weed to get onboard any boat. We used the Rhu pier quite a lot, particularly for sheep.

'Murdo's daughter now owns the business and it has expanded greatly. They have a large shed for boat work, and a shop and a tea-room, as well as many moorings and facilities for yachtsmen. They do a fantastic job. Ronnie started working for Arisaig Marine in 1979 and he was at first skipper of their old *Shearwater*. I suppose that was really the start of tourism on Muck. He is very much a part of our lives here and comes to most of our parties, ceilidhs, weddings and events. He brings nearly all the clientele for the craft shop during the summer months. During the winter when the tourists stop, Toby and Mary charter *Sheerwater* for their shooting parties and this greatly contributes to its success, and it also means when the CalMac boat is not running he often comes instead and transports other passengers who would have been stuck. Ronnie scarcely ever misses a trip. He has only had to cancel a few parties of guns since the shoot began, which is miraculous, given the bad weather we often have in winter. He is a superb seaman, with a lifetime's experience in these waters, and we view him as our lifeline.

'We also charter *Sheerwater* quite often for special events. Jenny organised a secret trip for my 60th birthday. That night we had a barbecue on the beach at Gallanach and lots of dancing on the sand to the strains of the pipes. A couple of days later I was told I had to go to Port for a coastguard exercise, and when I got there I was totally amazed to see the old *Shearwater*, with a bar on board, packed with people from Eigg and the mainland, as well as islanders. We then went straight to Tobermory, where the Reade family had organised another party at MacGochan's pub. I remember dancing on the life raft on the way back and Ronnie sending a message saying, "Get that man off there, it's dangerous."

'Ronnie has only once had a near-miss here on Muck, when he was coming in really slow in thick fog and hit a rock. Everyone had to be evacuated. But that is in all the years he has been coming here. We would be lost without him. And of course his knowledge of marine wildlife is incredible, so he is very good indeed for the tourism of the area.'

The Turf-roof Bothy

Strike out across the hill through the russet-coloured bogs, heading north-west from Gallanach, and you reach a tiny turf-roofed bothy, Bagh. It nestles next to the hillside close to the shore just a short distance from a tiny pink shelly beach a little further on where the determined beachcomber may find perfect little cowrie shells and other minute treasures thrown up by the sea. It's a lonely spot frequented by ministerial grey herons, the occasional otter, and snipe, curlew and other shorebirds. As children, Lawrence and his brothers and sister soon recognised the potential of a derelict building here and, as it was the nearest ruin to the farm, decided to put a roof on it. They eventually succeeded and, using driftwood consisting largely of Walker's of Mallaig fish boxes, managed to make a rough structure with crudely cut turfs on top. They frequently went there for picnics, but it leaked badly and later the turf was stripped off and the roof felted, with little more success.

In 1974, the Kennard family from Kent came to the island for a holiday. Vernon Kennard owned a music business in Canterbury. Lawrence describes him as an eccentric character. He became a regular visitor to Muck and, having seen the potential of derelict Bagh, proposed putting a proper roof on it. This was duly agreed, with the aim that he and his family could use it during their frequent visits. Another visitor, bookseller Alex Fotheringham, helped with the project and together they removed the central wall inside and put on a proper secure roof covered in turf. The plan was to share the use of the little bothy, however the pair fell out. Alex was then given another ruin on the Port Mor side of Muck, since known as Alex's bothy, and he did that up for himself instead.

'In 1981, despite the difficulties involved with transport, Vernon brought four pianos to the island on *Wave*. Young David Kennard came to Muck with his father and his uncle Vernon, and during his stay watched shepherd Davy Jones and myself working our dogs. Inspired, he decided to become a shepherd himself.

'Having begun working with sheep on Romney Marsh, David and his family eventually moved to the beautiful North Devon coast, where his father bought Borough Farm. They run a flock of 700 breeding ewes, as well as a few beef cattle. He has become renowned all over the country for his extraordinary work and ability to train his team of Border collies to the highest standards and also runs weekly public demonstrations on his farm. 'There is no good flock without a good shepherd, and no good shepherd without good dogs': these famous words were the guide for David, as he battled, like so many other livestock farmers, to retain his hard hill farm and to make it pay its way. Finally, it was his loyal dogs who were to prove the key to the problem and they have since become the subject of a hugely popular children's television series, *Mist Sheepdog Tales*, while a range of videos reveal not only day-to-day farm life but also that of a host of creatures, both wild and domestic.'

Described as the James Herriot of shepherding, David Kennard has a charisma and an almost telepathic bond with his collies. He is also the author of bestselling books and has a great deal in common with his close friend Lawrence, as he too battles with the constant abuse hurled off the wild Atlantic on a regular basis, and still visits Muck when time allows.

A Pig in a Poke

In 1814, Robert Henderson wrote in his famous treatise 'On the Breeding of Swine':

> *I would recommend it to the inhabitants of these islands (the Hebrides) that they should immediately introduce this stock into their respective abodes. Nowhere do I know a country so well adapted for rearing swine as the Western Isles, where there are large tracts of pasture lands, in which swine will feed all the summer months among their cattle and sheep, and will resort to the shores and pick up sea-weed and shell fish which are excellent food for them.*

Despite Henderson's recommendations, there is no tradition of pig keeping in the Western Isles, however Muck has a long association with it. When the island had a dairy farm from 1876 to 1913, they were kept for home use and fed on the excess whey from cheese making. A byre was built with a piggery alongside, however this proved to be too draughty, so they did not thrive. Lawrence's father was very keen on pigs, but he had rings fitted through their noses in a bid to stop them tearing up the fields too much. He kept a few breeding sows, but latterly he tended to have young pigs for fattening. He used to send his pigs in a special box to butcher Lachy Wynne in Fort William, who apparently was always keen to buy them, as they had been fed on an excellent varied diet, helping to make them exceptionally good eating.

During Davy Jones's time on Muck, he started off a new generation of pig keeping and built a piggery at Godag. He put some electric fences over part of his 80-acre croft so that they could be kept outdoors. He really liked pigs, but unfortunately he did not manage to sell them and had to sometimes take the weaners to Stirling market as a last resort. It was a time-consuming operation, and once he had paid for ferries, fuel and accommodation it proved financially unviable. Though the islanders helped him by giving him scraps for them, he still had to buy copious amounts of food, so it proved a non-starter.

'I like pigs very much and did up Davy Jones's old piggery. Julie MacFadzean, who lives in Godag House, looks after them for me. We keep the pigs for about six to eight months before they are ready for slaughter. Now we tend to keep Large White pigs, with a little Tamworth and Saddleback blood in them too. They do very well, and we often have litters of 15 or 16, but we don't overfeed our pigs; it is interesting that very fat sows just won't produce as many piglets. The meat is used for a large range of delicious home-made products. Mary makes vast amounts of sausages for Gallanach Lodge, and Jenny's wonderful pork pies feature as a most popular part of shoot lunches.

'There was the famous time I got a sow and a boar from Mull. They were in a box on *Wave*, but when we got to Muck and tried to lift the box out with the forks of the tractor it fell to bits. So we had to leave them penned up in the boat overnight. Next day I got a bulk bag and managed to entice them into it with food, and we lifted that out with the tractor forks instead. The pigs were very happy to go into the bulk bag, lured by pignuts. Pigs love to snuggle up and this cosy looking place appealed to them. Perhaps onlookers did not think much of us, hoicking out pigs in a bag like this, so we stopped doing it at Tobermory pier, where we used to send weaners to the Reades at Sgroib-ruadh. We had done it on other occasions with no ill effects.'

It really was a pig in a poke.

'At the time of my 70th birthday, I had just weaned a sow at Gallanach and it is usual for them to come in season as soon as the piglets have been taken off. So it was time for her to visit the boar. She was being very stubborn about going into the tractor transport box, so I had to walk her over to the boar at Godag, and Dave Barnden offered to help me. She followed me down the road, albeit rather slowly, lured by a bucket of nuts. When we got there, the boar got rather over-excited as I opened the gate and he lunged at me. One of his large teeth sank into my leg, making quite a tear. Despite the blood, there was no pain, but Dave was very concerned and rushed to Julie MacFadzean's house to seek help. I had just been in the wrong place at the wrong time. Julie, who was a nurse, was marvellous and cleaned the wound up. Everyone made rather a fuss about it, though I was not too bothered, but pig bites have a reputation for quickly turning septic. She did think it needed to be stitched, but really I did not want all that carry-on – we had planned a special birthday trip on *Sheerwater* to go over to Canna.

'Dr Weldon came over from Eigg and took a look at the bite. She felt that I needed to have a trip to hospital to have it flushed out and stitched, however I managed to dissuade her from this idea – I certainly did not want to go. In the end, I was most grateful to her, as she stitched it up for me here instead and reluctantly agreed I could stay at home. When it came to the Canna trip scheduled for the next day, I felt I had better not go or else the doctor might be cross with me, as I had already escaped a dreaded trip to hospital. It was all very annoying, except I did wonder, had I missed an opportunity for a helicopter ride?'

One wise guy on the island later regaled me with a slightly more flowery version of the tale. When he had finished, he added, 'I always wondered if the pig was all right. After all, Lawrence is not the cleanest person, is he?'

One of my recent Muck visits coincided with the killing of a pig for home use. Molly, my collie, is particularly keen on Lawrence and is always pleased to see him. Not only does she seem to genuinely like him, but she is also further lured by the fascinatingly delicious infusion of animal-based aromas clinging to his boiler suits. After he has been milking each morning, she seems to be all the keener, and she is certainly not one to cry over spilt milk.

Arriving late one morning at Gallanach Cottage to work on his story with me, Lawrence blew in with the gale, looking particularly sodden. Molly was delighted with the new aroma of porcine blood lingering on the aforementioned boiler suit. We worked all morning while the wind did the Highland fling to the tune of lashing rain. Once Lawrence had left, I let Molly out too, to complete her ablutions. She vanished. This was totally out of character, as she never wanders far from my sight. Due to the gale and the cottage's proximity to the now boiling sea below, I began to worry. I shouted and whistled to no avail, my voice drowned out by the irate weather, and so I set off to look for her. I headed to the farm first to ask Lawrence about it, then I noticed that one of the byre doors was ajar and thought perhaps he might be in there. Sticking my head in to have a peek, I saw Molly with her back to the door. With hackles raised like an irate porcupine, she had her legs spread out wide and her back pressed down, and she was uttering the strangest low moaning growl I had ever heard her make. When I shouted at her, she took no notice and did not even look around. Then she started growling even more. The byre was dimly lit and I wondered what on earth she was doing. Now cross that she was being so disobedient, I suddenly saw the reason for her insubordination. There in the passage was a large sombre looking pig's head. This pig was certainly not going to fly again. She reluctantly followed me out, tail firmly clamped between her legs.

Island Transport

Happily, cars on Muck are few and far between, something that immediately changes the atmosphere of any island. A handful exist, used largely for ferrying endless goods back and forth to the pier, and for taking visitors and their capacious volumes of luggage and provisions to holiday houses. In this weather-dominated land and seascape, with no shops, travelling light is not an option. Though some vehicles are new-ish and in the peak of health, others are MOT failures. If the vehicles stay on the island, they have no need for road tax and most of these are on their final mission. They cough and splutter their way down Muck's highway, prolonging their final departure to the scrap heap. With dog-chewed seats, defunct power steering, windows that either won't open or are jammed open, trips to the pier are hilarious events, as children, luggage, animal feed and soaking wet dogs all pile in on top of one another and we chug precariously down or back from Port. My departures and arrivals are ever thus and cause me to giggle for days after I am home again. *Top Gear* would do well to feature some of these stalwart vehicles, mostly Land Rovers and other 4x4s that somehow manage to outlive many of their luxurious mainland counterparts despite little mechanical attention and deep penetration from rain and salt. Muck has no place for posers with their flash wheels. In fact, most of the cars that the islanders leave at Mallaig for mainland trips are refreshingly nothing to brag about.

In December 2013, there was a massive storm the day before I sailed to Muck. When I reached the car park at Mallaig, I found it filled with shingle and sizeable stones, as well as copious amounts of seaweed. Some of the cars had been damaged – further proof that the elements still rule. Once Jenny arrived in Mallaig to find that her trusty Volvo had been washed right out of the car park and onto the road.

One evening when I borrowed a vehicle to go visiting at the other end of the island in a howling gale, my collie Molly got such a fright when it rudely backfired that she leapt over two rows of seats straight on top of me. As I lurched forward, I set off the windscreen wipers and the horn and nearly leapt out of my skin. I was lucky – some of the vehicles don't even have wipers: one peers out through a wet, fogged-up circle that has to be constantly wiped with an even wetter hand. But, driving at less than five miles an hour, you are certainly not going to come to any grief, though it is easy to put a car into a bog, especially if you have not mastered the muscle power to cope with heavy steering. It all adds to the joy and fun of visits to Muck.

'Shepherd Archie MacKinnon had the first car on Muck. It was an Austin Seven and it arrived on *Wave*, as did some of the early tractors. However, the road was awful at that point and I do not think he used it very much. Bruce Mathers got himself a Hillman Imp and we took that across on *Wave*, too. It was very amusing when we brought it over, as he held onto the door handle all the time, as if that would have kept it safely on board. I have never cared less about cars, but Bruce was very keen on them. We always went around the island by tractor with a transport box: if we were going to Port at night for a social event, we had good waterproofs and piled everyone into the box. A lot of the time the tractors had no headlights, but the road was a lighter colour, and it was possible to see, so I never worried. I remember there being lots of toads on the roads at night in the summer, but now we seldom see them in big numbers like that. We do still have toads around, as I find them in the garden sometimes, however oddly we never seem to have had any frogs. I wonder if it's the salty air . . .

'Tractors certainly do not like salt! You will remember the consequences when I forgot to put the handbrake on and the Ford 4000 took the plunge off the pier.'

Lawrence laughs rather uncomfortably.

Television

Tom Weir was the first person to come to the island to film for his popular television series, *Weir's Way*. His visit coincided with the MacEwens moving cattle from one side of the island to the other, providing a perfect visual opportunity for the needs of fickle TV crews. He spent time interviewing Bryan Walters about his lobster fishing and Bruce Mathers about his woodturning work. In view of their tragic ends, they seem all the more poignant and sad when watched today. When he interviewed Clare Walters, Bryan's wife, in the garden of Gallanach Cottage, she was very shy at first but later told him how much she enjoyed life on Muck and how their house was so close to the seals in the bay beneath that she could even hear them cleaning their teeth. Lawrence remembers that Tom was a very pleasant soul. Other television filming events have proved more onerous and demanding, and it is quite clear that though Lawrence enjoys being in the media spotlight he is at times a paradox. Like a hermit crab, he comes out of his shell in all his glory but quickly, when things get uncomfortable, likes to withdraw into a private world as well. And some of those working in the media are famous for their demanding and temperamental nature.

In most cases, media coverage helps promote the island, but at a cost. It has often proved to be stressful, particularly when trying to get on with the all-important work, when time is at a premium and the weather is good. Usually camera crews and presenters show up just at the wrong moment and it is sad that all too often the people who are filmed and provide entertainment for the masses end up with not a penny.

Though Lawrence liked Tom Weir, he is far less enthusiastic about his experiences with Selina Scott for the programme *Scot Free*. The crew arrived on Muck in August 1985 and as far as Lawrence is concerned wanted to portray Muck as a sort of kingdom, making him out to be the tyrant ruling over everyone. They interviewed him for an entire morning, pushing their angle for the story, and it took him all his wits to keep cool and avoid falling into a verbal tiger trap.

'Selina Scott had been filming at Pluscarden Abbey, near Elgin, before coming to Muck and that had apparently not gone well, as there she had endeavoured to find out about the sex lives of the monks. You can imagine that caused ripples. Well, she caused a few ripples here as well. To start with, they filmed her getting out of a dinghy onto a rock as she arrived, as if Muck was even more remote and difficult to reach than it is. The ridiculous thing was that in the background while all this was going on you could see the pier. A week later, we were taking lambs down to our boat and a few escaped. After we got them aboard and we put the engine astern, nothing happened, as we had grounded. We then had to wait for a couple of hours for the tide to turn. This had never ever happened before. Clearly, we were harassed by the intrusion. On the way back from taking them across to Arisaig we even ran out of fuel, another first.

'The crew went around interviewing everyone, but some of the islanders, including Davy Jones, did not like it and refused to get involved. Just as she was interviewing Bryan Walters, Davy drove past right into the camera shot with a dead cow suspended on the forks of the tractor. That was very funny indeed, though they didn't think so.

'Mr Schellenberg heard about it and came rushing over in his boat to invite her to film in Eigg, but she did not go, so he was bitterly disappointed and quite cross.

'There were ceilidhs at nights, so there was some fun, but it was all a lot of work. Eventually, Alasdair and I were invited down to Bristol to the BBC studios to see the film in their cutting room. When it appeared on television, it really was a bit of a let-down – it was nothing special at all. I suppose now the best thing about it is seeing the shots they took of the island from a helicopter, and how young we seem all those years ago.'

It is interesting that while I was talking about Selina Scott's visit to Colin, who is a much more private person and is less keen to have either himself or Muck in the spotlight, his first comment, said with a particularly large smile, is that they had grounded the boat not because they were hassled but because all the men were far too busy ogling the presenter and not paying attention to the job in hand. It certainly seems a far more plausible alternative.

The press at the time had some even more damning comments to make about Selina Scott's programme, in particular about the incomers who moan about how hard it is to live on an island. John Gibson, who described Selina Scott as 'as exciting as yesterday's potatoes', wrote in the *Evening News*:

It's not that I have no sympathy for them. I know how it must feel to be isolated on a Hebridean huddle without a Sydney Devine album . . . they weren't bundled on to a boat at Tilbury in the middle of the night and shipped up there in chains.

Funniest of all was another piece in one of the red tops:

[Scott's] vacuous voiceovers churned cluelessly on. She went through 'Time and tide wait for no man' and was just into 'No man is an

island' when I spotted the only sign of intelligent life on Muck. It came from the sheep who leapt off the miserable island apparently delighted to be going to market.

For many years, the MacEwens supplied milk to the islanders. 'To begin with, it was a perquisite for those who worked on the farm, as well as the teacher. Later on we had a system for islanders whereby they could help themselves to free milk from the dairy, though usually soon after milking we tried to transport it to Port to save them having to come to fetch it.

'Nick Nairn came to film on Muck during his series *Island Harvest*, when he toured several places in the Hebrides. On some islands he did the cooking, and on others it was someone local. We were rather disappointed that he did not cook for us; instead, he asked Jenny to make something. She did a marvellous spinach quiche. We all sat down and were filmed eating it and drinking lots of wine. It was very annoying indeed because the BBC was as tight as two coats of paint and they neither provided nor paid for the wine after all the trouble we had gone to. We were a bit miffed, but there was worse to come. I had worked hard to train one of our most attractive cows, Clarissa, to be hand-milked, so that when Nick came he could be filmed milking her. But he was having none of it and so I had to do it instead. I was filmed putting the milk into cans. When the programme came out, someone from the environmental health department spotted things and we were contacted soon after about providing milk for members of the public and from then on were no longer allowed to supply islanders. It was ridiculous because we were not charging for it. Health and safety rules and regulations finally hit Muck, and I felt very sorry about this. So filming is not always beneficial for us.'

For a more recent programme with the presenter Paul Merton, Lawrence is seen chauffeuring him up the road in his vintage tractor. The weather was particularly good and Muck looked beautiful, however little was said about the island; instead, the onus appeared to be on the much joked of 'Lord Muck', or the Laird of Muck, something they all get heartily sick of.

Pat & Gwyneth

'Pat and Gwyneth Murphy came from Preston in Lancashire. He worked for the Post Office, but he must have had a great interest in remote places, for when Lion Television advertised for potential castaways for *Castaway 2000* Pat and Gwyneth applied and were successful. However, what the company were actually looking for were abrasive, difficult characters who were eager to speak to the television monitor and cause ripples to bring about some exciting viewing. While of course not all the subjects fitted that bill, they certainly got it wrong with this couple. Both were eager to bond with the other castaways on Taransay, and Pat's highly practical bent must have proved invaluable on the island.

'After the programme was over, one of the other castaways, Des Monks, seeing the accommodation pods selling for a song, purchased one and had it transported back to the mainland for storage by the original builders. There was a problem finding a suitable site to have it erected, however, and eventually Des left to teach in Oman, so it was no use to him.

'Meanwhile Pat and Gwyneth, unable to settle back in Preston, were searching for another island to live on. Ben Fogle had made his mark – and not by being difficult, quite the reverse. He was working in television and had been to Bardsey Island off the Lleyn Peninsula in North Wales, and he advised them to go and have a look. It was on Bardsey that they met David and Libby Barnden, who were farming on the island. Pat took a job as warden and was of great assistance to the Barndens. The National Trust for Scotland were seeking a couple to manage their guest house on Canna, and Dave and Libby, finding it increasingly difficult to farm on Bardsey, decided to apply. They were only runners-up, but their name was passed on to Muck, as we were also looking for a new family. We chose them, as they seemed highly suitable. As you know, David is now a key player on the island.

'Pat and Gwyneth came to visit them and, though they really loved Muck, we had no spare accommodation for them at that time. However, there was still the Taransay castaway pod in storage and Des, eager to put it to good use, agreed that it could be erected and modified for them on Muck. Once they arrived on the island, they quickly became an invaluable addition to the community. Whilst Pat could turn his hands to most things and was adept with a paintbrush, Gwyneth was entirely responsible for the magnificent floral decorations at Ruth and Colin's wedding. She also kept all the islanders smart, with every type of haircut imaginable. When they left for family reasons, we were sad to see them go and miss them very much.'

Izzy

I am standing in the island graveyard, where a few of the oldest lichen-encrusted stones lean at precarious angles. A curlew calls in Port bay below, while sheep crop the slopes above. Otherwise the afternoon is totally silent. In the distance, the smudged shapes of the hills on Ardnamurchan peep out through low wisps of cloud. A small bunch of rain-drenched flowers bound with coloured ribbon lies on five-year-old Izzy's grave. Even being here fills me with the most desperate sorrow.

IZZY MARY FICHTNER-IRVINE
17 Sept. 2004 – 11 Oct. 2009

A Tiny Flower Lent, Not Given
To Bud on Earth and Bloom in Heaven

Nothing is worse for any parent than losing a child. Izzy, who everyone describes as the loveliest and happiest little girl on earth, tragically died suddenly due to pulmonary complications following a cold. There was little or no warning. This was the blackest day that Muck has ever known and even now speaking about it to anybody on the island causes waves of deep sadness. Her parents, Mary and Toby, discussed moving away from the island with their two sons, Archie and Jasper, when they lost Izzy, but eventually decided to stay put and try to come to terms with her loss here at home.

Words are inadequate to describe such a horror, but in his monthly contribution to *West Word* Lawrence's beautiful, simple entry following Izzy's funeral says a very great deal:

Farewell to Izzy
Her pony led by Ruth walked slowly up the hill in the sunshine. (Little Jasper went running behind and had to be constrained before he reached the pony's fetlocks.) Alan Lamb, the minister, came next, followed by the little white coffin carried by four islanders. Then came the long column of mourners. At the graveside Alan committed her spirit into God's keeping and Bryan read 'Do Not Stand at My Grave and Weep'. Then it was quickly filled in and soon it was covered with the loveliest flowers ever seen at an occasion like this, many reflecting hours of work by Gwyneth. Sandy placed a little cross above her head – and it was over.

Earlier in the garden in the tent we had sung her favourite hymns or sat in silence while Alan gave us words of comfort, words of hope. Lawrence read from the Bible and Colin read 'God's Lent Child'. Sarah gave us 'Izzy' and Mary bravely told us a little of what she had packed into five short years. And in the evening hot air balloons soared heavenwards into the sunset to mark the end of a day we will always remember, a day that was 'Farewell to Izzy'.

The Green Shed

In the middle of Port Mor, a small green tin tabernacle, like its near neighbour, the craft shop, is an emporium filled with the islanders' artistic talents. It was once used as a generator shed and now for much of the year is stocked with fresh Muck-grown vegetables and eggs, as well as an astonishing array of crafts. When Dave and Libby Barnden came to Muck from Bardsey Island in 2007, they made felt rugs using a peg loom and sheep's wool. At first these were displayed in Jenny's shop, but soon more space was required and Colin gave them the old shed, together with tin for its repair. They then began experimenting with needle felting to decorate their rugs in an arduous process using a barbed needle to paint with wool. For colour, dyed merino is added to the base of rich brown Jacob-Cheviot wool. Since Libby left the island, Dave and his stepdaughter Vicki Tubb have continued to produce the rugs, creating a wealth of designs from puffins to sheep and horses, and beautiful game birds, the latter popular with the visiting parties of guns. They also take on commissions, decorating the rugs with favourite animals using photographs, particularly of dogs and horses. Other islanders were encouraged to provide items for the Green Shed venture and the result is an array of treasures, from baby shoes to hand-made wooden toys, preserves, jewellery, paintings and soap. The children sell hand-made cards to help raise funds for their school.

Dave is, as Lawrence says, a great asset to the island, a hard-grafter who helps with just about everything. When he arrived on Muck, the MacEwens had long promoted an ethos of self-sufficiency and he quickly commandeered unused gardens, as well as putting up polytunnels, for an impressive vegetable-growing enterprise.

Originally from a game-keeping and forestry background, Dave is currently the island's part-time gamekeeper and as such has become the important right-hand man for Toby and Mary. He is also an ornithologist and keeps a record of the birds on Muck, including any passing rarities. He has recently embarked on a further venture, with a state-of-the-art game-bird processing shed, complete with plucking machine, adjacent to the lodge, where he prepares pheasants, partridges and ducks for table and supplies local restaurants and hotels. Since this business has really taken off, he wonders how he will ever find the time to grow the copious amounts of vegetables, as he did previously.

One of my arrivals in Muck coincided with the last shoot of the season and the beaters' shoot. My return to windswept Gallanach Cottage was on a particularly icy January day. The cottage, having been empty for a while, was colder than usual, as the Raeburn had only just been lit. Then the gas ran out and the electricity decided to do the Highland fling, tripping on and off at frequent intervals. At twilight, I went down to the farm to see if there was any more gas and fell in with Dave and a party of beaters tidying up at the end of their last hard day. Their spirits were high after a successful season, and this driven soul who clearly takes his work very seriously must have been feeling some kind of euphoric relief at a job well done. We had a brief chat and, as I was shivering profusely and must have appeared more than usually jaded after a ridiculously early start and no sleep, he foisted a generous measure of some amber liquid from the back of the game cart in my direction: 'That'll warm you up,' he laughed. Going with the flow as I always endeavour to do on Muck, I downed this mysterious elixir. By the time I reached the farm, I was floating in a haze of oblivion. I felt a glow of delicious abandon as I waltzed in to find Lawrence chatting to his cows in the byre. A few nights later, still giggling about the potency of that amber liquid, I was invited to join the beaters' party at Gallanach Lodge and accepted with alacrity.

The new lodge is awe-inspiring and has without doubt one of the finest views in the Western Isles. It also shows a totally different aspect of Muck, being incredibly modern and well-designed to cope with outdoor visitors who appear frequently sodden to the skin. Luxurious and tastefully done in every way, Toby runs a tidy ship and his thickly bedded, immaculate gravel yard outside is in stark contrast to the island's mud. Everyone old and young who had anything to do with the shoot was there, from those that end up with their arms in the sink to the youngest children who join the beating squad. The atmosphere was carnival, as faces glowed due not only to past days spent out in the savage weather but also to Toby's opulent liquid refreshments. Food and drink flowed like a highland burn in full spate. We congregated at a beautiful long dining table. I had been on Muck the day it had arrived on the CalMac boat to be met by an army of island men to lift it aboard a trailer. Made by Sandy Fraser on Rum, the elm came from Toby's family farm in Aberdeenshire. Dave, in his role as under-keeper, sat at the end of the table and began a priceless résumé of the season's events, awarding forfeits by way of more exotic nectar for the shoot's best moments. It was a night of hilarity and camaraderie further bonding Muck's tiny community. My return walk to my cliff-top eyrie seemed somewhat more circuitous, and as seals on the skerries serenaded me with Hebridean laments, the shadowy forms of cows and calves on the beach came and went in the darkness. I quickly fell into a deep sleep as a whisper of a breeze mingled with the cries of a curlew.

Colin & Ruth's Story

The importance of finding the right wife for Muck is paramount and, as is illustrated in the following tale, has been very much uppermost in Lawrence's mind all these years. He once said to me, 'It is important to have a wife who feeds the pet lambs.' This sums it up, albeit simply.

'Father was good-looking, social and very naive, as my tale will reveal. During the period between mid-November and mid-March, he and his mother, older sister and Meg, his cousin, used to go to 9 Douglas Crescent in Edinburgh. During the 1930s, he got engaged to Doff, the daughter of an Edinburgh surgeon, and her ideal wintering ground was Egypt! A date for the wedding was chosen and presents began to arrive. At the eleventh hour, Father's older brother Alasdair (who, as they say, had married well to the daughter of the owner of a thriving Inverness tweed business) chartered a yacht and took Father around Islay for a cruise. During that time he spelled out exactly what being married to this girl was likely to mean. As soon as they got back, all the presents were returned and Father blotted his copybook badly with Edinburgh society by breaking off his engagement. Not so many social invitations came after that. I only tell you this story because it points out the hazards to the continuity of island ownership that changing generations and marriage can bring.' We both laugh loudly and Lawrence continues to chuckle for some time.

Ruth, like her mother-in-law Jenny, is well suited to Muck life. She first got together with Colin in 2001, following a friendship at the University of Edinburgh studying agriculture. She is a strong and cheerful character, with a zest for life, and like her husband has an incredible work ethic. More often to be found on a quad bike with their young daughter Tara strapped onto her back and their son Hugh sitting beside her than hoovering and polishing the farmhouse, she is away out to the hill to feed the stock accompanied by an entourage of collies and her much-adored little black cocker spaniel, Chloe.

A farmer's daughter from Whitby, North Yorkshire, with a passion for sheep, Ruth witnessed the full horrors of foot-and-mouth disease when most of her father's sheep stock of 1,500 ewes and lambs was lost in a contiguous cull in 2001. Before returning home to Muck, she and Colin travelled widely, visiting Venezuela, Columbia, Ecuador, Peru, Argentina, New Zealand, Australia and India, and then both worked for four years on the mainland. Neither of them appears to have any qualms about returning to the island to farm.

Colin is far more like his mother in character than his father. He does not enjoy publicity and tends to shy away from the press and media, preferring to keep his head down and work hard. He is highly popular and has the same benevolent streak so often witnessed in both his parents. He chose Christmas Day 2009 to propose to Ruth; they decided that they would get married on Muck rather than in Yorkshire because, as Ruth says, it has the 'wow factor' and by then it felt like home.

'Colin and I talked about getting married in September, but by then everyone tends to be so jaded, as the community have been so busy with summer visitors. So we decided on 1 May, but this did not give us much time for preparations. We still had 9,000 trees and hedging plants to put in for a Rural Stewardship Scheme, as well as lambing to get through, and so many other important jobs, before we even started the preparations. We had all the sheds to sort out, but we were so lucky because the community as ever gave us such a massive amount of help. We had 220 people coming. The holiday houses were all empty then, but even with them we can really only sleep 50 comfortably. There are about 100 beds on the island if families on the island help out, so the older generation got priority for beds and the rest camped.'

An amazing book of pictures bears witness to an event that Ruth says far outlived all her expectations. The normally chaotic and work-like sheds were transformed into an awesome wedding venue, with miles of horticultural fleece stapled and then draped around to completely cover walls and ceilings. The farm steading was whitewashed, the lower reaches painted by children, completing the metamorphosis of the old byres. Colin and a squad of islanders worked tirelessly, while Ruth concentrated on the lambing. Colin even re-baled round straw bales to make them into small bales for the 'church pews'. Jenny busily stitched 100 yards of bunting, and everyone was consumed making mountains of incredible food. This was a fine example of Muck's teamwork at its most superb. The Walters family – Clare, Emma, Ishy and Marcus – were responsible for the brilliant wedding photographs that record a quite extraordinary weekend.

Minister Alan Lamb, who has played an important role over the years in Muck's sorrows and joys, came over to marry them. Ruth, who is as far removed from a girly-girl as it's possible to be, is still incredibly excited when she describes the turn of events.

'The highlight came at the last minute. Emma Walters and her partner Graham Moss had asked Mary if she thought I would like to sail from Port Mor to Gallanach with the bridesmaids in *Mascot*, an old classic yacht, which Graham was helping to manage at the time, and then we would be rowed ashore. When Mary mentioned it, I leapt at the idea, though Jenny thought I was totally mad, given the problems of getting in and out of boats in a wedding dress. So away we went to Port dressed in our finery, and the bridesmaids and I were taken around to the bay in this wonderful yacht. Then we climbed into three dinghies and were gallantly rowed to the beach. It was just amazing. I cannot describe to you how wonderful it was because all these handsome men in kilts took their shoes and socks off and waded out to pull the dinghies onto the shore so we would not get our beautiful clothes wet in the sea. Then up we went to the byre that had been transformed into a church, and there was Colin and everyone waiting for us. It was such a fabulous day, and though it was a little cold, and I noticed that people put more and more clothes and hats on as evening wore on, everyone had such a great time and agreed we were so lucky with the weather.

'The day before the wedding, as always happens, things started to go wrong; we even had a poor cow with a prolapse that had to be quickly sorted. Sandy Mathers, who has inherited his father's joinery skills, made a proper bar area for us in the shed, and there was also a huge hog roast and masses of wine chilling in boxes. The cheese board was the biggest I have ever seen. We had to use picnic tables as well, as we had so many people. Robert Nairn, who is only in his 20s, led the band – he is a crofter and fencer from Acharacle, and when you speak to him on the telephone he sounds so much older, so it is quite amusing. They played just about everything you could imagine and we just danced and danced.

'On the Sunday, we had a lovely sunny day. Muck looked just like paradise and Ronnie in the *Sheerwater* did a terrific job ferrying all the guests safely back to the mainland. It was a weekend I shall just never forget and, as with all events here, everyone young and old joined in and helped. We are so lucky, as you do not get that elsewhere.'

Since she married Colin, there has been little time for anything other than work. Colin is rather reticent but agreed that during his childhood he was lucky because his father was very good at taking time off and taking them for various expeditions in the boat.

'Yes, I think Dad was much better at this than me. There was always a boat full of random visitors and other children, and we would go off over to beaches on Rum and have great days out. I am grateful for that. Mary and I had a wonderful childhood here. I think I will be a lot stricter with my children than Dad was, though, on the safety front, certainly when it comes to boats.'

At times the strain of a heavy workload shows; during one particular visit I witnessed their terrible disappointment and frustration when an important calf sale was missed due to the weather, which led to the inevitable loss of revenue. 'Living here, we really cannot play the market at all, so it really alters the way we sell things and the way we have to work as farmers. Previously, we relied on our own boat to take lambs off, and often we would take animals before sales and had to leave them in a field at Arisaig, where there was seldom enough grazing. Sometimes it could be up to a week before the lambs reached the market in Fort William, and by then they would have lost condition and would also look filthy. Now we get a wagon to come to the island directly on the CalMac ferry. We usually use Sandy Taylor from Dall, Loch Tayside. He is very good with stock. We can then get a good number of animals off in one batch, so that is much easier, but of course we cannot predict the weather, even for lorries coming. I know compared to my father I get a lot more stressed about it. I know how lucky we are to have our own boat too, but *Wave* does need a huge amount of maintenance – all boats are very costly to run, and scraping and varnishing is very time-consuming, and has to be done every summer. If I have to go over to the mainland with, for example, the wool clip, this takes me pretty much the entire day – and that's a lot of time that I am unable to work on the farm.'

Colin is currently working against the clock to renovate the bunkhouse, with the help of two islanders, Barnaby Jackson and Gareth Moffat, a job that he would like completed before lambing time, when he says he won't have a moment to work on anything else. It was an old tin bothy, once lived in by Katie and Charlie MacDonald. Lawrence and another couple who came to live on the island, Ian and Stella Stevens, converted it during the 1960s, when its role was as the first bunkhouse, the debut of more organised tourism for the island. The old tin shed, complete with Raeburn and wood-lined living area, became a popular venue for those seeking cheaper accommodation. Keeping abreast of tourism demands is a vital part of the island's economy, but has also to be fitted in with the agricultural calendar.

Ruth agrees with Colin: 'Life is so dominated by the farm, and there is always a job to be done, and even when you have done the essential stuff there is always drainage or fencing or trees to plant, and the three holiday houses are always needing something done to them too. If we are not careful, it can be really hard to stop. We love it, but we aren't very good at taking time out.'

For such a tiny community, there is seldom a week goes by without both of them participating in a range of hugely diverse events. Their two children, Hugh and Tara, run free between their own house and their grandparents' next door, and Jenny is always there to help look after them when farm work dictates. However, it seems that it won't be many years till they too are out in the sheep fank helping; they will grow up well-equipped to deal with life, not strapped to a computer, tablet or television.

Everyone on the island has many roles. Ruth is in the fire service, Colin in the coastguards, and they step into various jobs when needed. Ruth and Mary, together with other islanders, campaigned tirelessly to get a much-needed new community hall built at Port Mor. An award-winning architect designed what Lawrence describes as a 'gold-plated' building; the spec had to be considerably lowered when the tenders came in, as most were way higher than anticipated. It took several months to knock off the 'gold plate' and make a hall far more functional for Muck's needs. The hall committee had help with this from Kishorn Development Ltd (KDL), who won the contract. In comparison to many other building projects, it was relatively straightforward, though funding was a constant concern. Amongst other things, Mary and Ruth arranged a fund-raising ceilidh in a church hall in Edinburgh, with all the food taken to the event from Muck, and a raffle of prizes including holidays in self-catering cottages on the island. The community hall was eventually completed in time for Christmas 2012.

Ruth is full of praise for the builders who worked on the hall. 'KDL did an excellent job in completing, despite various complications. The weather was terrible both at the beginning of the project in 2011 and during the work, and it played havoc with getting freight and workmen to the island. But they stuck at it. They were a really super team, and included Charlie MacKinnon, a joiner whose father, Archie, was shepherd here many years ago. They all became part of the community whilst they were on the island.

'The first event held in the community hall was appropriately Jasper Fichtner-Irvine's fourth birthday party. Then on Christmas Day Lawrence led a lovely service in the upstairs meeting room. Various islanders did readings and we all sang carols, and then had mulled wine and food. It has given us a wonderful spacious area for various events, even just for the children to run around, and is available 24-7. We can also play indoor hockey, badminton, football and table tennis, and have Scottish dancing, a sports club, Toddlers group, parties and games there, and we also hold ceilidhs, theatre productions, talks and training events too. Upstairs we have the meeting room, a heritage area and a library. We are very grateful to our funders, the BIG Lottery, Scottish Rural Development Plan (SRDP), the Highland Council, the Robertson Trust and the Hugh Fraser Foundation. Meanwhile our side of the deal was to help by digging trenches for various cables, as well as working to landscape, fence and paint, so there was indeed a great deal of community involvement.'

Mary & Toby's Story

Being in a 'class of her own', as the press reported when she became the only pupil left in Muck's school, has doubtless had repercussions, but whatever problems Mary encountered at school and through being a lone pupil for a short time, the end result is a highly driven soul and a seriously hard worker. As Lawrence frequently says, Mary has the MacEwen determination. And she has needed it.

'I was never very academic, unlike Colin, who just sailed through school and basically loved it. When we had teachers in Muck that really did not suit us very well, he could always catch up, while, looking back on it, this always put me on the back foot. He left a year early and went to Merchiston, where he excelled, and for a time I was the only one left in the school. By then the teacher was Barbara

Graves and actually I did not mind too much, as she was a very nice person. Before that all my school companions were boys, including Colin, but they had all moved to school on the mainland, so I was used to being in male company. I remember I had a group of sheep that I used to feed each morning on my way to school and I loved that too. Then our new school opened and this coincided with the arrival of a new family, the Smiths from Wakefield, who had six children. Surprisingly, it didn't help much because they were so un-countrified and I had little in common with them; I suppose I was very set in my ways. Eventually, I was sent to St Leonards in St Andrews, but I really hated that because I was not at all suited to this sort of school. I suppose my parents just didn't realise, and eventually I was asked to leave. The only option really was the outdoor-orientated Rannoch School and I loved that. That was where I met Toby in 1997. There was plenty of sport and everything was organised around the outdoor life, so that was far better for me.

'After school I started training as a nurse at Queen Margaret's in Edinburgh and during that period nursed in a hospital in the Borders. I have always loved helping people and really enjoyed it, as I felt I was making a difference in people's lives. I soon found that everyone has a story to tell, too. Toby trained as a land agent and worked for Strutt and Parker for a while, but he always knew that I wanted to eventually come back home. For a while, we lived in an estate cottage at Straloch in Aberdeenshire, close to his family farm. When I was expecting Archie, I decided to give up my job, even though I would have loved to continue, but it was just the way things worked out. The family also needed help back home. Before this Toby and I had been running a small shoot at Old Meldrum, and I spent the weekends beating on local estates. We always wanted to return home to raise and educate our children. Growing up on Muck I believe sets you up for life and all that it has to throw at you. The only problem was that we had to work out how to make a living.

'Archie was born when Toby was still at university, and then when he was one I moved to Aberdeenshire, as Toby was working nearby as a factor at Glen Dye and Fasque Estate in Kincardineshire. Then Archie and I went back to Muck to help Mum run the craft shop, as by then she was heavily involved with her catering enterprise at the Siding in Fort William. It was four years later, when Ewen gave up Port Mor House, that we had the ideal opportunity and decided to lease it and start a small shoot on Muck, using the house for guests. Colin came back at much the same time, and I remember it was a glorious spell of weather and we came over in *Wave* with 70 pheasant feeders piled in. We then began to put a few pheasants down on the island. To begin with, we tried some ex-layers and gradually built the numbers up each year. Eventually, we both agreed we would really like to be in a position to be able to educate our children at boarding school, so we knew there was a lot of hard graft ahead. However, we have always been workers and believe that you should work hard when you are young.'

Toby is a huge bear of a man, by anyone's standards. At the shoots, he appears in nearly all weathers dressed in his tweed plus-fours with only a shirt and waistcoat, while the rest of the team are wearing storm-force protective outer clothing. He seems always to be smiling and has the perfect warm manner for dealing with guests; he is famous for his generosity as host. And everyone likes him. He and Mary are a good team and have built up their extraordinary island shoot remarkably fast. Eventually, they found they needed to offer far more; Port Mor House required extensive alterations, so instead of going ahead with these, they decided in typical MacEwen style to take the plunge and built Gallanach Lodge. While in summer the lodge is available to tourists, in the shooting season there is a long waiting list for parties of visiting guns. They run between 18 and 20 shoots for parties of eight guns. This brings in valuable winter income for the islanders, as well as opportunities for beating, catering assistance and now with their new lodge housekeeping as well. Mary does the cooking and, like her mother, has acquired all the culinary skills to make any repast a memorable occasion. The MacEwens have long been largely self-sufficient. Even when deliveries fail due to inclement weather the catering remains second to none. It's a real family affair, and their two sons Archie and Jasper are very much a part of the team.

Having put so much hard-won investment of both time and money into the business, there comes the inevitable pressure to suc-ceed. As well as pheasants, partridge and duck, there are a few snipe and woodcock, and wild-goose chases at dawn and dusk add to the excitement. Goose numbers have expanded greatly in the Hebrides in recent years and are the subject of much controversy, due to the damage they inflict on crops. The guns come from far and wide and claim that it is not only the sport that proves exciting but also the logistical adventure of reaching this small windswept island. They also say that the seascapes and craic here cannot be found anywhere else in the world. Toby and Mary always ensure that they are well aware of the risks and that if Ronnie is unable to return to fetch them in the *Sheerwater* they may end up stuck on Muck. Few seem to care, and some I spoke to say indeed they hope that will be the case.

Toby explains: 'Lots of small birds have really increased since we started planting game crops, more trees and hedges, as well as the increased feeding of grain. Sparrows and starlings that are scarce elsewhere are thriving and we seem to have more finches as well. Peregrines breed on the island and we have large numbers of rock doves, but we also have very large numbers of rats and wage a con-stant war on them, and the hoodies and great black-backed gulls. There have apparently always been a lot of rats on Muck.'

Though Lawrence's maxim that a wife should be able to feed pet lambs cannot perhaps be applied to Toby, there is no doubt that he, like Ruth, is well suited to island life, being resilient and innova-tive. Archie will soon be leaving Muck for boarding school on the mainland and will be sorely missed during shoots, where at 11 he has already made his mark. Meanwhile, his younger brother, Jasper, who his grandmother Jenny describes as an absolute scream, is already to be seen rushing out as soon as school is over to help his father with shoot work. As a family, they make a terrific team.

Sarah

I was nearing the conclusion of my role as narrator for Lawrence's story when I finally met Sarah, Jenny's daughter – the missing link in the tale. Despite her absence from the island, I had heard a great deal about her and quickly noted that she is held in the same high esteem as her mother, and clearly has a very similar nature.

Our meeting came about since Ruth had been to the mainland to have a badly broken ankle fixed for the third time. A desperately needed operation had been squeezed in between the end of winter and lambing, and having been in Edinburgh for this, she was now recuperating for a few days with Sarah before returning home. Everyone from Muck uses Sarah and her husband Willie's home as a base when they are in the area. She is the islanders' home from home, and as such is hugely valued.

An unseasonal blast of hot air had sent the world and his wife to a commercial garden centre with thoughts of spring, and its cafe where we met, near Stirling, bustled with activity. Ruth on a crutch was hopping about with the speed of a kangaroo fleeing a bush fire, taking things in her stride as usual. Sarah was just as I imagined her. Incredibly similar to Jenny, cheery and with a wonderful sense of humour; her kindness shines through instantly. We chatted while she showed me an ageing photograph album. 'There's the combine squeezed onto that landing craft, and there is Davy Jones driving it up the beach,' she explains. There were dog-eared images of family picnics, nut-brown children on white sand digging happily, weddings, pet lambs and boats. Having started her school days in a mainland convent for a very brief spell, she then was the only pupil on the island of Soay and was initially schooled by her mother in a barn there. Then Jenny began to lobby Highland Council, who finally agreed to refurbish the island's dilapidated school, and Sarah finally joined Duncan Geddes's children there. She was eight when she moved to Muck with her mother. Her companions at Muck school were Davy and Nessie Jones's girls and they have remained friends ever since. Jenny later told me that poor Sarah used to go to school with an odd assortment of things for lunch, and often had to take items such as cold chops. She also told me that from a very early age she was a serious bookworm and, particularly on torrentially wet winter days, much preferred to stay inside with her head deep in a tome than battling against the elements to help feed sheep or hens. Sarah remembers that Lawrence always read to her and in particular she loved *The Black Stallion* and *My Friend Flicka*.

'I always remember how much he adored children's parties, too; in fact, he still does, and he loves games and won't miss any of the grandchildren's birthday teas for anything. Of course, he has always loved cake! You know, it all amounts to so much more with him than just running the island. I have a wonderful memory of him being very tiddly one Christmas and hiding from Jenny under the Christmas tree.'

Sarah and her husband keep a small wooden chalet on Muck tucked in behind the farm and come for holidays as often as they can. Their son David is so good at maneuvering sheep that Lawrence calls him the 'dog with a brain'. He is particularly keen on the island and all it entails and loves to help with the farm work. Ruth, who is younger, is currently less interested in the outdoors.

Jenny laughs when she talks about the relationship between Sarah and Lawrence. 'Sarah speaks of Lawrence as "Dad" and has always viewed him as such. She is wonderful with him, and is much more patient than I am. She always makes him lovely puddings when she comes home. She also helps me a lot in the craft shop. When she was little, she particularly adored beachcombing and we often went off on Sunday picnics to Camus Mor and Fang Mor, where there was always plenty to find. We put panniers on a pony and she used to ride over there with us. She had a little Lhasa Apso called Tisha that she adored.

'Looking back, when Sarah finally went away to school to Kilgraston in Perthshire, and when we went over to see her, we often had Budget Renta-vans and turned up laden with things like loos and baths on board. I remember she was always very embarrassed by us. I also remember that while we were on Soay I made her a duvet and stuffed it all with old pillows. It had a nice cover and she adored it. However, when we left Soay in the boat after our wedding, I used it to cover Ewen when he was so drunk and it got soaked and ruined by seawater. I don't think she has ever forgiven me for spoiling such a treasured possession.

'She is such a helpful person, and it was she who brought the famous Merino tup up in the back of her Volvo and met us at the market in Fort William. She actually went to Edinburgh University to do an agricultural course and specialised in soil, though she has not used her degree.'

Needless to say, I liked Sarah just as much as I like the other members of the family. As Jenny so aptly says, 'Sarah is an absent part of the island, but plays her role on the mainland.'

Land and Seascapes

It is time for me to reflect on some of my finest moments spent on the island. I have a lifetime of someone else's treasured memories adding to my own. I am looking for Lawrence. The sun has appeared fleetingly from behind a world of dense grey, and extraordinary light quality so typical of the Hebrides is transforming the scene into a perfect vibrant patchwork. I can hear his quad bike heading slowly up the hill, as Molly and I set off in hot pursuit. Eventually, we catch up with him feeding hogs at Camus Mor. Ardnamurchan and the silhouette of my most favourite hill on earth, Ben Hiant, glow silver in the gathering light. We chat about the hogs, then Lawrence points to a great turret-like crag on the shore, Spichean, by the steepest side of Beinn Airein. 'That is the cliff that Catriona and I scaled as children,' he says wistfully, as the hogs jostle for position at the trough. 'And around that corner is the cliff overhang where poor Blackie and her companion got stuck and rolled down to the rocky shore. You must go out there and walk around during the next spring tide and you will see what a tricky place it is.' He brings his hand up to his face and I note a tinge of emotion.

We set off back up the greening field, passing young trees battling to hold backs straight against incessant shoving from boisterous Atlantic gales. We are heading up the hill, winding our way through the heather onto the northern slopes of Beinn Airein to feed ewes. They gather, watching his approach against a sky of smudgy blueblack. Molly and I follow on foot. Stray rays of sun come and go; there are rainbows over Rum's peaks and beams like stage lights over different islands. Soon we are on a flat face where sheep troughs are lined-up. The ewes are like a parcel of scurrying clouds racing towards Lawrence, eager for food. On the crest of the hill, herring gulls watch us, their plumage snowy white against the strengthening light. The sky is clearing, a blue vista spreading before us. It's a scene that takes place every day – sheep rushing to the trough; an elderly man bent over, pouring sacks of sheep nuts in all weathers, a job he has done so many times he has long lost count.

But there can be few more dramatic settings for the scene of the story that has gradually been revealed. 'I want to show you Queen

Victoria and Pug's cave,' he says as we leave the sheep and the gathering cobalt-coloured view, and head around the vertiginous craggy corner. 'This is the place where we sometimes used to camp in summer. You see it's quite small, but we could wriggle in without too much bother. If you stand here, you will see that from this angle the rock above looks just like Queen Victoria's head on the early penny black stamps.' There is a child-like quality to Lawrence's voice, as he excitedly shows me these special places.

There is silence. We inhale the view. For the first time in days, a wealth of islands loom in the distance: Mull, Iona, Treshnish, Coll, Tiree, Barra Head, Mingulay, Sanday, Vatersay, Barra, Eriskay, South Uist and Benbecula. The remote and lonely Hyskeir lighthouse, like the gulls, shines with a brilliant dazzling whiteness.

'Are you going to go up to the top of Beinn Airein?' he asks me, but I sense that his dodgy knees won't stand the climb today. I nod and take off up the heather-clad slope with Molly racing in front. From its summit, the Western Isles, and the drama of the surrounding mountains, is almost too much for the soul to bear. It's one of those moments where the whole world seems to stretch before me. The lighthouse on Britain's most westerly point, Ardnamurchan, like Hyskeir, glistens too. It's not only the wind that brings a tear to my eye.

The day turns into the finest I have had here after weeks of gales and lashing rain. Molly and I do a fast island tour, for another storm is waiting in the wings. On the island's southern side we walk from Port Mor around the shore to the castle – Caistel nan Duin Bhan, a fortified rock that has an ancient house site on its top used during the Iron Age. It's an atmospheric place. Sheep crop the short turf scattering as we approach; redshank and curlew call from the shore. We pass a lonely dwelling – Alex's bothy – and eventually at low tide we find Mermaid's Pool. It was so named by Lawrence's cousin, Meg Dewar, an artist who tragically died young before he was born. She made quite a mark here and, as well as leaving many wonderful paintings and being a close companion to Lawrence's father, she clearly loved Muck as much as Lawrence does. It's a place that has meant a great deal to family and island visitors, a picnic spot and swimming pool, a lagoon of gin-clear water in an oasis of bronzed weed, framed by dark barnacle-covered rocks and a tiny patch of sand. Ewen took his mother here shortly before her death, as she loved it so much. For Lawrence, every stone has its story. I know that when I see him later he will ask me for every last detail, so I linger to absorb it all. We round the headland as the sun, a watery grapefruit, slides low to the water, casting its glow into the Atlantic. Gold rays mingle with purple and pink as the wind sighs in the tawny grasses tenaciously clutching the headland. Camus Mor is spectacular, sheer drops tumble to the rocks beneath. A peregrine passes fast overhead, wings streamline against its perfect body as a clatter of rock pigeons explodes from the cliff face. Molly takes off inland after a pheasant.

The wind is now building up and the light fades fast. We are going to one of my favourite places, the stone circle and the old MacEwen burial ground, overlooking Rum and the tidal Horse Island, where the hogs are wintered each year. Snipe ping from the heather-covered headland. A small patch of sand uncovered at low tide is a favoured spot for flocks of starlings feasting on invertebrates and small flies in the rotting seaweed. Sometimes there are parties of hooded crows here, too. They island hop, travelling back and forth, taking advantage of whatever is available. Like yobs on a street corner, they jostle for position, flexing their wings before taking off warily. I watch a pair of ravens carrying nest material in the direction of the crags on Beinn Airein. On nearby Lamb Island, greylag geese are joined by a handful of barnacle and a Greenland white-fronted goose – recently someone saw two snow geese. A sleety shower obliterates Rum and it's time to head back to the cottage on the cliff. For me, it has been another memorable visit.

Horseplay

Early spring, and everyone on Muck is working flat out. Celandines are smiling from the verges and hillsides, with primroses just beginning to appear too. The sharp points of flag iris are emerging like green yacht sails in a regatta. It's my first evening back after a month. As I walk through Wire Park heading to Camus Mor, I see some hoodies and an evil-eyed greater black-backed gull pecking hard at the wet corpse of a premature lamb. A dark-coloured ewe stands sentinel, stamping her foot. This is just one of the usual trials that herald the start of another lambing season, due to commence next week. This time Molly and I are staying in a new venue on the edge of one of John Low's woods, in Seilachan Cottage. It gives a completely different aspect to Muck – the loud dawn chorus of house sparrows is impressive, given that on most of the mainland they are becoming scarce. Spring is definitely in the air if their rampant activities on the roof are anything to go by. Bees hum soothingly in the pollen-laden pussy willows, and mallard quack incessantly with thoughts of nesting; a chiffchaff has arrived. In Gallanach Bay, shelduck have joined the parties of cooing eiders, and there are three great northern divers: their eerie calls have a haunting melancholy. At night I sit in the garden, listening to one of nature's most evocative sounds, drumming snipe. They rise and fall by the light of a silvery new moon on its back over the pine trees.

I walk across the fields to Camus Mor and sit on the cliff top; a pair of golden eagles takes to the air from a crag on the opposite side of the bay. I am treated to one of the finest eagle displays I have seen for some time. The duo ride the thermals, with barely a wing beat, and then descend with broad wings swept back before clutching each other's talons in mid-air, grappling, tumbling and falling before separating and rising high into an opaque sky. One cruises low over the hogs to land in the heather, picking up a brittle stalk and lifting off effortlessly with it in its talons. I watch as the bird passes it to its mate and catch my breath at this awesome display. Lawrence says that eagles have never nested on Muck before. It's getting late in the year for them to start now, but these are probably prenuptials in the build-up to their adulthood. They prospect the cliff face for a perfect site. Muck's burgeoning game bag is not only to the liking of the shooters. There is eagle fodder aplenty here, and it would seem likely that by next year nesting may be a possibility. They are a fabulous sight and punctuate my daily walks with brilliant exclamation marks; sometimes they are dwarfed by a passing sea eagle.

It's a week of spring tides and Lawrence suggests I walk around to the spot where Blackie came to grief on the far side of Spichean. Typically, he describes the route skirting around the bottom of the bastion of Gothic-esque crag as 'not too bad' – 'quite straightforward during a spring tide'. The golden eagles are around and make numerous entrances and exits, as Molly and I walk out towards Spichean. Wheatears have newly arrived from sunnier southern climes and their sweet song mingles with the salt sea tang as they announce their presence from the tumbled remains of an old dyke running down towards the sea. When we reach the bottom of Spichean, the tide is still dithering on the retreat and we have to clamber over the lowest part of this rock cathedral to reach the sheep track above. The wind rudely tugs at my shirt; progress on rocks as slippery as ice is precarious. My heart is in my mouth especially when I reach the path above a sheer guano-greened grass face only to find that most of it has eroded badly in winter's storms. I don't wish to return the way I have come. I daren't look down, though the eagles above are doing just that. I must appear clumsy as I cling on, crouching low to avoid the worst of the gusts while endeavouring not to slip. For Lawrence's two heifers coming the other way and down this route from the top, it was indeed treacherous. It's hard to believe that they escaped largely uninjured. The view from the summit is spectacular, and once I am in the lea of the hill and my thumping heart has stopped drowning out all sound, a skylark's sweet Hebridean Overture carries high above me. It was worth the white-knuckle scramble.

Lawrence has another plan, a sort of grand finale. His family are sceptical; however, the tides are going to be low enough to venture to Horse Island to retrieve the hogs after their winter there. Everyone else is too busy to help, so he is borrowing Ruth's young dog Shona. My friend Mark Stephen, BBC presenter from Radio Scotland's *Out of Doors*, is here and, as always, is game for anything. So it will just be the three of us; plus one young dog, and my untrained dog. Molly, though, is as keen as mustard. Everyone seems to be laughing and I feel they are taking bets to see if we will succeed – these will be heavily stacked against rather than for. Lawrence has been advised against it but is as solid as Spichean. And as I have already mentioned, there is that MacEwen determination – and it seems particularly prevalent over this issue.

I bump into Colin the day before, and he does his characteristic eyebrow raises and laugh, saying that even with good dogs and several extra willing assistants it is no easy task. 'I certainly do not think you will manage it. Dad is very lame, and Shona is not his dog, and well, I am not sure about your dog, but maybe if Mark is going too . . .' he grins. It is a gauntlet and Lawrence has taken up the challenge. Jenny adds that if Lawrence breaks his leg on the slippery seaweed she will be very fed up. Tension mounts.

I can tell that Mark is thinking that he may get some very good radio out of the expedition and is raring to go. Mary adds, 'Do make sure you understand the plan before you get to Horse Island because Dad is notorious for not giving any instructions and expecting every-one to know what they are meant to be doing.' Lawrence, jaw set, leaves on a quad; we are to meet him at Lamb Island. There is a lot of giggling as Mark and I are furnished with sticks; everyone wishes us luck. I am beginning to feel apprehensive, as if there is something they know that I don't. I try to cover up by saying several times that I have always wanted to go to Horse Island and it will be lovely to see it whatever, even if mission is not accomplished.

The light is flat and silvered, the sun lurking behind hazed cloud. There is heat in the air, but sea and sky are of hammer-marked grey. However, there is nothing muted about the colours of the newly exposed seaweed, the brilliant pinks, purples, greens and bronzes of waltzing weed and uncovered rock pools, each a magical marine garden. And the brilliance of Lawrence's mood is alone worth this epic. We set off like intrepid explorers as the tide retreats further. Even the swift caprine skip that I occasionally adopt when crossing a dense bog is useless. Every footfall has to be slowly and carefully placed. Lawrence leads on, his limping is minimal and I wonder if he will pay for this later.

Finally, we have crossed the channel, and in one piece. Horse Island is a dramatic place. There is a feeling of total seclusion. It is a haven of birds, and rats. In autumn, grey seals breed on the beach, while soon it will be alive with the cacophony of hundreds of sea and shore birds. The hogs have not seen humans for six months and take off steadily up the hill in front of us. It's no place to send a dog out wide if you do not know what lies in front. The cliffs are sheer and dogs and sheep could vanish into the sea, and indeed in the past have done so. The plan goes vaguely as instructed and there is minimal shouting, and no bad language, except perhaps did I hear one stray *'bloody dog'* carrying on the wind from the lips of the maestro? My face turns puce as I retrace my route up the steepest part several times to ensure none of the hogs are lurking behind the rocky outcrops there. Worse than failing would be to leave a few behind. It takes patience to stop the young sheep breaking back in an explosion as they gather near the rocky shore. Eventually, a first brave beast takes to the narrow gap in an old stone dyke and the rest eventually stream through like sand in an egg timer. Molly has a great eye and knows exactly what she should do, though Shona does most of the work. Before we know it, the flock is heading across the rocks towards the broad channel of seaweed. I rush ahead to take photographs of the spectacle, and Molly stays with the boys and Shona, as they slowly edge them across. Lawrence is beaming and saying we are now almost home and dry – literally – and commenting that it was not that hard. I am wondering if this is a little premature. A far trickier part is to get them down a steep cliff on Lamb Island and onto the shore on Muck. Mark is helping to ease them down, microphone in hand and running commentary to the fore. It takes some time, but eventually another hurdle is overcome.

Lawrence is now wearing the smile of a teenage boy, and I think I know exactly what all this means to him. Mark, whose wit is as sharp as a tack, suggests that there are two ways we can play it on our return: telling everyone a long protracted saga of derring-do and chivalry in which we battled through hell and low water to get the sheep home, or merely giving a nonchalant shrug, telling them that actually it was all *just a piece of cake*. Either would be appropriate . . . but then it all goes slightly astray – at least the hogs do. Lawrence, relaxed and riding the crest of a wave, is so busy chatting to Mark that he forgets where we are supposed to be taking the prodigal hogs. I point out the fact that Shona is sending them towards the Beinn rather than down through the farm gateway, but Lawrence is on a roll. Mark looks up and smiles, as he also spies what is happening. Lawrence chats on, and waves a huge hand at us to say, *It's all just fine*. It is with difficulty that we finally have a last fling around the hill, Mark and I acting as two extra dogs, chasing the confused hogs back down, and there is now quite a bit of shouting from the head shepherd, and Shona is thoroughly confused too. The small flock turns around but descends to the farm the wrong way. Heading straight for the gateway where the cows have been fed all winter, they race on through the bemused beasts, straight into the deep quagmire of mud and dung around the ring feeder. It's as glutinous for the small Cheviot hogs as flypaper for a bluebottle, and has a similar effect. And this is the moment that our victorious return goes belly-up. Mark is proving his true worth and for the second time on his trip to Muck is up to his knees in mud, hauling sheep out of the mire, microphone in one hand and a handful of wool in the other. I am afraid to admit, but I am now weak with laughter. Ruth appears clutching Tara and Hugh, as well as her crutch, and politely peers over the gate, enquiring in a falsely controlled and high voice, 'Goodness, what on earth made you bring them this way, Papa?' Fear of Mark's omnipresent microphone has made her use a polite translation of what she really wanted to say to her father-in-law! It is a hilarious moment in time, yet nonetheless glorious for this mud-larking, and soon all the sheep are safely gathered in. Lawrence's face is a picture, and perhaps just a little of the wind has gone from his sails. But only a little.

The End, or the Beginning

For so small an island, Muck has an enviable work ethic. Despite the abuse that the climate frequently hurls, and the problems of getting to and from the mainland, this is a thriving community that works exceedingly well – a microcosmic example of the importance of fine leadership. When Lawrence and Jenny finally take a back seat, then they will be leaving Muck in safe hands with the next generation of MacEwens. The island is moving with the times, yet unlike so many others it remains unspoilt by over-commercialism; 2014 sees the arrival of a Marine Harvest fish farm off the island's north-east coast, but Lawrence is relieved it will not be visible from any of Muck's houses. This deep-water site will not only bring work for the islanders but there will also be three new houses completed at Port for fish-farm employees. Being situated in an area of fast tides and currents will mean few, if any, disease issues. Colin and his squad have finished a new bunkhouse, and there will be a new teacher and her husband, a plumber and heating engineer, shortly installed, too. Lawrence is particularly happy about the prospect of the latter. Another family will also be chosen for Carn Dearg.

My time on Muck with Lawrence begins to draw to a conclusion, and like so many others before me this island has unwittingly wheedled its way into my psyche in such a way that my departures are now becoming increasingly difficult; I want all this to last forever. For the past 18 months, I have lived and breathed the island; the painting above my bed is no longer a mystery of imagined characters in a land and seascape that I do not know. It's tangible; the places and people all mean something to me. In the annals of my mind, there lies another folder of private stories that will never be told but that have formed part of the whole and helped me to understand the island's human side.

In his *West Highland Survey*, written in 1955, naturalist-writer Frank Fraser Darling wrote of Muck:

The island is of tertiary basalt and extremely fertile, especially as there has been influence of blown shell sand on the north. There is a small anchorage in the south-east corner of the island. The human population is about 30 souls held together by tenacious and benevolent private ownership. Without that regard it is doubtful whether the small area and poor boat shelter of Muck could hope to hold a community, despite the richness and easiness of the land. Muck is in the ocean, not in the narrow seas.

It seems clear that his writing some 60 years ago still rings true today. Lawrence says, 'This may be paternalism, but it has been better for me to control things here. I certainly never wanted to sell anything on the island. I want to die here, too. One of the reasons why the graveyard at Port is unfenced is because I would like to have the cows walking over my grave.' He is leaning against the byre door, having just brought his beloved cows in for the night. His hands, huge guiding hands, safe hands, have kept Muck an island apart from all others. Their lines and scars are ingrained with truths and a thousand tales, and his smile reveals so much about a man who has become a legend in his own time. Hugh and Tara and a posse of dogs rush out of the farmhouse gateway, 'Papa! Papa!' they shout, and he takes hold of their little hands and heads off in the direction of the newly arrived hogs to make sure they are all coming to the trough.

Lawrence's Parents

Lawrence's father, William Ivan Lawrence, was born in 1892 and lived with his parents in Edinburgh, though the family spent much of the summer holidays on Eigg. His uncle, Lawrence Thomson (MacEwen), bought Eigg in 1894, and then Muck in 1896. After prep school at Ardvreck School in Perthshire, he was sent to Dartmouth College at the age of 13. He had clearly been earmarked for a naval career from a young age but left the navy in 1922.

Lawrence's mother, Edith Alice Traquair Nicol, was born in 1902 in Edinburgh. She was always keen on agriculture and natural history. Her father was a university professor and lectured in chemistry at Birmingham. He was very skilled with his hands and built some of the first horse-drawn caravans, and the family set off for long holidays all around Scotland to places such as Kintyre, Knapdale and Glenogil. This was highly unusual during the early 1900s, as the only people travelling like this were tinkers, as they were known at the time. They would stop on various farms, staying to help, particularly during haymaking time; Edith revelled in this kind of work. Like her son Lawrence has proved to be, she was mad about farming and had, like him, an incredibly tenacious and determined spirit. Though an intensely practical person, Lawrence claims she was not very demonstrative. When the Nicol family were on their peregrinations, the mail used to chase them wherever they went. It was simply addressed to: *Prof. Nicol, Caravan, S.W. Scotland*. Sooner or later it seemed to catch up with them. Later Edith trained as a marine biologist and lectured at St Andrews University. She completed a thesis and detailed study of brackish water lochs in North Uist and Orkney, and had various papers published on the subject.

Edith and William married relatively late in life, but they had spent a lot of time together and knew each other well, as they were second cousins. Their wedding took place in Edinburgh in 1937 and they then moved straight to Muck. The 'Commander', an appellation used for him all the time, rather than his Christian name, had been to the East of Scotland Agricultural College and had worked on a farm in the Borders to gain experience. Up until the time he was married, he had always had a farm manager for the island. Lawrence remembers that his father was a particularly kind and meticulous person, and someone whom he admired.

Timeline

1937: William Ivan Lawrence MacEwen and Edith Alice Traquair Nicol married, Edinburgh.

1939: Alasdair MacEwen born, 18 May.

1941: Lawrence MacEwen born, 24 July.

1944: Catriona MacEwen born, 15 July; Jenny Davies born, 2 May.

1946: Ewen MacEwen born, 6 October.

1947: Lawrence attends school on Muck with Alasdair; first tractor, Fergie TE20, arrives with coal puffer.

1953: Lawrence sent to school at Aberlour House.

1955: Lawrence attends school at Altyre House, Gordonstoun.

1956: Muck gets the telephone.

1959: Lawrence leaves school, July.

1960: Lawrence gains farming experience at Mersington, Greenlaw.

1961–62: Lawrence to Aberdeen University and Glen Dearg, Galashiels, for practical farming with Haig and Peggy Douglas.

1963: Lawrence's final year at university.

1964: Fergie 35X tractor arrives in March. Lawrence leaves university in June. Lawrence leaves aboard SS *Canberra* for Australia, Tasmania and New Zealand in November. Johnnie and Hector MacDonald drowned, 9 December. First car arrives on Muck.

1965: First mail delivered to Muck. Fatal Accident Enquiry for Johnnie and Hector MacDonald, 4 February. Sheriff congratulates the modest heroine. *Loch Arkaig* calls at Muck for the first time.

1966: Lawrence returns to Muck in July. Alasdair at the helm, Lawrence doing the cattle and lobster fishing.

1967: Commander MacEwen dies in January. Lawrence and Alasdair meet Tex Geddes.

1968: Lawrence's mother, Ma, buys Hardiston Farm at Cleish, Kinross. Catriona's wedding to David White, 21 June, on Muck. Lawrence's first trip to Soay, where he meets Jenny Davies.

1969: Work begins, wiring up Gallanach for electricity. Alasdair marries Fiona Style in Jersey. Alasdair announces he no longer wants to farm on Muck; Lawrence takes over the farm.

1970: Port Mor and Gallanach wired up for electricity, and two generators bought. Island has electricity for first time with generator.

1971: Sarah Maitland (Jenny's daughter) born, 2 February.

1972: First Luing bull arrives. Ewen home from Patagonia.

1973: Ewen starts building Port Mor House. Bryan and Clare Walters arrive.

1974: Bruce and Sandra Mathers come to live at Boatman's Cottage. Peter MacRae dies in tractor accident at the pier, 21 March. Fatal Accident Enquiry follows. David Jones arrives as trainee shepherd.

1975: Colum Beagan arrives. Local authorities tar the road.

1977: Mrs Edith MacEwen, Ma, dies.

1979: Lawrence and Jenny Davies married on Soay, 26 September. *Loch Arkaig* sinks at Mallaig pier.

1980: Colin (Lawrence and Jenny's son) born, 31 July. Ewen finishes Port Mor House.

1981: Craft shop opens, 23 May.

1982: Mary MacEwen (Lawrence and Jenny's daughter) born, 7 March.

1988: David Jones killed in boat accident. Bruce Mathers drowns off Ardnamurchan, together with crewmember Roderick Murray from Mull. Charlie MacDonald dies, 24 February. *Wave* gets a new engine.

1989: Sandra Mather's mother, Katie MacDonald, dies, 17 November.

1990: Alasdair dies. Dr Hector MacLean from Eigg retires. Planning begins for wind-power scheme.

1992: Construction starts for new school. Wind-power committee formed. Power cables laid. Wheelhouse fitted on *Wave*.

1993: Sarah Maitland marries William MacRae. First block for wind turbine is cast. Wind Harvester in liquidation.

1994: New school opens. Last puffer, *Eilean Easdale*, comes to Muck for the final time.

1996: David MacRae (Sarah and William's son) born.

1999: Another wind-power scheme commences.

2000: Princess Anne calls in for unscheduled visit. Work on new pier commences. MV *Loch Nevis* launched in Troon, May.

2001: Ruth MacRae (Sarah and William's daughter) born.

2002: Archie Fichtner-Irvine (Mary and Toby's son) born.

2003: Brian Walters dies at sea, September.

2004: Izzy Fichtner-Irvine born. New pier opened by MSP Nicol Stephen. CalMac's *Loch Nevis* comes to the new pier for the first time, 5 March, no further need for the flit boat.

2005: Second wind turbines arrive, but not installed.

2007: Mary MacEwen and Toby Fichtner-Irvine return to Muck. Jasper Fichtner-Irvine born. Mary and Toby take over Port Mor House and start shoot. Colin MacEwen and Ruth Harland come back to Muck and take over the farm.

2009: Izzy Fichtner-Irvine dies, 11 October.

2010: Work on new hall begins. Colin and Ruth are married, 1 May.

2011: Hugh MacEwen (Colin and Ruth's son) born.

2012: Tara MacEwen (Colin and Ruth's daughter) born. Ambitious building project begins on Gallanach Lodge. New hall officially opens.

2013: Opening of Gallanach Lodge. Final electrification of Muck, 22 March.

2014: Colin building new bunkhouse. Mary MacEwen and Toby Fichtner-Irvine married, 17 May. Marine Harvest start building three houses for fish-farm employees. Fish farm opening off Muck, August 2014.

The Isle of Muck – a Brief History, According To Lawrence

As Muck is the most fertile of the Small Isles and there are clear signs of Mesolithic settlers on neighbouring Rum, it is probable that settlers were also here at that time. The use of skin-covered coracles for sea transport made it fairly straightforward to travel between the islands and the mainland.

Further substantial evidence of more recent settlement include a Bronze Age dagger uncovered by a plough during the 1950s, and the fortified rock, Caistel nan Duin Bhan, with a house on top at the entrance to Port Mor, being attributed to the later Iron Age.

Two crosses from the graveyard at Port Mor bring us into the Christian era, one of which can be seen in the craft shop. For a written account of Muck, we have to go to 1549, when Donald Munro, High Dean of the Isles, states: '. . . ane verie fertile fruitful ile of cornis and girsing for all store, verie gude for fische, inhabite and manurit, with ane gude falcon nest, pertaining to the Birshop of the Iles, with ane gude hieland heavin in it, the entrie at the west cheek of it.'

The influence of the Church was written large across the Western Isles, but all was to change with the Reformation, and already the MacIan of Mingary Castle in Ardnamurchan was running Muck for the Church. Then in 1617 the Bishop of the Isles feued Muck to the MacLeans of Coll, who evicted the MacIans and took over the island. MacLean control lasted until 1857. During this period, it was often a son who actually lived on Muck, though, with birlinns powered by sail and oars, travelling between Muck and Coll would have been fairly easy.

Interesting events during this period included the imprisonment of the Catholic priest in 1770 (Muck was around 50 per cent Catholic) by Mrs Hector MacLean. Approximately 20 years later, the islanders were vaccinated against smallpox at an astronomical fee of 2s 6d per head. By now, Britain was at war against France and the price of kelp was rising, as it provided one of the raw materials for munitions. Kelping was labour intensive and it was therefore in the MacLean interest to allow the population to rise through subdivision of holdings.

The widespread introduction of the potato allowed a steep rise in food production per acre. Then came Waterloo. The ensuing peace brought a steady decline in the price of kelp. Soon the MacLean tenants were in arrears. Bad weather helped little, and by the 1820s the MacLeans were buying meal to help feed a starving population, particularly on Rum, where the land is poorer. Muck was overpopulated and the solution was emigration. The MacLeans chartered the *St Lawrence*, which left Tobermory in July 1828 with a load of immigrants from both Muck and Rum. The few that remained lost their land and had to build houses at Keil above Port Mor and fish for their living. The craft shop was originally Keil House. Keil was probably the nearest to a village on the island, as it had a school, and its foundations are still in place.

Before the Education Act, schooling was intermittent, but the Society for the Propagation of Christian Knowledge and the Gaelic Missionary played a part. As far as we know, there was no church. All that remains of the old Keil village is now heaps of lichen-covered stone ruins, showing that there were numerous tiny dwellings. Even though the occupants could fish, they too left fairly quickly. When we dug the cable trench for the electricity, we found some worn out quern stones and red peat ash in places, as well as shells and other remains. Keil always held the island graveyard and, though in the early days no gravestones were used, the cross in the craft shop was found there.

By 1835, Cheviot sheep had arrived from the Borders, a lucrative enterprise, with the price of wool up to five shillings per pound. In 1845, the Thorburn family, originally from Dumfriesshire, had arrived. Before coming to Muck, they had been tenants of Treshnish Farm in Mull, and Achateny in Ardnamurchan. They were hard grafters and set about improving the island. The lazy beds were flattened out over the best areas of land, and dykes and drains were built using stones from the old houses. The stone barn and the horse gang at the 'square' went up, and Muck at last had a small pier.

In 1857, Hugh MacLean, the last MacLean on Muck, sold the island to Lt. Thomas Swinburne, who already owned Eilean Shona, an island in Loch Moidart. Eager to support the community, he purchased fishing smacks to be crewed by islanders (some of whom returned from Tobermory, where they were living) and he built Pier House as a salt store, as this was the only method available to preserve fish prior to refrigeration. He also extended the farmhouse.

By 1878, sheep farming was in decline and Australia was dominating the wool trade. Thomas, the last member of the Thorburn family, finally gave up the lease. By then, a new type of farming was spreading north from Ayrshire: dairying, and this meant cheese. Soon the Weir family from Kintyre had taken the lease of the farming operation. This necessitated another major building programme; twin byres with a piggery on one side, and the dairy and cattleman's house on the other, with a midden in front. David Weir was tragically drowned in a boating accident off Horse Island and, coincidentally, almost immediately a major event occurred in the story of Muck: the island came on the market.

Lawrence Thomson MacEwen (he had dropped the MacEwen for

reasons unclear, but he may have been involved in financial irregularity) was the son of an Edinburgh solicitor but spent much of his early life overseas selling armaments, first in South America and later in Japan as agent for Cammells, the Tyneside builder of warships. He was also foreign correspondent for *The Times* and an enthusiastic collector of Eastern artefacts. Eccentricity was the hallmark of the Thomson era, and possibly the generations of MacEwens that have followed. He mainly resided on Eigg, which he had purchased two years before Muck, and it is recorded that when Japan defeated the Russians in a major naval victory in 1906 he had a beacon lit to celebrate. He had sold many of the warships manned by the Japanese.

On Eigg he always had a place at table laid for absent guests. He went for long walks at night alone and kept his coffin under his bed; he had his grave built on Castle Island. He suffered from diabetes and died in 1913. Diabetes at that point was untreatable. His main legacy on Muck was three barns to store the farm crops during an era of corrugated iron. When he died, Thomson left Muck to his brother John, but as he always had a great liking for his nephew, William Ivan Lawrence, my father, there appears to have been a gentleman's agreement that he was the one who would finally inherit the island.

A career in the Royal Navy was intended for my father, but when the Great War was over and the Washington Agreement led to savage reductions in naval ships and manpower, there were major cutbacks. Meanwhile Muck was in the hands of trustees, having been let to John MacDonald of Glenbrittle, Skye. Cheese-making had ceased in 1913. For Father, who had an island to go to, a career change seemed obvious and he took a bounty of £300 and left the Royal Navy for the East of Scotland College to study agriculture. With guidance from noted horticulturalist and author Sir Osgood MacKenzie, creator of Inverewe Gardens, my father planted the island's three oldest woods prior to taking over the lease from John MacDonald. He also engaged the youthful Charlie and Alick MacDonald, who had recently left school to work on the farm. Absent from Muck for much of the winter, Lt. MacEwen, my father, also employed Sandra Mathers' great uncle, Lachlan MacDonald, as farm manager. Lachlan was part-time and also farmed on Loch Awe side. He made monthly visits to Muck. By now the island was noted for its livestock, and was breeding Highland bulls and tups mainly for the Department of Agriculture, who leased them to crofters all over the Highlands and Islands.

In the 1920s and 1930s, Father had a fairly relaxed lifestyle, keeping the farm books and collecting stamps. He had a 12-metre sailing yacht, with hands-on farming largely involving things such as haymaking and working in the sheep fank.

In 1939, war broke out again and Father, who was in the Royal Naval Reserve, was called up and posted to Lerwick in Shetland, and later St Christopher, the inshore training base at Fort William. My mother Edith – or Babs, as she was more commonly known – was running the farm. Labour was in short supply and there was rationing. The Ministry of Food kept prices at low levels and, unlike during the First World War, it was a bad time for farming during the second war. When peace returned, the opposite was the case. The government determined that never again would the country be on the brink of starvation and did much to boost British agriculture, with a generous subsidy system and grants to modernise fixed equipment and dwellings, something that Muck was to benefit from.

On Muck, too, it was all change: with four children in the coop, it was no longer possible to spend four months of the winter away in Edinburgh and the family's two townhouses were put on the market. In fact, my parents became somewhat reclusive. A motorcar, though present before 1939, was not in our possession and we travelled by train or bus. I well remember standing on Arisaig station holding tightly onto Father's hand while a Gresley 'K' class locomotive roared into the station with the train for Glasgow. Even more surprising was the lack of a wireless in our house: world news came through the weekly *Scotsman*. I certainly had never heard any pop music, as the only music until I was 12 was from my aunt's piano. Little surprise, then, that when I arrived at prep school at Aberlour House relating to my fellow pupils was very difficult.

Father, who shared County Council duties with Doctor Hector MacLean on Eigg, was less isolated and a much more frequent traveller. One must also remember that until 1956 there was no telephone on the island. All this isolation helped to engender a powerful love and absolute dedication to Muck, which has stayed with me all my days.

Lawrence MacEwen
Isle of Muck
April 2014